Traffick

Traffick

The Illicit Movement
of People and Things

Gargi Bhattacharyya

Pluto Press

LONDON • ANN ARBOR, MI

First published 2005 by Pluto Press
345 Archway Road, London N6 5AA
and 839 Greene Street, Ann Arbor, MI 48106

www.plutobooks.com

British Library Cataloguing in Publication Data
A catalogue record for this book is available from the British Library

ISBN   0 7453 2048 1 hardback
ISBN   0 7453 2047 3 paperback

Library of Congress Cataloging in Publication Data applied for

10   9   8   7   6   5   4   3   2   1

Designed and produced for Pluto Press by
Chase Publishing Services Ltd, Fortescue, Sidmouth, EX10 9QG, England
Typeset from disk by Stanford DTP Services, Northampton, England
Printed and bound in the European Union by
Antony Rowe Ltd, Chippenham and Eastbourne, England

Contents

Acknowledgements

Writing books can be a painful business – by the time you are able to piece together the narrative, you are all too aware of how little you know. At the same time, getting to write as part of my job can feel like a privilege, particularly when the world is so troubling. The last few years have been distressing times for many of us, so I have been pleased to have this chance to have a think about things.

While writing this, I benefited from discussions with colleagues and students at the universities of Jadavpur and Dhaka. I thank both institutions for their hospitality. Thanks also go to everyone at Pluto Press, for their encouragement and patience throughout this project.

As always, I am indebted to a whole host of people. Especial thanks go to my students at the University of Birmingham, with whom I first discussed many of these ideas; to Matt Waddup, who won't remember, for a conversation about the left's addiction to conspiracy theories that is in the background of much of this work; to Khademul Haque for our discussions of the impact of globalisation on various parts of the developing world; to Stanheed Butt for our ongoing debate about global events and local political choices; to Manju who reminded me that the moment when the powerful are most insistent about asserting their absolute power may be the moment when that power is crumbling; to Sonali for all of our shared horror at what has been happening around us and our discussions about how this could be explained and linked to other recent events; and, most of all, to Dilip who kindly and diligently read the draft of this work, despite his antipathy to extended prose. I hope you feel like I finally learned something worth knowing.

I
How Did We Get Here?

When I first started to plan this project, in the summer of 2001, few people I met seemed to agree with my suggestion that we were living through a step-change in the rhythm of globalisation. I wasn't yet confident about the parameters of the book, and the account I could give of the tangled interconnections between the trades in arms, drugs and people seemed as old as human trade itself. Nothing new in that seedy world, certainly no sign of a new phase of globalised relations. Then, from September 2001, everyone started to talk about the need to regulate global movements, of the dangers of untraceable transnational transactions, of the urgent need to put a break on globalisation. It has since been hard to escape the suggestion, made by all kinds of people in a whole range of places, that we are in a new era where we must learn to regulate and contain the excesses of our insistently interdependent world (for some examples see Amin, 2003; Brennan, 2003; Mertes, 2004). We may not have agreed a method for doing this, or a membership for this imagined regulatory body, or even an ultimate goal – but that first shift in consciousness, the one that says that there are dangers in leaving global processes to regulate themselves, has hit home hard. What follows is an account of how we come to this place.

Sometimes, when reading famous attempts to narrativise the tumultuous events of the nineteenth century that seek to register what it felt like to be alive in this best and worst of times, I have wondered what it must have been like to live through these world-changing processes without any sense of where things are going or how they might end. We present-day readers approach these documents – the novels and the political treaties, the famous essays, the diaries, the amateur investigations that form the basis of social science as we know it – with the lazy seen-it-all-before of our hindsight. We have no doubts about how it ends. Of course, it ends with us.

The massive social changes that swept across Europe in the nineteenth century seem to us to be no more than the building blocks of our everyday reality. The transitions to becoming urban, industrial, literate, governed by the state, internationally networked and nationally identified – all of these cataclysmic changes now represent no more than the most tedious and predictable components of contemporary life in the West. For the contemporary reader, it is hard to imagine that the world has ever been anything otherwise.

But something is lost in that easy acceptance of what is. Certainly, our imaginative grasp of the process of change is dampened by an unwillingness to consider that things could have been different, and, by all accounts, once were so. How can we understand epochal change unless we have some way to access that breathless uncertainty, the mixture of fear and anticipation, the jitters and rejiggings that come from things being as yet undecided? This work argues that we are all living through some wondrous and horrific world changes – and that attempts at understanding what is happening must make space for both the wonder and the horror of our times.

When I first read Marshall Berman's groundbreaking account of cultural change, *All That Is Solid Melts Into Air*, I was struck by the sense of high excitement that pervaded this study of the cultures of modernity. Although this cultural production emerges from the most turbulent times, and runs parallel to immense and intense barbarism, there is something important about acknowledging that sense of excitement. Most of all, I took that elation as a sign that things were not yet decided. Berman himself writes in this vein of the modern voice:

> It is a voice that knows pain and dread, but believes in its power to come through. Grave danger is everywhere, and may strike at any moment, but not even the deepest wounds can stop the flow and overflow of its energy. It is ironic and contradictory, polyphonic and dialectical, denouncing modern life in the name of values that modernity itself has created, hoping – often against hope – that the modernities of tomorrow and the day after tomorrow will heal the wounds that wreck the modern men and women of today. (Berman, 1982, 1988, 23)

That heightened sense of simultaneous possibility and danger is Berman's chosen subject. His argument that modernity, in all the many varied processes that this term includes, at once renders us hopelessly broken and endlessly powerful, always torn between mourning what has been lost and welcoming what could be, embodies the doubleness of modern experience. The suggestion that all that is solid melts into air is both a threat and a promise. Everything known and certain in the world, the good, the bad and the indifferent, drifts away leaving us without any of the comfort of knowing where we are or of being at home. Yet that uncanny sense of rootlessness also promises that the shape of the world and our destiny in it are yet to be written. Anything can happen and there is no way of knowing whether that anything will be good or bad – only that our modern consciousness tells us that it is ours to shape:

> To be modern is to find ourselves in an environment that promises us adventure, power, joy, growth, transformation of ourselves and the world – and, at the same time, that threatens to destroy everything we have, everything we know, everything we are. (Berman, 1982, 1988, 15)

We are now passing through a time of similarly tumultuous change. I am not making a case here for the end of modernity, and neither is this a belated addition to the fractious debates about postmodernity (see for example Bauman, 1997; Crook, Pakulski and Waters, 1992). Rather, the parallel I wish to draw is with that feeling of living through huge and unpredictable change. Perhaps this is an extension of the same long process, with all that is solid still melting into air. It is certainly arguable that the multiple processes that are gathered together as globalisation represent a continuation of the seemingly endless refinement of modernity. That long discussion is beyond the scope of this project. Instead, my interest is in our ability to register and understand these changes as we live through them. I hope that what follows goes some way towards registering this moment, and offering some clues towards its understanding, while recognising that its end is not yet decided.

Inevitably, this work shows the influence of the anti-capitalist movement, and especially of the intellectual renaissance that has emerged in resistance to globalisation (Gills, 2000; Klein, 2000; Mertes, 2004). However, the present study is not quite in the tradition of these anti-corporate critiques. There is a resonance with this other work, and some points of political agreement, but my primary goal here is to construct a framework for understanding. There is something uncomfortable about identifying your enemies too easily and too quickly. The teacher in me is concerned that we register the complexity of the situation, even as we line up in our respective teams. In the end, I want to argue that understanding needs to be, in part at least, distinct from political allegiance, although I hope that there will also be some informative relation between the two.

The other characteristic that distinguishes this work from much other related literature is my wish to register something of the excitement of the globalising process. The chapters that follow focus on various extremes of human hardship and danger. The underbelly of globalism is not a pretty thing, except in the terms of the exploitative anti-glamour that gets off on death and suffering. But there is something missing from any account of the global integration of the shadows that does not make space for the sense of adventure and possibility that is also apparent. For this reason the discussion to come tries to register both the horror and the elation of what we are living through.

CHAOS AND ORDER

The strange and exciting processes of globalisation can be characterised as an ongoing and irresolvable battle between forces of chaos and forces of order. Of course, the discussion of globalisation has more often concentrated on the apparently chaotic aspects of this era. So we learn, with some sense of relief, that the era of increasing global integration decentres us all. No more master subjects of empire, now even the rich and powerful have become vulnerable to forces beyond their control (Sardar, 1998).

This is the account of globalisation as 'accidental'. Here the economy grows in unexpected and unplanned ways and we have no choice but to live with the consequences of this cultural earthquake. Here globalisation has not been subject to planning or conscious development by any party; it is portrayed as an anti-human force, resistant to control or intervention. In this telling, the various attempts by human beings to co-operate at an international level – be this in terms of political agreement or economic contract – come to be seen as the antithesis of globalisation.

Against this, I shall argue that the globalisation we encounter today is a product of earlier and ongoing international aspirations. The chaos has been a byproduct of one style of ordering. In fact, the chaos ensures that the order can be maintained.

Many of the debates about globalisation have seemed to assume that it is akin to a natural disaster, a strange event that happens to us and which we can only hope to survive. Although some brave souls have attempted to suggest that perhaps these happenings are not inevitable, the notion that globalisation could be halted or turned back has been ridiculed as unrealistic and Luddite.

My interest is not in halting or reversing these processes. Whatever the many and extreme deprivations that have resulted from movements within the global economy, it is not the case that the poor were better served by what happened before this. There is no state of grace to which we can return, as usual. Instead, along with many others, my interest is more in the possibility of adapting and reshaping globalisation in order that it might better meet the needs of ordinary people all over the world. This is one of those pesky lessons of modernity – any better tomorrow must come out of the debris of today.

However, the main focus of this book is the notion that the global structures we inhabit have not emerged spontaneously, inevitably, and without historical context. In fact, others have argued quite the contrary, namely, that globalisation represents a plan for world domination. Mark Rupert, for instance, argues that the whole debate about globalisation and its emergence has been conducted in deeply ideological terms that mask the political project of a particular neo-liberal vision of global integration:

> There is no reason to believe that liberal globalization is ineluctable. Contrary to much of the evolutionary imagery or technological determinism which is often invoked to explain it ... globalization has been neither spontaneous nor inevitable; it has been the political project of an identifiable constellation of dominant social forces and it has been, and continues to be, politically problematic and contestable. (Rupert, 2000, 42)

While I agree with some aspects of this account, in that the formal institutions and processes of economic integration have been part of an explicit plan instigated by a self-proclaimed interest group, the implication that the multi-layered processes of globalisation can be explained away as a conspiracy by the powerful is problematic, to say the least. Technology may not be determining, but technology has played an important role in shaping the manner of global integration. It may be true that the metaphor of an unstoppable evolution has formed part of the propaganda of neo-liberalism, but global integration has been shaped by more complex and contradictory forces than this embodiment of capitalist will. Even if the powerful have a plan, history will always complicate its implementation. We have been living through a time when the forces of globalisation have seemed to belong exclusively to the rich and powerful. As the world changes, it can feel as if ordinary people everywhere have no choice but to suffer – there is little sense that we can shape the new day that is arriving: that privilege belongs to someone else. Yet even the unstoppable juggernaut of globalisation can be rattled by unplanned complications. In particular, recent rumblings from international institutions have suggested that there exists a criminal and illegitimate set of global networks that threatens to destabilise the more celebrated transactions of the global economy proper. It is this parallel world that forms the focus for this volume.

In the discussion that follows, I want to return to some old and seemingly forgotten arguments.

AN EDUCATION IN CURRENT AFFAIRS

When I began thinking about this book I wanted to pull together a number of key debates, and to provide some kind of route map for the complex suggestions coming from different disciplinary fields. In this sense, then, while I am entering these debates very much as an amateur, my hope is that a cross-disciplinary approach may open up connections and insights to a wider audience.

As a teacher, I have found that students are highly engaged with debates about the nature of globalisation and its impact on our everyday lives, and are eager to think about the emerging political context and challenges that are facing us all. However, much of the material that discusses the emergence of contemporary globalisation remains somewhat remote from their concerns. In my most recent courses I have found that students share my concern to understand contemporary events as they unfold before us. This desire to develop some critical insight into the confusion of recent happenings, most especially when what happens is so very frightening, has been shared by my students and myself.

As a result, this work has been motivated by a strong belief that education can help you to understand your world, however quickly that world may be changing and however alarming those changes may be. I also think that these turbulent times offer excitement as well as alarm, and that the adventure of social change is a story well worth telling. What follows, then, is an attempt to pull together some disparate threads in the bloodcurdling but eventful adventure tale of recent global events. There has been a strange tension in many spheres of social science discussion in recent years – good sense tells us that there are no sustainable metanarratives, just broad conceptual frameworks that must be filled with local detail to bring any insight;

yet the new catch-all of globalisation theory seems to promise a welcome return to our dreams of totalised knowledge. Everyone seems to be looking for some story that will link the disparate confusions of our world and, despite its varied chapters and approaches, the saga of globalisation appears to offer this longed-for handle on all human life. It is hard not to be painfully aware of the allure of this promise. In response, this volume also tries to link the segments of some diverse globalising trends while remembering that this is not a new universalism. Most of all, what follows is an attempt to describe the collection of events that have come to be known as the most recent phase of globalisation as historically particular, as the events of a particular context rather than as a new master narrative for all time.

GLOBAL INSTITUTIONS AND THEIR IMPACT

The remainder of this chapter will review the formation of the Bretton Woods institutions, such as the IMF and GATT, and the project of global economic integration that has been undertaken through these structures. That is one theme in this discussion – the formative role played by international economic institutions in the creation of what we now regard as the global economy. Alongside this, there is the role of foreign policy decisions that are not easily mapped onto pure economic interests. I hope that what follows shows something of the manner in which these two forces shape and contain each other, and lead us to the encounter with contemporary forms of globalisation.

The return to more economically informed modes of analysis that comes with the widespread take-up of globalisation-speak is welcome. Better to know than not about the stitch-ups of trade agreements and the unstoppable calls of national and transnational interests. Without some awareness of this not-quite-visible element of all our lives, it seems impossible to understand anything of the changes we are living through. However, there is a danger that a desire to understand the workings of economic life can become an acceptance of one account of what economic life could and should be. Much of the discussion that portrays globalisation as an unstoppable force in one direction, as an inevitable linking of the world into a particular form of global market, accepts the free market as the natural state of economic life. Somehow the market will out, regardless of the actions of individual actors. Samir Amin has mounted a long-running critique of the apparent naturalness of the terms of capitalist development and the seemingly magical powers attributed to that mysterious entity, the market:

> 'The market', a term referring by nature to competition, is not 'capitalism', of which the content is defined precisely by the limits to competition implied by the monopoly of private property (belonging to some while others are excluded). 'The market' and capitalism are two distinct concepts. (Amin, 1997, 15)

The concept of the market has taken on a talismanic status in debates about the global economy. The market will provide solutions to economic and even social problems. The market is something that must be enabled to build prosperity. The market represents freedom and capitalism and its imperatives cannot be denied. Encouraging markets stops being seen as a limited economic strategy and instead is vaunted as an end in itself, because the market is the epitome of capitalist freedom (see, for example, Mihevc, 1995). In the process, places that are being subjected to such restructuring are denied the safeguards and protections enjoyed by the marketeers of the affluent economies.

In this process, some of which has been orchestrated for openly political reasons, it has become much harder to see markets as just another mechanism in the complexities of social life. Instead, the market has come to be portrayed as the basis on which all other institutions must be built. Diane Coyle discusses this phenomenon in the context of recent debates about economic management and concludes that the celebration of the market as an abstract concept has been the province of a very particular politics:

> It is only during the decade or so of high Thatcherism and Reaganism that free markets were ever understood as standing somehow outside social and political institutions. The radical neo-liberal agenda hijacked the idea of markets to mean a very specific set of institutions, namely the minimal, night-watchman state. However, economists dating back to Adam Smith, the founding father, have understood that markets work better in some contexts than others. (Coyle, 2000, 26)

The long-standing debate about the impact of context on market functioning has been muffled by the more amplified propaganda of contemporary neo-liberalism. Increasingly, however, contrary voices have been questioning the inevitability of this version of global integration (Green, 1999). Presenting a certain model of international trade and economic relations as the abstraction 'the market', and pretending that this system is self-creating and self-sustaining, has been one of the more successful propaganda campaigns for Western interests.

MORE THAN ECONOMICS

Throughout this work, I try to argue that economic forces are important and yet are not the only shaping force in the creation of the global economy. My other key theme considers the role of changes in international relations, and the impact of these political shifts on the contemporary map of the world.

Both strands of the analysis begin from a sense that we are living in a moment of great change. Whatever contracts of global relations have operated previously, we seem to be in a moment of all-round reassessment. In the fields of both economic policy and international relations, contemporary debate stresses the need for change, either to regain some lost dream of stability or to finally realise the longed-for vision of global co-operation. Whatever we may feel about the causes or the consequences of this moment of change, there is clearly a widespread agreement that something is indeed changing.

I do not propose any particular theory to explain this period of crisis. My approach is to suggest that global integration has proceeded through complex and multiple events, and that this complexity can lead to unforeseen consequences. I have taken some guidance from the suggestions of Samir Amin and his account of chaos as the normal state of capitalist relations. He writes of recent shifts:

This evolution is not leading simply to a new world order characterised by new forms of polarisation, but to global disorder. The chaos which confronts us today comes from a triple failure of the system: (i) it has not developed new forms of political and social organisation going beyond the nation-state – a new requirement of the globalised system of production; (ii) it has not developed economic and political relationships capable of reconciling the rise of industrialization in the newly competitive peripheral zones of Asia and Latin America with the pursuit of global growth; (iii) it has not developed a relationship, other than an exclusionary one, with the African periphery which is not engaged in competitive industrialization at all. (Amin, 1997, 2)

While I agree with Amin's account of the failures of the global economy as it stands, this volume does not regard inequality as the principal cause of turbulence. In fact, Amin himself argues that this chaotic inequality is a key characteristic of global capitalism, not an anomaly but an instability that is central to its perpetuation. What I do take from Amin's account is this sense of precariousness. The very business of integration relies on activities that endanger the integrity of global institutions. Much recent discussion about the failures of globalisation has suggested that the entire system is corrupt, no more than a huge and complex scam through which the rich world screws the poor, endlessly until death (Chossudovsky, 1997). Despite my sympathy with much of this work, in the interests of understanding I try here to suspend my distaste and instead appreciate the vision and promise that the creation of a globally negotiated economy once had. Some will be irritated by the discussion that follows, couched as it is in terms of the possibility of a global capitalism that creates prosperity. But I hope that others will be convinced that the best critique is one constructed from within, and that all students, whether academic or activist in their inclination, must learn the logics of their enemies.

The moment of change that I am identifying is precipitated by a sense of crisis in international institutions. The machinery of Bretton Woods, structures that have been in constant flux since their creation, now appears unsustainable. This, in part, is the argument made by Amin:

> The present international monetary and financial system, put together at the end of the Second World War and managed by the IMF, is no longer functional. It should not surprise us that the long post-war period that began in 1945 eventually came to an end in 1990, or that the world system which will evidently succeed it will be qualitatively different from what we have known for nearly half a century. (Amin, 1997, 46)

Much of the discussion that follows is an exploration of what 'no longer functional' might mean. Despite the assertion that the long post-war period came to an end long before 1990, and with it the international monetary and financial system created at Bretton Woods, the much discussed process of globalisation only began to enter public consciousness in or around 1990. To celebrants of the new regime, globalisation is the fortunate nirvana that takes over from the incomplete project of Bretton Woods. However, what we recognise and describe as globalisation has clear roots in the terms of the post-war settlement. There is no clear break between what happens before 1990 and what comes afterwards. International events may cause the escalation of certain economic trends, but, largely, we are still in the long aftermath of 1945.

The ever-growing industry in globalisation-commentary has continued to circle around some enduring themes, central among them the question of when globalisation begins and whether its prime motor is economic, political or cultural (Rennie Short, 2001; King, 1991; Steger, 2003). For the purposes of this discussion I want to concentrate on the period since the formation of the Bretton Woods institutions until the present day. Although there have been greater and lesser levels of integration in the global economy at different times, the formation of these institutions marks the beginning of the new formal incarnation of globalisation. This moment is important for a number of reasons. Firstly, I am interested in the level of intention involved in the creation of this global framework. There is nothing accidental about the emergence of these global phenomenon and their formation represents one active strategy for managing the turbulence of international relations. Secondly, there is the very twentieth-century belief in the power of economic planning, a power that promises to contain the dangers of political disagreement and potential violence. Thirdly, and this is the discussion that forms the main substance of what follows, there are the more recent and largely unintended consequences of the powers and interventions of these international institutions.

CREATING INTERNATIONAL FINANCIAL INSTITUTIONS

Although these events are well known and have come to form part of popular folk memory, it is worth spending a few moments reviewing the circumstances and intention behind the formation of these still powerful bodies. The Bretton Woods conference, held in Bretton Woods, New Hampshire, USA in July 1944, met in anticipation of the world order that would emerge when the war was finally and conclusively over. It was explicitly an attempt to use the insights of Keynesian economics as a tool to enable world peace. Importantly, the conference assumed that prosperity was the surest route to social stability and international co-operation. Whatever the impact of their later actions, the institutions that were formed from this conference – the Bretton Woods institutions or international financial institutions

(IFIs), the International Bank for Reconstruction and Development, the International Monetary Fund (IMF), and the International Finance Corporation – were designed to disperse the benefits of economic planning across the world. This meeting also saw the creation of the General Agreement on Tariffs and Trade (GATT), planned to be a debating forum for international trade negotiations.

The international financial institutions have two key areas of responsibility – they are designed to induce international discipline and exchange-rate stabilisation and they are empowered to oversee international economic relations and to foster the expansion and balanced growth of international trade. The two areas complement each other. The first task is to establish and police the terms by which trade occurs, making sure that stable and predictable exchange rates can be maintained because everyone is subscribing to the same model of strict economic management. The second task, encouraging the growth of international trade while avoiding the turbulence of currency crises, needs the agreed practices of the first. For some of the world, this system works pretty well for a while. What is of interest to us here is how and why this is.

The International Monetary Fund is charged with the specific task of assuring the stability of exchange rates and with the responsibility to oversee the orderly adjustment of exchange rates if and when this becomes necessary. In the plan to remake the terms of the global economy, this is the bad-cop role. Whereas the World Bank is able to guarantee loans and play a supportive role to restructuring nations, the IMF sets and enforces the rules of international economic engagement. Most particularly, this entails keeping a strict hold over the system of fixed exchange rates – because confidence in this system is what guarantees international trade.

The IMF continued with this task until 1971 – when most of the world's currencies were floated following the United States' abandonment of the gold standard. The move to floating exchange rates altered the role of international financial institutions. There were still two complementary areas of activity, but now the stick-and-carrot management of the international economy became more interventionist.

In the terms of Bretton Woods, the IMF is the regulatory body of the international economy. Even after the demise of fixed exchange rates, the IMF continues to have responsibility for determining the rules and regulations governing the activities of member states. Initially the Fund was created to provide short-term balance-of-payments assistance for members who were having trouble with their external payments. After 1971, stabilising balance of payments problems became a much more complicated exercise. The highly contentious and interventionary role that the IMF has today developed as a response to these new circumstances.

As just noted, the World Bank has had a different role. It was empowered to provide financial resources for countries recovering from the ravages of the Second World War and for the economic growth of developing nations. Over time, co-operation between IFIs has become more institutionalised – so that the IMF relies on the World Bank's evaluation of the appropriateness of a country's medium-term investment programmes.

THE RISE OF NEO-LIBERAL ORTHODOXY

The heated debate about the evils and inequities of globalisation has focused on some quite particular aspects of trade and development, largely ignoring a whole range of globalised outcomes, the not-yet-decided impacts of cultural seepage and transnational migration, of all those global flows that do not take place through corporate means, not to mention the wayward interpretations and everyday appropriations of global culture that are emerging in so many places. The central criticisms of globalisation have not really focused their wrath on this diffuse culture of the global. What more immediately enrages the various forces of the anti-globalisation movement, as evidenced in written comment and protest venues, is the working of the global economy and the institutions which ensure that this economy continues to privilege richer and more powerful nations.

In fact, the particular set of relations that is critiqued by anti-globalisers is the outcome of a shift in the approach of international financial institutions. From the late 1970s, the IMF and the World Bank started to pursue policies informed by neo-liberal economic theories – known as the Washington Consensus. Reflecting the location of both IMF and World Bank, this idea of consensus indicated the close alignment between the government of the United States and the supposedly independent IFIs. The key components of the recommended policy certainly echoed the favoured development strategies of US policy makers – curtailing public expenditure, tax reform, financial liberalisation, competitive exchange rates, trade liberalisation, opening to foreign investment, privatisation, deregulation and protection of property rights. It was this ideological mission, carried out through the coercive use of economic assistance and advice, that has been identified as the enemy of the poor, the veil for remaking unequal global relations in our time. This was also the dogma that came in for attack from a host of former adherents to the project of pursuing global affluence through liberalised trade.

The Washington Consensus has become another of those bogeymen of recent debate, so much so that it is difficult to remember how anything like consensus was reached. For the purposes of understanding, it is worth reviewing the terms and background of this approach.

Through the 1970s the unspoken assumption that the Keynesian-influenced management of national economies and the terms of international trade was the best and only way came under attack. The attack was fuelled by a combination of ideological and intellectual fervour and dismay at the apparent failure of previous approaches to economic management in the face of new demons such as stagflation and other indicators of economic crisis. The next chapter will discuss the demise of Keynesian orthodoxy and the impact this has had on conceptions of economic management. This shift in economic orthodoxy extends to the activities of the IMF and the World Bank, and arguably has had its most resilient impact in the international arena. As a result, all kinds of austerity measures that have short-lived currency in advanced economies continue to be advised for developing nations (Chossudovsky, 1997).

The central characteristic of the Washington Consensus is its distrust of state-led development. This has been seen as inefficient for three main reasons. The first is the belief that protectionism damages local economies – protecting domestic producers reduces competition and creates inefficiency. Resulting goods are of a high cost and low quality and this is passed on to domestic consumers. The second is a concern that states do not create structures that are vulnerable to corruption or other self-serving activity at the expense of economic efficiency – state intervention is seen to encourage unproductive income-earning activity deriving from state regulations. The third is a doubt about the ability of the state to plan effectively for development – state regulations have the effect of discriminating against some sectors while protecting others, in a manner that may damage overall growth.

The remedy for all three potential problem areas is proposed through one consistent approach – the encouragement of the private sector and the liberalisation of economies. This conclusion is strongly informed by an ideological distrust of the state and a belief in the market, and, as a result, the advice given to economies in crisis calls into question the role of government in economic recovery. The three key proposals made to nations seeking help, regardless of any local factors, have been currency devaluation, rolling back the state and liberalisation of international trade.

These measures have been regarded as the route to economic health – a way of achieving low and stable levels of inflation alongside sustainable economic growth that would, eventually, trickle down to enrich all sections of society. All of this was in response to the stagflation suffered across the global economy in the 1970s – which was seen to be exacerbated, if not created, by state interventionist economic policies and the failures of Keynesianism. However, although much has been made of the shift to neo-liberalism, others have suggested that the Bretton Woods institutions have continued to pursue some consistent goals:

> The historic bloc pushing contemporary transnational liberalism nonetheless retains a fundamental continuity with the political project of the postwar hegemonic bloc. While the growth-oriented 'corporate liberalism' of the postwar decades and the hard-edged neoliberalism of more recent times may disagree on the terms of international openness, both share an underlying commitment to a more open world economy based on private ownership of the means of production and generalized commodity exchange. (Rupert, 2000, 44)

Despite changes in strategy, the key goals of global integration have remained – peace and prosperity through international trade. What has changed is the manner in which poor nations are cajoled into participation in the global economy. The Washington Consensus gave rise to the infamous structural adjustment programmes (SAPs) – and through this process the developing world increasingly learned to distrust the advice and motives of the international financial institutions.

The programmes of action propagated in response to the failures of Keynesian approaches resulted in fairly extreme economic effects. Whatever was hoped for in terms of future prosperity, the immediate impact of such measures was the infamous shock treatment:

> Shock therapy is a three-part cure. First, prices are liberalised, the exchange rate is lowered, and the economy is opened up to competition. Secondly,

credit and subsidies to loss-making industries are cancelled. This immediately cuts back the rate of growth of the money supply, reduces the budget deficit, and allows the imposition of fresh taxes based on money transactions. Finally, the main source of the excessive money-supply growth – the bloated public sector – is shut down or sold off for whatever price it will fetch. A country which accepts shock therapy would be entitled to foreign help to meet the 'transitional' costs of restructuring the economy, including the restructuring of its foreign debt. The crucial requirement for success is also the most difficult: a strong and legitimate state. The crisis needs to produce a new government, or a new regime, armed with the authority to tackle the problems which caused it. (Skidelsky, 1995, 141)

Skidelsky is writing primarily about the experience of the former Soviet Union, but his remarks describe the unhappy impact of shock therapy in many places. The economic tactics amount to a deflation so rapid it is almost immediate – pulling the plug on the various uncompetitive and inflationary activities that buoyed up economic activity. These packages of measures have come to be known as structural adjustment programmes – plans to restructure economies for effective participation in the global economy. Structural adjustment is the process by which the World Bank and the IMF base their lending to underdeveloped countries on certain conditions. The conditions must be agreed before any loan – so economic policies must be drafted with implementation plans that are regarded as acceptable by the IMF. In practice, this has tended to force a move to more market-orientated economic policies. For critics of structural adjustment and the Washington Consensus, this is another indication that an illogical and ideological obsession with the market overrides any concern for human welfare or social impact (Adepoju, 1993; Mihevc, 1995).

Structural adjustment programmes have been a highly coercive method of shunting national governments into such market-led policies. Previously there had been some adherence to 'policy dialogue' – with the World Bank advising countries on economic management and adjusting the funding of development projects according to the response to this advice. Structural adjustment programmes, on the other hand, have demanded much tighter 'conditionality' – in effect the IMF shapes the management of the developing economy for the period of the programme.

Another criticism of structural adjustment programmes has been that they adopt too uniform and formulaic an approach to all situations, without proper regard to the particular histories and issues of each location, and it is certainly true that programmes have concentrated on five key areas of reform, in what some would describe as a dogmatic fashion. The five areas can be summarised as:

1. allowing markets to work by allowing the free market to determine prices;
2. reducing state control on prices so that prices can reflect scarcity values;
3. moving state-held resources into the private sector;
4. reducing state spending as much as possible;
5. reforming state institutions towards the growth of the private sector.

In order for such objectives to be met, trade reform must be organised to eliminate import controls, reduce tariff levels and reduce existing restrictions on foreign investment. The exchange rate must be adjusted to ensure the profitability of export industries, that is at a level that renders domestic products sufficiently cheap to the international market, and interest rates must be set above the rate of inflation to reduce and then eliminate the excess demand for credit. All regulations of the labour market (such as minimum-wage controls or entitlements to job security) must be removed, along with any other protections of certain industries or goods. State activity must be privatised as much as possible.

In effect SAPs have forced the poor countries of the world to open their economies to the forces of the international market with no protection, have taken away the powers of national governments, and have allowed unmanaged privatisation of services while preventing state investment in essential services. The result has been extreme and biting poverty for many – in pursuit of a model of economic health that does not register this human cost.

RESISTING NEO-LIBERALISM

Given this experience, it is unsurprising that critiques of SAPs have been sustained and well developed, with many commentators and civil organisations arguing that structural adjustment has become another means through which the rich world can exploit the poor (Chussodovsky, 1997). Among the more well-known examples was the cross-country report produced by SAPRIN (Structural Adjustment Participatory Review International Network) – a work that eventually appeared as 'The Policy Roots of Economic Crisis and Poverty'. This project began in 1996 as a network of civil organisations working with the World Bank and national governments undertaking a multi-year investigation into the impact of SAPs. However, in August 2001 the World Bank withdrew its support and participation following a disagreement over the draft report. The SAPRIN report was the outcome of this research, published under the auspices of civil organisations without World Bank patronage.

The findings of the report question the effectivity of structural adjustment as a plan for development. More than this, the central claims of the SAP approach are shown to be, at best, not fully achieved, and, more likely, downright wrong. For our purposes, there are some key themes to review.

In terms of overall economic growth and well-being, SAPRIN found that in the countries studied, there had been an increasing dependence on imports. Even in countries where exports had increased, the import sector had experienced greater growth. Overall, there had been an increase in trade and current account deficits, leading to higher levels of foreign debt. Given that the whole point of structural adjustment is to make countries into sustainable businesses that can make money, not further increase debt and dependency, this is not a good outcome. To add to the problem, SAPRIN found that in many of the countries studied it was transnational corporations which benefited most from any export growth, and that domestic producers suffered accordingly.

SAPRIN identified few successes arising from the structural adjustment process. In terms of the impact on ordinary people, the findings showed a series of dangerous trends. Levels of employment worsened, real wages decreased and income distribution became even less equitable. The employment that remained was more insecure and employers gained more flexibility in their employment practices, and were therefore more likely to use hourly-paid contracts and other forms of employment that minimised benefits to workers. Women did badly as a result of labour market reforms, and there was an increase in the amount of work carried out by children and older people, as households sought to increase their dwindling incomes in any way possible. The reforms of the agricultural sector also exacerbated inequalities and led to a decline in food security. Overall, the promised improvements in productivity and competitiveness had not been achieved. Instead SAPs had become identified with drastic 'reforms' that appeared to yield few if any benefits to the general population, and which brought both suffering and social unrest to the countries under treatment.

THE WORLD BANK AND NEW MEASURES OF DEVELOPMENT

The widespread dissatisfaction and distrust created by the experience of structural adjustment programmes has entered popular and policy debates about development. When the IMF and World Bank are vilified as the tangible incarnation of a satanic people-eating capitalism, it is primarily SAPs that have caused such outrage. More recent moves towards encouraging country ownership and participation could be regarded as something like an attempt to put right previous mistakes (Thomas et al., 2000). This shift is most clearly embodied by the initiative of Poverty Reduction Strategy Papers (PRSPs) – although already this process has been described as a continuation of structural adjustment by some commentators (see Dembele, 2003). PRSPs emerged as a response to the criticisms of the tight conditionality of structural adjustment programmes which, in effect, left countries with little control over their own national economic policies. Partly in response to this criticism, the IMF and the World Bank presented PRSPs as an approach that would increase country ownership and empower participants in the development process. However, as others have pointed out, concepts such as ownership and empowerment are difficult to quantify, and the experience of previous contact with international financial institutions has led to a situation in which countries shape their policy and statements to anticipate IMF requirements, because it is easier to tell the Fund what it wants to hear in the first place than to go through a supposed process of negotiation in which individual countries have little leverage against the policy demands of international institutions (Stewart and Wang, 2003; Dembele, 2003).

The World Bank and IMF argue that PRSPs represent a number of important principles:

- country ownership and broad-based participation
- a pro-poor perspective that is orientated towards results
- a recognition that poverty is multidimensional
- a long-term poverty reduction perspective.

Although it is not stated explicitly, the underlying message is that this process will focus on reducing everyday poverty, not on creating an abstract notion of economic soundness which may fit certain ideological criteria, but which exacerbates the suffering of the population in the meantime. Understandably, critics have argued that these warm words may speak of the importance of poverty reduction, but still maintain a neo-liberal model of the world economy and of economic life in general. However, for our purposes, what is important to note is that such a shift in rhetoric and policy has taken place. The bullish arrogance of the Washington Consensus has undergone some adaptation, however slight that may be. This work seeks to understand the pressures that give rise to such changing perspectives, even among the most unchallengeable and powerful of global institutions.

Very recently, the World Bank has argued that development must be evaluated in terms of quality of impact, and not only in terms of the absolute extent of economic growth. This calls into question previous approaches to aid and development and opens a whole area of discussion about the relation between economic growth and everyday well-being. Most of all, it suggests that, despite all the efforts of Bretton Woods, participation in the international economy may not be the best or only indicator of improvements in ordinary people's lives. Even the World Bank is starting to express doubts about the social value of so-called free trade (Thomas et al., 2000).

OTHER IDEAS ABOUT GLOBALISATION

Although this is not a discussion of theories of globalisation as such, some central themes from the larger debate about globalisation and its impact on everyday life shape the work that follows. Here we shall take a short detour through debates that examine the cultural and social impact of globalisation. There is no attempt to provide an exhaustive account, only a few indicative points from a larger debate, selected for their relevance to later chapters.

The first theme is the suggestion that globalisation is something that cannot be avoided, whatever some may wish. The influential social theorist, Zygmunt Bauman, provides an overview of ideas about globalisation starting out from this theme:

> For everybody, though, 'globalization' is the intractable fate of the world, an irreversible process; it is also a process which affects us all in the same measure and in the same way. We are all being 'globalized' – and being 'globalized' means much the same to all who 'globalized' are. (Bauman, 1998, 1)

Bauman is speaking of the manner in which globalisation has become the descriptor of our time, of what it means to be alive right now. The present work takes that sense of intractability and irreversibility as a starting point: globalisation is the only game in town. There is no way under, over or around it, for any of us. The chapters that follow look at what that inevitability creates – a world where even the least equipped regions must enter the global maelstrom somehow or other. However, for people and places with little power and few resources, the manner of this entry is decided elsewhere, on other people's terms. This volume argues that being globalised does not mean the same to all. On the contrary, where and who you are will shape your experience of being globalised to such an extent that it can be hard to chart the continuity between different moments.

My own background is in the field of cultural analysis, and my contact with ideas of the global has been mediated through this arena. Unlike the more deterministic accounts of financial institutions and economic agreements, discussion of global integration in the cultural sphere has focused on mixed-up and multi-directional flows and on the roles played by ordinary people and their tastes and habits in reshaping the global. Central to this has been a consideration of the impact of migration on everyday life for all kinds of people and in all kinds of places. In his influential account of the cultural impact of globalisation, Arjun Appadurai identifies the lived experience of diaspora as a key component of global cultures and consciousness.

> The story of mass migrations (voluntary and forced) is hardly a new feature of human history. But when it is juxtaposed with the rapid flow of mass-mediated images, scripts, and sensations, we have a new order of instability in the production of modern subjectivities. As Turkish guest workers in Germany watch Turkish films in their German flats, as Koreans in Philadelphia watch the 1988 Olympics in Seoul through satellite feeds from Korea, and as Pakistani cabdrivers in Chicago listen to cassettes of sermons recorded in mosques in Pakistan or Iran, we see moving images meet deterritorialized viewers. These create diasporic public spheres, phenomena that confound theories that depend on the continued salience of the nation-state as the key arbiter of important social changes. (Appadurai, 1996, 4)

The emerging canon of globalisation literature has identified the spread of global media and technology as a key aspect of what differentiates our era from earlier periods of global interchange

(Castells, 1996). Now, people from many places can imagine themselves as part of a larger world, dream the dreams of many other locations and communicate with others who live different lives in faraway places. Whatever the intentions of international agreements and institutions, the practice of global integration is a haphazard and human process. The setting of exchange rates may play a central role in trade and stability, but it is the movement of people that has enabled many of the opportunities of the global, including the much vaunted economic opportunities. Media and technology allow the development of a global consciousness, so that we move through the world intensely aware of our connections to a larger global sphere, but it is the movement of people that has animated that consciousness. Without migration and the unpredictable adaptation and sharing that it brings, no amount of imagery can make us feel globalised in the particular manner of our time, a manner that infuses our everyday consciousness with such intensity. Others have described this intensity of experience as a mixture of technological and economic change. Will Hutton and Anthony Giddens, both famous for their ability to read the key symptoms of social change, describe this moment in these terms:

> What gives contemporary change its power and momentum is in the economic, political and cultural change summed up by the term 'globalisation'. It is the interaction of extraordinary technological innovation combined with world-wide reach driven by a global capitalism that gives today's change its particular complexion. It has now a speed, inevitability and force that it has not had before. (Hutton and Giddens, 2000, vii)

This is the contemporary equivalent of everything solid melting into air, a rapid world-shift that seems to encompass all spheres of life. The cultural accounts of globalisation tap into this sense of urgency, which is both exciting and alarming – the feeling of being caught in a whirlwind where many things are possible, but little is stable. These are processes of change that may not be new, but which have taken on a new significance, because now the changes are so quick and unavoidable and pervasive. 'Globalisation is so powerful an idea because of the sense of there being no escape. It's coming down the tracks straight at you.' (Hutton and Giddens, 2000, 4)

This, unfortunately, represents another theme of the debate – the sense that globalisation is beyond human control, or at least the control of ordinary individuals. This aspect of the discussion contributes to the feeling of impotence and helplessness that suffuses so much of the commentary on globalisation, as if we are all caught in the headlights of global processes, transfixed by what we cannot avoid and cannot change. These are the two broad areas of emphasis in the debate – one suggesting that globalised consciousness is a matter of everyday cultures that meld migration and new technologies, the other viewing globalisation as a process determined from above by forces beyond our control. Perhaps predictably, this work agrees with aspects of both accounts – recognising that the structures of globalisation have been formed by larger and resilient forces, but maintaining that the manner in which we react to such structures is always open to human innovation.

In fact, the culturally inflected accounts of globalisation also identify economic change as the motor of all this extensive change. Something has shifted in the processes of the global economy, and while this shift may not be one guided or controlled by international financial institutions alone, it is one that has a wide-ranging, if not universal, impact:

> The transmission system for all these changes is a market capitalism, combined with global advances in communications, which is now unchallenged as the means through which the world organizes its economy and society. The collapse of communism, which for all its grotesque defects and brutalities had the unsung merit of taking the more brutal edge off capitalism in its effort to triumph in its great ideological battle with its enemy, has allowed a resurgence in a tougher, harder and more global capitalism. The quest for markets is as relentless as the growth of private corporate power; inequality has widened, especially in the Anglo-Saxon economies in the vanguard of globalisation, as the rewards for managerial and technological skills have exploded while those at the bottom have been exposed to an emerging world market in labour. (Hutton and Giddens, 2000, viii)

Not all accounts take the collapse of communism as a founding moment for the advent of a freshly unbridled capitalism. More celebratory accounts focus on the momentum of capitalist development – the possibilities of new technologies, the accelerating pace of transactions, the increasing mobility of capital – and sometimes suggest that the demise of the Soviet Union is another victory for this unstoppable motor of progress. This volume takes the break up of the Soviet bloc as a key moment of change – most of what is discussed here can be traced back to the end of the Cold

War – but remains agnostic on the question of whether the demise of the Soviet Union was a cause of this change, or another example of the extent of the change. Either way we all enter a time when capital becomes so flighty that it loses all ties to and responsibilities towards a place, and as a result previous strategies for tempering the excesses of the profit motive no longer have the same bite. Instead, power becomes much more closely linked to the ability to move around. Previously, resistance to exploitation has relied upon the leverage of place, whether that be workplace or locality. 'In the post-space-war world, mobility has become the most powerful and most coveted stratifying factor; the stuff of which the new, increasingly world-wide, social, political, economic and cultural hierarchies are daily built and rebuilt.' (Bauman, 1998, 9)

Bauman argues that the ability to be mobile at will and of your own volition is the defining characteristic of privilege and power in this new age. The poor and the excluded must stay put, or move when forced, with little control over the nature of that movement. Mobility is the attribute that allows people to make the most of global integration and to ride globalisation as an opportunity and an adventure, rather than a disaster that must be suffered.

> There is a new asymmetry emerging between the exterritorial nature of power and the continuing territoriality of the 'whole life' – which the now unanchored power, able to move at short notice or without warning, is free to exploit and abandon to the consequences of that exploitation. Shedding the responsibility for the consequences is the most coveted and cherished gain which the new mobility brings to free-floating, locally unbound capital. (Bauman, 1998, 9)

Capital has become transnational, without loyalty to any place or constraint from any state. This means that previous models of economic management, including the ideas that inform the Bretton Woods institutions, can no longer be relied upon. National governments have far more limited influence over the domestic economy as capital becomes more mobile – attempts to protect the interests of the population through taxation or labour rights or management of spending levels can now all be circumvented by corporate interests that choose to move. As a result, the business of national government increasingly consists of an ongoing negotiation with global economic forces, with the maintenance of market confidence becoming a key consideration of any policy decision.

Linked to this process, there is a wider reworking of the scope and influence of the state. Although globalisation has not abolished the nation-state, the authority of the state has been adapted in relation to other forces. Armed conflict combined with failures of economic and social infrastructures has wiped out any recognisable state in some places, as shown by the unhappy experiences of Somalia, Sierra Leone and Congo, among all too many others. In other places, even powerful states find their power curtailed by new global actors. In his discussion of what he terms 'the New Century' – meaning the world that begins after the short twentieth century is brought to an end by the fall of the Berlin Wall – the eminent historian Eric Hobsbawm links this shift not only to economic influence, but also to that most treasured of state powers, the right to wield force:

> I think that both this reversal in the process of strengthening nation-states over several centuries and the disintegration and effective disappearance of some states are linked to the sovereign state's loss of its virtual monopoly over coercive force. (Hobsbawm, 2000, 36)

A later chapter will discuss in more detail the emergence of new forms of wars and the role of non-state actors in armed conflict. However, it is the larger suggestion that the state is, after centuries of ascendance, in retreat that centrally informs this work. When the international community expresses panic and concern about the shadow trades that take place alongside globalisation, it is these spaces of disintegrating states that are regarded as the sources of danger. Hobsbawm argues, as do others, that these disappearing states uncover the never-settled boundary and sovereignty disputes of an earlier imperial order:

> ... the disintegration of states in these regions of the world is mainly the result of the collapse of the colonial empires, of the end of the era in which the great European powers controlled large portions of the world, where they had found non-state-governed societies, and had imposed a degree of external and internal order. (Hobsbawm, 2000, 36)

Despite the residual imperial tone of this account, this is a reminder that the twentieth-century map of the world includes borders and states that have been imposed by the retreating imperial powers. The power-play of the Cold War maintained a kind of order in these uncomfortable structures, often through the patronage of one authoritarian regime or another. The end of this uneasy ordering brings on a fresh phase of unravelling states:

> This creates serious problems in relations with the other parts of the globe where this is not occurring: Europe, America, and Eastern Asia. It raises the question of interaction between the world where the state exists and the world where it does not. (Hobsbawm, 2000, 37)

This interaction could be seen as that between formal and informal aspects of global integration, between places that appear to be playing by international rules and those that cannot. Ultimately, this is the connecting theme of the whole book – the fearful possibility that this interaction will allow the unstable, fragmented and unruly business of failing states to seep into the rest of the world. The irony is, of course, that everyone knows that this is how globalisation works. 'The idea that all nation-states are to some extent bedeviled by globalized movements of arms, moneys, diseases, and ideologies is also hardly news in the era of the multinational corporation.' (Appadurai, 1996, 19)

GETTING INTO GLOBAL NETWORKS

Much of the discussion surrounding the formal institutions of the global economy seems to assume that there is one route of entry into this activity that is open and suitable for all, one route to development, one route to prosperity, one route to freedom. Although fashions have changed in terms of whether this route is to be enabled by economic planning or a loosening of trade barriers, the idea that there is one international market and one manner of participation in it has gone almost unchallenged.

My interest in this volume concerns the alternative routes to economic participation that emerge in the nooks and crannies of globalisation. Whatever the hype, it is pretty clear that many regions of the world enter the realm of international trade through various unorthodox and half-acknowledged practices. In some ways, this rush to reach the market whatever the consequences would seem to support some of the most celebratory contentions of globalisation-speak. 'Look, this really is irresistible and there is only one path to development and global trade is it.' Yet the route that is taken by significant portions of the poor and less rich world is nothing like the models of development put forward by the IMF or the World Bank, in any of their incarnations across the years.

One of the most noticeable characteristics of this unorthodox route to globalisation is that these processes are not led by states or even by nations. This is the arena of those new heroes or anti-heroes, the non-state actors. There is an extensive debate about the challenges raised by these new global players, and some of this literature will be reviewed later (see in particular Higgott, Underhill and Bieler, 2000). The other linking characteristic is the propensity towards the more dangerous kinds of trade – the kind of commerce that is often illegal, or, even when just about non-criminal, the kind of business that is risky, dirty and hard to make respectable on any terms. So, as always, the poor world absorbs risk for the rich. We may all be interlinked and interconnected nodal points on an enormous global network, but for some this entails huge amounts of danger.

Policy makers have identified this interconnection between different aspects of dangerous trade, but largely as a challenge for law enforcement. We have all learned that there is a chain of association between the drug trade and the gun trade, between organised crime and the traffic in illegal migrants, between forced labour in the urban centres of the West and the desperation arising from global integration. These interlinked spectres have come to animate the anxious imagination of the globalised West. If we picture globalisation proper as a series of branded goods – all trainers, burgers and fizzy drinks – then the dangers of these other illicit commodities are always lurking in the shadows. If globalisation has been an exciting adventure, then these are the bogeymen that threaten to spoil it.

The discussion that follows focuses on the most obvious examples, the stories that have already permeated popular consciousness and policy discussion. These are not the only forms of dangerous illegality that can be fostered unexpectedly within the crevices of global integration – part of what is being described is the desperate innovation of places that cannot compete on the terms of the formal economy. The chapters that follow are organised around key themes in the developing mythology around the dangers of the globalised poor – the fear of organised crime, of the drug trade, of the trade in arms, of the movement of people. The anxieties of the rich world reveal a sense of threat, centred around these same depictions of crime, drugs, arms and immigrants. This sense of pervasive fear suggests that there may be an alternative logic to globalisation, where even the winners in the global economy fear that this skewed arrangement cannot go on.

Since the demise of the Soviet bloc there has been a growing interest in the role that organised crime might play in any transition to a market led economy. For a time it seemed that gangsterism might be rehabilitated, regarded as little more than a slightly over-enthusiastic form of entrepreneurialism, perhaps even an example of an indigenous take-up of a market. This was all in the immediate aftermath of Soviet decline, and probably represents yet another example of the brash triumphalism that seeped into too much economic commentary during this time. Since then the unfurling disarray of so much of Eastern Europe has tempered hopes that transitional economies could become the new miracles of capitalism. Instead there are fears that these Mafia-style practices have become so powerful in this region that they will seep into the financial dealings of other parts of the world.

Similarly, the drug trade is portrayed as a transnational traffic in evil, exploiting the vulnerabilities of the young across the developed world. It is clear that the renegotiated boundaries of our globalising world have enabled the drug trade to become a truly global industry. It is not at all clear that it is possible to fight a successful war against drugs and, at the same time, promulgate a version of global integration that meets only the interests of rich nations.

The trade in arms has undergone significant adaptation with the end of the Cold War. While many saw this moment as an opportunity to reverse the long escalation in the arms race, in practice the arms industry has remade itself for new circumstances. The emergence of non-state actors as buyers of arms has rendered this trade in carnage an unruly and unpredictable business – no longer even constrained by the imperfect rules of international diplomacy. As a result, deadly small arms and even deadlier 'weapons of mass destruction' circulate the world freely, leaving all too little trace of their journeys. As attempts at arms control have relied on states to police such activity, it seems that the new arms trade defies even such minimal regulation.

My previous research has been in the politics of race and of sexuality. I've been interested in the ways that these structures of human life are imagined and represented, and in charting the ways in which material changes are registered and represented in the iconography of popular representation. Through this earlier research, I became increasingly aware that a variety of stories about the illicit movement of people were forming an alternative strand in the literature of globalisation. Such work identifies new forms of migration and the cultural impact of these movements, or documents the unhappy stories of women trafficked for sex work as an unforeseen outcome of global restructuring. Alongside the broad macro-stories of economic processes and political realignment, these more everyday concerns about bodies and identities, about sex and race, about stock and contamination, continued to animate everyday understandings of the global. The present work is my attempt to chart some connections between the abstractions of international economy and the irrational fearfulness of everyday global living.

In part this remains a work about representation. I remain convinced that the manner in which fear is articulated can offer a route into understanding the material context of that fear. As a teacher, I want my students to understand that these new monsters do not arise from nowhere, that there is some correlation between real events and these media caricatures. Equally, I try to show them the continuity between the scare stories of previous eras and the hysterical demons that haunt our popular imaginations. What follows relies on the scholarship of many others, but I hope that my collation of this disparate material will introduce new audiences to these ideas. I also hope that the juxtaposition of debates from very different areas may lead to fresh insights and an extension and popularisation of these important issues.

Unlike some other commentators, I do not long for a return to the time before globalisation. And although I may wish and pray for the emergence of a new revolutionary subject who is equipped for the struggle against global capital, I am also sceptical about these totalised narratives of redemption. I know that there are no saviours to come galloping over the hilltop of history, no inevitable victories, no unified struggle that can link us all in all times and all places. What I do think is that horror must throw up resistance and that people will always struggle for some better way of living, using whatever resources are available to them. One strand of this book began with a conversation I had with my father. I asked him, because he knows more about these things than I do, whether structural adjustment programmes had worked anywhere in the world? After a little thought, he replied that no, he didn't think they had. However huge the disparity in power between international institutions and poor nations seeking help, that just didn't seem sustainable to me. Somewhere somehow something had got to give.

As I read more in this area, I realised that that sense of having reached the precipice was being articulated in many places. The most well-known exponents have become darlings of the anti-capitalist movement. Yet other sources in more unlikely locations echo the suggestion that globalisation cannot go on in its present form. This is not at all to suggest that globalisation cannot go on. Only that it cannot be like this indefinitely. The chapters that follow outline some key areas of anxiety in the global economy – areas that capture the imaginations of both public and policy makers and which give rise to a range of sometimes desperate responses. None of this means that a new world is assured; but it does suggest that what exists now is more fragile than we realise.

2
Underbelly of the Global

The official institutions of globalisation have their own public relations machine. The pronouncements of First World governments, policy statements from a range of organisations and the media commentary of various experts all combine to perpetuate a certain account of global integration. This largely celebratory account is the one that has entered popular discourse, although an array of anti-globalisation campaigns are in the process of challenging it. Here I want to suggest that this institution-led integration is real and substantial, but is not at all the only story in town. In fact, this official globalisation has relied upon another parallel set of processes, an undercurrent of less celebrated activities that buoys up and supplements the official economy.

In his wide-ranging scholarly snapshot of the world at the turn of the century, Manuel Castells identifies a parallel world that emerges alongside the flashing lights and high jinx of the informational economy, a set of processes that consigns large parts of the world's population to what he terms the black holes of social exclusion. This is the so-called Fourth World, a non-network of impoverished regions that includes major parts of the 'Third World', but which also exists in the pockets of poverty that exist in every country and in every city.

Against this absolute exclusion, where some people and places fall out of this new networked world altogether, Castells also identifies another parallel universe. Or, if not quite parallel, then in the shadows – the underbelly of globalism. Castells calls this phenomenon the global criminal economy, but similar processes are identified by other writers as the shadow economy, or even the informal economy (Fiorentini and Peltzman, 1995; Jung, 2003). And although he does not make this argument explicitly, there is an implication in Castells' work that this is the alternative to the poverty of the Fourth World.

In Castells' telling, this criminal economy is characterised as one interconnected industry: 'the criminal economy has expanded its realm to an extraordinary diversity of operations, making it an increasingly diversified and interconnected, global industry.' (Castells, 1998, 174) Castells goes on to outline the varied activities of this global industry of transnational organised crime, identifying the themes which also inform the structure of this book. However, rather than view this criminal economy as one firm or cartel of firms, I want to argue that this range of activity represents an alternative route into the global economy. If the emerging networks of global capital consign some to exclusion from participation in all the good things of life, then the criminal economy seems to offer reintegration for these lost black holes.

It is nevertheless true that this shadow economy consists, largely, of a range of criminal activity. Here we see the illicit traffic in drugs and arms, the trafficking of illegal immigrants, the trafficking of women and children for sex work and other forms of bonded labour, the trade in body parts and the laundering of money, all variations of the trade in despair somehow made respectable. However, what distinguishes this global criminal economy is not its criminality as such but its ability to connect this illicit trade to the formal networks of the global economy proper. In fact, not all aspects of the shadow economy are illegal, as the later discussion of the arms trade will show.

If anything links these different kinds of business, it is that age-old dream of easy money, accompanied by the equally age-old risk to life and limb that goes along with anything too profitable. Here I want to consider what is peculiar to these dangerous and profitable endeavours in the era of the global. Clearly, there is nothing particularly new about any of these kinds of business. Human desperation has given rise to new opportunities for profit for as long as commerce has existed. Similarly, the trade in drugs or arms is nothing new. The globalised reach of organised crime builds on the national and regional successes of earlier incarnations of the Family. There is not a single aspect of this underbelly of globalism that cannot also be found in previous times.

What then, is the point of this discussion? What I am trying to describe here is the extent to which the transnational expansion of these dangerous trades has come to form part of the essential machinery of globalisation as we know it. This is the activity that has been enabled by the intervention of international institutions, so that programmes for economic recovery that push for marketisation at the expense of all else make new spaces for the entrepreneurial skills of the criminal. That is one strand of the discussion that spans the volume, the idea that a certain model of economic liberalisation cannot help but free illicit trade as it frees all other barriers to trade. The other strand is less often discussed. This is the suggestion that what we call globalisation is the outcome of some very particular recent historical events, most importantly the settlements around international institutions that emerged at the end of the Second World War. Although the Bretton Woods agreement placed economic stability at the heart of global co-operation, with trade forming the basis on which peace, diplomacy and international law could thrive, the recent past shows us that the economy alone does not determine all other structures of international interaction. Something like political or territorial considerations retain some autonomy from purely economic imperatives, and the decisions taken in this other arena also give shape to global integration as we know it.

The rapid expansion of globalisation-speak has led to a revisiting of the discourse of economics in a wide range of popular, policy and academic debate (Goddard, Passe-Smith and Conklin, 1996; Klein, 2002). After a period where the recourse to economic analysis when examining social or cultural phenomena was regarded as a stuffy and anachronistic hang up with Marxism, now almost all commentaries on contemporary events require some level of economic literacy. The opening of world markets has reminded us all of the role of international trade in determining everyday life. I have been among the people who have welcomed this return of an economic analysis, after such a long period of signs without referents and culture without determinant. I like the idea that to understand Hollywood you must also understand the IMF. However, I am concerned that we are in danger of falling into a new form of economism, where a mythical and monolithic version of the economy is portrayed as the monster that shapes all other aspects of life, while it itself is shaped by nothing other than its own motor of expansion. The global economy that we now experience has emerged through the interaction of a certain geopolitics and a certain brand of economics. In addition, some of the inevitably unexpected events of history have reshaped this interaction, so that what we now experience is nothing much like what was imagined at Bretton Woods. The second important strand in this work discusses the place of superpower foreign policy in the world that emerges after the Cold War. By this I mean both the legacy of Cold War strategies and the new doctrines that are coming to animate contemporary global politics.

GLOBAL INTEGRATION BY OTHER MEANS

In the previous chapter, we outlined the most optimistic dreams of globalisation. This is the world in which international institutions really do create and sustain a peaceful global community. Many of the critiques of globalisation begin by dismantling this myth (Germain, 2000). The interventions of the IMF and the World Bank clearly have failed to make poverty a thing of the past. Although there are variations within these two organisations, and quite a wide disparity between the approach of the IMF and the Bank, increasingly both have come to be portrayed as the villains of the piece. Far from helping the poor, these big institutions are seen to make interventions that exacerbate poverty and suffering. It seems important for us to remember how far this is from the original dreams of Bretton Woods.

The one aspect of that Bretton Woods fantasy that does appear to have come true is the integration of the world economy. Although trade continues to be very far from free and fair, and long-standing inequalities of power and resources continue to shape transactions between nations and regions, almost all nations now look to participation in the global economy as a route to prosperity. Of course, the question is how this participation takes place.

In order to participate in a fantasy of free trade as depicted in the Bretton Woods agreement, or even more recently in the agreements reached through the World Trade Organisation, states must have a certain level of infrastructure and control over the economic activity within their borders. The conception of what can constitute a healthy economy has been shaped deeply by the vision of the IMF. Any nation wishing to participate in the world economy with the support of international institutions had only to look to the five concerns at the heart of the IMF – here was a checklist of what was expected in an ideal economic world. Although the chorus of convertibility, exchange, currency, credit and adjustment are identified as lubricants for international trade, these criteria also represent an only thinly-veiled prescription for national development. This has been the framework for the unhappy structural adjustment programmes – but even without this direct and coercive intervention, poorer nations could not help but tailor their ideas of development around at least some of these themes.

A key question for any nation aspiring to development has been the issue of international trade. Despite the deep belief that self-sufficiency was an essential component of the struggle against colonialism, few countries were able to approach economic planning without making some provision for international trade. While there may have been resistance to the suggestion of convertibility and exchange – because both rich and poor nations were reluctant to relinquish the leverage of controlling their own currency rates – the relative stability offered by the dollar standard seemed to answer everyone's needs.

Of course, for most of the poor world international trade represented little more than a necessary evil. The catchphrase of decolonisation is self-reliance, not global integration (Winters, 2003). Formerly colonised nations were painfully aware that they had been made into hyper-exploited outposts of the occupier's national economy. In this context, international trade is recognised already as yet another version of business as usual. The rich world buys on its terms, and equally sells back on its own terms as well, in its own currency and within its own framework of trade. Yet newly independent nations could not give up on international trade altogether. The best that could be hoped for, especially if self-reliance was ever to be reached, was to enter international trade on less destabilising and disempowering terms.

This defensive engagement with the global market entailed strategies that echoed the prescriptions of international institutions. Newly independent nations valued their access to foreign currency as a useful tool for internal economic management. However, the prescribed strategies were not always readily achievable. Instead, for some regions, criminal trade offered a more effective and developed form of local business. Castells explains the development strategies of Latin American drug cartels in these terms:

> They aimed essentially at exports to the United States, later to Europe, then to the whole world. Their strategies were, in fact, a peculiar adaptation of IMF-inspired export-oriented, growth policies toward the actual ability of some Latin American regions to compete in the high-technology environment of the new global economy. (Castells, 1998, 173)

TRYING TO MAKE DEVELOPMENT WORK

Although the terms of international institutions have been defined tightly from the viewpoint of the more powerful nations, the poor and developing world has done its best to make development work. After all, who could be against development? To be against development is to be against prosperity and security, to accept that lifelong poverty is the inescapable destiny of some parts of the world. There seem to be few other options for nations seeking to better the lives of their populations, although there has been a considerable and convincing critique of both the concept and the practices of development in recent years (see Rahnema and Bawtree, 1997).

However, it would be a mistake to forget too quickly the investments that the poor world itself has had in the vision of development. Emerging into the new global relations that were created in the aftermath of the Second World War, nations that were newly independent and nations still struggling for independence, as well as nations broken apart from the processes of war, all aspired to progress through development. Even the 'winners', those among the allied nations who retained some infrastructure at the war's end, termed this a period of reconstruction. For a while, development was the only game in town. In his review of the post-1945 histories of the Third World, Mike Mason describes the prevalence of a trade-and-industry conception of development: 'You couldn't be developed, or be developing, if you didn't have industry and proper trade. Communists poring over five-year plans and fascists boasting of trains running on time were alike concerned with orderly development.' (Mason, 1997, 5)

Although development focused on economic matters and, more importantly, prioritised certain conceptions of national economic development above any more nuanced reading of everyday living conditions, the promise of progress proved impossible to refuse. It is all too easy to dismiss this as yet another indication of the global power of a mythically unified capitalist class. But I think it is worth reminding ourselves that national liberation movements across the poor world, movements that spanned a wide range of political influences and allegiances, all viewed the economic betterment of their populations as a central goal (Mason, 1997). While there have been competing accounts of the exact manner in which wealth was extracted from the colonial relation, there has been a great deal of consensus about how the effects of colonisation might be overcome.

The only alternative has been to build national economies – almost exclusively through assorted attempts to industrialise, to capitalise on natural resources and local industries, and to harness the nation to technological development as a route to economic progress. Newly independent nations were looking for their own industrial revolution, their own leap from variously functioning agrarian

economies to mass-producing industrialisation that could compete
with the economic power of their former colonisers:

> Its [the Third World's] ideological core was the notion of state led
> industrialisation. This drew its inspiration from nineteenth-century economic
> nationalism, first elaborated in opposition to Britain's 'free-trade imperialism',
> to which was added a belief in Soviet-style planning. The strategy would
> enable poor countries to escape from neocolonial domination. (Skidelsky,
> 1995, 8)

Despite Skidelsky's mocking tone, his summary is apt. Industrialisation is seen to offer a means of creating affluence within nations
and as a route to international participation, hopefully with defences
against the intrusions of neo-colonial corporate domination. In
practice, of course, we have seen that attempts to nurture national
industrialisation, and, at the same time, safeguard against the
creeping colonisation of foreign companies, have not proved sustainable. International institutions, while in thrall to the so-called
Washington Consensus, have suggested that the state protection
designed to allow the development of indigenous industry stifles
the innovation and efficiency necessary for competition. Yet the
proposed solution of liberalising economies and dismantling all
protection of indigenous firms has led to a wholesale destruction of
this economic infrastructure. Such restructuring has led to unfortunate outcomes across the poor world, from the crisis of agriculture
in Somalia to the resurgence of infectious disease and destruction of
the health system in Vietnam to the impact of international debt in
Brazil (Chossudovsky, 1997).

It is also true to say that much of the attempted industrialisation
of newly independent nations has not been able to produce goods
that can compete in the global market. This raises the question of
whether, quite apart from the ideologically inspired pressures exerted
by international institutions, it is possible for any nation to get along
without engaging in international trade.

POOR-WORLD NATION-BUILDING – APPROACHES TO DEVELOPMENT

Attempts at development have been largely state-led – developing
nations may be doing their best to accommodate the various
demands and specifications of international financial institutions,

but this accommodation has taken place through the vehicle of state management:

> Central to the economic achievements of the South was an activist state or public sector. In some countries, the state sector was the engine of the development process. In others, state support was critical to the success of domestic businesses wishing to compete against foreign capital. While private ownership of land, resources, and enterprises was the rule in most of the newly independent societies of the South, and economic exchange was largely mediated by the market, government intervention in economic life was pervasive, and the state had a strategic role in economic transformation. (Bello and Cunningham, 1994)

What is missing from this account is any acknowledgement that this approach has not been limited to the South. Europe was remade in the aftermath of the Second World War through precisely these forms of Keynesian-style state interventions in economic life. Even the United States, which emerged from the war as the unassailable economic power in the world, followed these principles of economic management and development in the post-war years.

Given this, it is unsurprising that nations wishing to emulate the relative affluence of the West employed similar tactics of economic management. In fact, it is precisely this belief in the power of the state to shape the economy that drove the dream of development in newly independent nations. If the state does not have this ability, what value is there in independence? We will go on to discuss the suggestion that formal independence can mask the continuance of other forms of domination in a later chapter.

PERVERSE DEVELOPMENT

Much of what follows reveals the weaknesses of state attempts to manage and control their economies. Some parts of the South employed versions of Keynesian economic management to some positive effect, and became, if not rivals to the West, economic powers within their own regions. Our later discussion of the rivalry between India and Pakistan demonstrates one example of this process. Others, however, barely developed the machinery of a state, let alone executed plans for economic development – it should come as no surprise that this includes areas of long-running conflict such as Afghanistan and Somalia.

For these places that are not equipped for state-led development – either because there is no effective state, or because what state there was has collapsed or dissolved, or because conflict disrupts all effective government – different patterns of economic development emerged.

> There is no doubt that the criminal economy represents a sizeable, and most dynamic, segment of Latin American economies in this end of millennium. Moreover, unlike traditional patterns of internationalization of production and trade in Latin America, this is a Latin American controlled, export-oriented industry, with proven global competitiveness. (Castells, 1998, 194)

In a sense, this is a confirmation of the power of the market. Regions that find themselves unable to compete in mainstream forms of industry and trade diversify into more risky forms of business. However, although this may be industry that is initiated in the region, it is rarely organised through the state. More often, the perverse economy bypasses states which are already weak and ineffective, in the process setting in motion a form of development that exacerbates the erosion of the state. The criminal economy highlights the weakness of states in key areas – maintaining law and order, controlling and guiding economic activity, providing effective government or services. In a previous era, these failings could be disguised through the international recognition that came from superpower patronage – the population would suffer, but the pretence of functioning government could survive:

> The idea of states, and of nations, is now globalised. Successor states are created by colonisation and by the anticolonial struggle for control of the colonial state and territory. Some poorer third-world states depend for their existence on the fiction of sovereignty, on international recognition within a state system and on international aid including military aid. The end of the Cold War removed a strategic motive for great-power propping up of otherwise fictional states. (Pettman, 1996, 80)

CREATING AN ALTERNATIVE GLOBAL ELITE

As formerly colonised nations have pursued their various conceptions of development, there has been an escalating discussion of the possible drawbacks of aping Western economies and cultures.

Strangely, it is the cultural argument that is better known and, perhaps, more widely accepted. The experience of decolonisation has focused attention on the role of culture – because even when direct political control ended, it was clear that the cultural impact of colonisation continued to shape the possibilities of independent nations (Tomlinson, 1991).

The resulting critiques of Westernisation and cultural imperialism have gained considerable credence. Looking at the Western-educated elites of the developing world, at the cultural and educational infrastructures that retain the shadow of colonial influence and the slow-drip of transnational media into everyone's consciousness, who would not accept that cultural processes can maintain colonial relations by other means? We have come to accept that the cultural products and aspirations of the West will shape everyday consciousness in many parts of the world.

But surely economic development is another matter? Transnational media may encourage us all to want too much – too much stuff, too much variety, too much that is unattainable – but discussion of economic development has not been led by this kind of consumer-dreamland demand. Economic development – the development that cannot be refused – has been concerned with the life-and-death issues of food distribution and infant mortality, of dignity and well-being for all throughout their lives. How can such aspirations be dismissed as an imposition of Western culture?

It takes some audacity to argue that planning for economic growth is a continuation of imperialism by other means. Of course, there have been flashes of this audacity in anti-colonial struggles, such as the Gandhian conception of self-sufficiency. However, despite the warnings of such thinkers, when faced with the challenges of meeting national aspirations there seemed to be few alternatives to rapid industrialisation by any means possible.

This process of quick and sometimes desperate restructuring in order to develop economies on a Western model has led, some argue inevitably, to a variety of tensions. Most problematically, it is not at all apparent that this approach has improved the situation of the poor. National economies may have grown, but the benefits of this growth have not been felt throughout societies (Douthwaite, 1992).

Some of the most unforgiving critiques have suggested that this is no accident. Economic development on the model of industrialisation, growth and exportation recreates the national elite as a national bourgeois class – even if these are people who gain power and influence from older social structures. At its worst, the poor swap one form of domination for another and may never register the difference that independent nationhood makes. The elite, on the other hand, purport to pursue the national interest, yet become increasingly tied into a global class interest. In this account, the economic development that is driven by the elite is little more than colonial exploitation by proxy. There may be progress for those close to the governing class, but for everyone else, it is just business as usual.

DEVELOPMENT AND THE CREATION OF A NATIONAL ELITE

Against this very stark account, others have suggested that there has been substantial improvement in the living conditions of many in the previously poor world. Paul Krugman has argued that there came a moment sometime in the 1970s when the lower wage costs of developing countries suddenly become a sufficient incentive for some manufacturers to move their production. Until then, cheap wages had not been enough to compete with the developed world:

> The entrenched advantages of advanced nations – their infrastructure and technical know-how, the vastly larger size of their markets and their proximity to suppliers of key components, their political stability and the subtle but crucial social adaptations that are necessary to operate an efficient economy – seemed to outweigh even a ten- or twentyfold disparity in wage rates. (Krugman, 1999, 16)

Then somehow this changes, for some industries at least. In his discussion of recent currency crises and what they can teach us about the shape and dynamic of the global economy, Krugman considers the moment at which some developing nations become exporters of manufactured goods and acknowledges that we do not know exactly how this change comes about – perhaps some combination of better communications technologies and cheaper travel, and a lowering of tariff barriers. Whatever the reasons, some countries that have previously exported only raw materials, now enter the international trade in manufactured goods, most notably clothing and sports shoes. This change is not at all pleasant. We are talking about the industries that provoke anti-sweatshop campaigns and criticism of the failure to maintain international labour standards (Klein, 2000). However, Krugman argues that, despite these drawbacks, these new export industries lead to 'unmistakable improvement in the lives of ordinary people' (1999, 17). Most tangibly, this foreign direct investment improved average calorie intake and life expectancy in countries such as Indonesia where economic success could be measured by such basic issues as who was hungry and who could stay alive, and this improvement is presented as an example of what capitalism can achieve when it works (Krugman, 1999, 18). After all, none of this is as a result of aid programmes or socialist economic planning: 'It was the indirect and unintended result of the actions of soulless multinational corporations and rapacious local entrepreneurs, whose only concern was to take advantage of the profit opportunities offered by cheap labor.' (Krugman, 1999, 18)

The resulting rise in incomes and living standards for some parts of the world may not signal an end to global poverty but, equally, it does not represent no progress at all. What is more questionable is the extent to which such forms of development change lives throughout society – against the accusation that this is yet another route to affluence for only a few.

A major criticism of international financial institutions has been that they have fostered the creation of a new form of patronage economics. Once again, in a theme that recurs throughout this work, part of the problem has arisen from the structures and practices of these institutions. Whatever the intention, the IMF and the World Bank have demanded a certain structure of response from nations – an elite is interpolated as the subject of this international address. Various recent commentaries on the workings of such institutions have revealed how coercive this relationship can be (Stiglitz, 2002). More tellingly still, other recent events – such as the dismantling of the Mexican economy under successive governments and IMF guidance, leading to a crisis in the value of the peso – indicate how vulnerable national governments can be if such patronage is withdrawn or altered (Martin and Schumann, 1997). However, we may be witnessing a new backlash against such interventions. Popular democratic movements in various poor-world settings now regard co-operation with the IMF and the World Bank as a sign of government corruption – another indication of how far so-called leaders are from the people. Naomi Klein summarises this feeling in relation to recent experience in Argentina: 'Argentina, as the obedient pupil for decades, miserably failed by its IMF professors, shouldn't be begging for loans; it should be demanding reparations. The IMF had its chance to run Argentina. Now it's the people's turn.' (Klein, 2002, 55)

This explicit resistance to the project of institutionalised globalisation is one cause of the nervousness within international institutions. Although local populations have been resistant to structural adjustment in the past, and have shown their ingratitude through riot and unrest, the widespread naming of the IMF in particular as the incarnation of Western imperialism upsets the attempts to hail compliant local elites.

In the main, popular resistance to the IMF has not been fuelled by any particular desire to live beyond the frippery of Western consumerism. Although politicised faith movements may mount an ideological critique of the whole basis of economic development, more often political turbulence occurs where populations are disappointed by the empty promises of development. Life has not become better as promised – or the gains have been short-lived and fragile. All of which calls into question the legitimacy of the national elite. What, after all, is government for if not to govern the economy?

THE RISE AND FALL OF KEYNESIANISM

Since the creation of the Bretton Woods institutions, there has been a process of economic change in many regions. For some parts of the poor world, including some newly independent nations, there has been development and economies have grown. Some, such as the now out-of-favour miracles of South Korea, Taiwan, Singapore and Hong Kong, even appeared to have benefited from an adherence to IMF-style orthodoxy, albeit with large amounts of unacknowledged state intervention. Yet almost everywhere the benefits of growth have been confined to a few. Neither Keynesian nor neo-liberal versions of economic management have delivered growth and stability, let alone the longed-for nirvana of endless prosperity for all. There may be widespread calls for greater regulation and management of the global economy, but few ideas of how we might avoid the mistakes of the past.

In the previous chapter we skated over the fall from influence of Keynesianism – and also outlined the formation of the Bretton Woods institutions, some of the most enduring and controversial legacies of Keynesian thought. However, to understand the tumultuous events that led to what we know as the global economy, a little more needs to be said about the influential role of Keynesian thinking in shaping ideas of economic management. In their account of the shaping role of Keynesian thought on the economics of the twentieth century, Luigi Pasinetti and Bertram Schefold argue that the analytic agenda set by Keynes continues to prove relevant: 'Keynes's preoccupations and claims re-emerge and appear re-confirmed again and again. The real world keeps on, so to speak, revealing itself more on the side of Keynes than on the side of orthodox economic theory.' (Pasinetti and Schefold, 1999, 13)

Keynesian thought gained currency because it fitted the circumstances and requirements of its time. In the face of mass unemployment, Keynesianism offered a method of economic management that could restore prosperity and safeguard social order. In his account of Keynesianism as a response to social conflict, Massimo De Angelis summarises the Keynesian revolution as a matching of the problem – unemployment – to a means of resolution – economic growth – to be achieved through an identifiable instrument – monetary and fiscal policy. In the face of seemingly intractable problems, Keynesianism reaffirms our ability to shape our world through human agency. Economics is the sum of human actions, not an independent force subject to its own unchangeable logic – Keynes reminds us that this force can be tamed.

Until the unprecedented slump that followed the First World War, economic orthodoxy held that large-scale unemployment would not last for long. Economies would find their own equilibrium in a manner that ensured full employment. The invisible hand of the market would lead, inevitably, to the optimum distribution of all resources, including labour. The role of government was to enable the effective working of the market – and if that isn't working, there isn't much else to do. This was where the world was in the aftermath of the Great War. When economies expanded through war activity entered a peacetime that could not replace wartime levels of demand, the newly acquired productive capacities had insufficient markets in which to sell. The resulting levels of unemployment confounded the expectations of existing economic thinking – and did not disappear as economies spontaneously achieved equilibrium, but instead increased as demand entered a downward spiral. By the end of the 1920s, key trading nations were experiencing an unprecedented global recession, and neither individual governments nor arenas of international co-operation offered any hope of a solution.

Unfortunately, through the Great Slump no alternative method of economic management could be imagined. The economic orthodoxy remained that of non-intervention and a belief in the self-regulating abilities of the free market. Governments continued to do the only thing that they knew how to do – deflated hard, protected the gold standard, sought to balance their budgets and minimised state spending. All in the hope that private enterprise would become reinvigorated and rebuild economies. Of course, these measures increased the pain suffered by ordinary people, and led to a distrust of established governments and parties. As a result, the doors were opened to less established methods and parties – benefiting both the Roosevelt government and its experiment with the New Deal and the authoritarian, nationalistic and aggressive regimes emerging in Germany and Japan.

These very different moves against economic orthodoxy yielded some benefits. Most notoriously, Hitler introduced a combination of extreme authoritarianism and a programme of public works that transformed a German economy that had been almost destroyed by the terms of the peace settlement that followed the First World War and the impact of global recession on its weakened state.

Ironically, it was the Second World War that reinvigorated the world economy. Germany and Japan used military investment as one method of job creation throughout the 1930s. The strict government control of resources and intensive investment in military capability of the war years counteracted the deflationary spiral of the depression, despite the pressure on the borrowing levels of individual nations.

When Keynes published his seminal work *General Theory of Employment, Interest and Money* in 1936, what was offered was a method of managing levels of demand in a national economy, and through this, managing levels of employment. By the time that the end of the war was in sight, key players on the Allied side were convinced of the benefits of such an approach, both within national economies, and, more importantly, as a blueprint for future management of the world economy. This sense of agreement shaped the discussion at Bretton Woods and framed the economic policies of the developed world for the decades that followed the war, whatever the political leanings of their governments. For parties with an ideological objection to welfare spending, a favoured alternative was military expenditure.

In the United States in particular, it was this form of military Keynesianism that has been the favoured approach of successive governments – learning the benefits of the war economy even in peacetime:

> Whereas Keynes was comparatively neutral with respect to the two blades of fiscal policy – increasing spending or the cutting of tax rates – practising postwar Keynesians in the United States have favored tax cuts over non-military spending increases. If federal expenditures were to be expanded, they have usually involved military spending or non-military spending under a military label, such as the National Defense or 'Eisenhower' highways. (Turgeon, 1996, 81)

This reliance on military expenditure as a legitimate, non-welfare avenue for public spending can obscure the extent to which even governments that present themselves as antagonistic to state intervention have adopted Keynesian methods of economic management. Even the much-vaunted monetarism of Reaganomics backed up an attempt at supply-side economics with huge military programmes.

Of course, the reason for this adherence to Keynesian approaches is that they worked, at least for a time. In the post-war period, the populations of developed economies came to expect the state to take responsibility for key aspects of their welfare – people expected to have work, access to basic services, a safety net for when times got hard. Most of all, they expected their lives and the lives of their children to get better. Governments of all persuasions concurred with such expectations and, necessarily, presented plans for economic stability and growth. There was an acceptance by all parties that such matters were the responsibility of government.

As with so many other aspects of our story, the event that called all this into question was the abandonment of the dollar standard. National governments still clung to their Keynesian habits, often in the form of military spending, but the rules of the game of world economy changed irreversibly.

By 1971, the United States had been fighting a draining and unpopular war in Vietnam for six years. The global economy was undergoing a (not yet recognised) crisis of profitability (Desai, 2002, 232–4). When Nixon announced that the United States was no longer willing to guarantee the price of gold and, as a direct result, that the dollar could no longer serve as the stable peg for all other currencies, it was a declaration that even the mighty United States needed the flexibility to adjust its exchange rate. Before long, and often despite the best efforts of other governments, other currencies were floated as well.

Although floating exchange rates did allow governments more flexibility in their monetary policies, because there was no longer an imperative to maintain a currency level regardless of all other local economic factors, the overall impact of ending the dollar standard was to limit the control that governments had over their economies.

While exchange rates were set against the dollar and its guarantor status, there was a widespread belief that the internal management of national economies could be kept separate from participation in international trade. There is the need to maintain growth and stability in the domestic economy – a task made possible by the insights of Keynesianism and its accompanying strategies of increasing government spending or cutting taxes to get over periods of economic sluggishness. Until the 1970s, no one thought for a moment that such activity might cause other problems, such as inflation, and no one believed that such domestic policy would have any impact on how successful or otherwise a country might be as an international trader. Why should it? These forms of domestic policy did not change exchange rates, so there was no necessary impact on the price of imports or exports. If anything, boosting general levels of activity within the national economy should help any firm that is not solely dependent on international trade, and a buoyant national economy should help firms participate in international trade. It is much more common, after all, for there to be innovation, creativity and investment when times are good. All in all, Keynesian demand management seemed to be an all-round winner – a way of fending off recession with no discernible costs to other aspects of economic life.

Once exchange rates were floated, this tidy partitioning of domestic and international activity was no longer possible. Now every aspect of internal economic management could have an impact on the price of your currency – which in turn would impact on your ability to trade and borrow. No more cost-free injections of cash into economies that needed more jobs and general oomph, because spending your way out of recession now had other costs.

This was the crux of the dilemma of national economic management after the demise of the dollar standard. The manageability of national economies, such as it has been, has rested on the availability of a number of measures. Without some leverage of government borrowing and spending, some flexibility in the setting of your exchange rate, some influence on the rate of interest, and perhaps, latterly, an ability to control the money supply, the dream of Keynesian economic management is not workable. In fact, as we are learning, this dream has been far more limited and short-lived than anyone expected.

What changed all the rules was the advent of a speculative financial market. If the price of currencies fluctuated like that of other commodities and currencies could be bought and sold for profit, then it became possible to make money by betting on the ebbs and flows of the currency market. What we know as the financial markets – a whole new way of making money for nothing – emerged with the new possibilities that were unleashed by the death of the dollar standard.

No model of economic planning or management prepared us for the additional consideration of speculation. Economic management becomes quite a different thing when it is possible for people to gamble on the outcomes of your policy choices – and to become rich by confounding the plans of individual countries through speculative behaviour. For less powerful nations, the impact of speculation, or the potential impact of speculation, becomes another unequal hurdle. Paul Krugman suggests that this new requirement to bolster investor confidence damages developing nations disproportionately:

> Floating exchange rates do work pretty well for First World countries, because markets are prepared to give those countries the benefit of the doubt. But since 1994 one Third World country after another – Mexico, Thailand, Indonesia, Korea, and, most recently, Brazil – has discovered that it cannot expect the same treatment. Again and again, attempts to engage in moderate devaluations have led to a drastic collapse in confidence. And so now markets believe that devaluations in such countries are terrible things; because markets believe this, they are. (Krugman, 1999, 111)

Somehow the appraisal of the market, that fictional entity that is no more than the combined and self-interested activity of speculators, can determine the economic future of entire nations. Any attempt by national governments to engage in economic management threatens to become a signal of weakness that can be exploited by speculators. As a result, the need to maintain investor confidence becomes one of the most important considerations of national economic policies.

FRANKENSTEIN FINANCE

An increasingly prominent sub-plot in the larger tale of disappointment and doubt in the arena of international financial institutions has been the suggestion that some of the central tenets of economic liberalisation and integration lead to instability in the global economy. The central demon in such an account has been speculation – most of all that international financial speculation that heats international markets and increasingly forms the most mobile and profitable arena of trade. This global casino has led to a number of consequences.

The theoretical benefits of international trade – I get what I want, you get what you want, the mechanism of the market allows effective planning and pricing – are, to put it kindly, somewhat distorted by the effects of financial speculation. Factor in the impact of speculation on exchange rates and managing a national economy comes to seem like an impossible task. All national governments who are in any position to attempt the management of their economy borrow in order to fulfil their objectives. Judicious control of the balance of payments may be a compulsory electoral pledge, but not borrowing is not an option for contemporary government. Whatever is said in public about the benefits of a mythically self-regulating market, the Keynesian-style use of government borrow and spend has become a non-negotiable aspect of national rule. Yet with the rise of financial speculation, the management of such domestic issues as government borrowing rates can become a market signal with potentially detrimental effects for a national economy.

Others have suggested that this apparent loss of autonomy in national economic management is illusory. The Bretton Woods framework institutionalised the power of the United States over other economies. Tying currencies to the guarantee of the dollar also tied economies to the health or otherwise of the US economy:

> ... a key role was played by the United States, as macroeconomic 'manager' and security guarantor of the free world. During the 'golden age' proper, only the United States enjoyed the luxury of an 'autonomous' macroeconomic policy. Under the gold-exchange standards set up at Bretton Woods, the United States was on the gold standard, other countries held most of their reserves in dollars. (Skidelsky, 1995, 85)

The first decades of the Bretton Woods project coincided with a period of stability and growth for most developed economies – which allowed the United States to wield its authority with a relatively light touch. At the point at which this arrangement no longer seemed viable, the United States itself changed the rules. As we have discussed, this period of stability was also the time of Keynesianism's greatest influence, a time when it seemed that the economic crises of the past could be avoided through careful management of demand. The promise of political stability through economic stability seemed to be achievable.

Keynes' ideas were shaped by both the spectre of human suffering due to economic mismanagement and the threat of political disorder in response to hardship and inequality. If governments are not able to manage economic stability, other forces may threaten social order. After the rise of Hitler and the Second World War, this was understood as a warning against fascism. However, in the earlier part of the century, such political anxiety was concentrated by the new possibilities unleashed with the Russian revolution. Massimo De Angelis explains the entire Keynesian project as an exercise in avoiding this form of social conflict. He argues that the Soviet revolution shifted the parameters of effective government, because now the 'aspirations of the working-class had to be integrated within the process of accumulation'. This is argued to be not only a response to a changing economic context, but also an outcome of political struggle, 'since economic liberalism has been defeated by people's refusal to act as non-human commodities'. De Angelis argues that Keynesianism was an attempt to combine economic and social management: 'Keynes' theory thus represents the scientific attempt to *acknowledge* and *recuperate* (co-opt and subsume) this power of the working class.' (De Angelis, 2000, 7)

Working-class organisation can scupper the smooth running of the domestic economy, and may threaten to replace the government, unless some attention is given to the needs and well-being of workers. While capital is relatively immobile, such a compromise is no more than good business. However, with greater capital mobility, such an accommodation with national governments is no longer necessary. Developments such as transactions via new communications technologies and the greater role of finance capital in the international economy herald this shift. Mark Rupert stresses the benefits that new technologies bring to capital: 'the new historical structures embody an enhancement of the social powers of capital, and especially finance capital, which can effectively pre-empt expansionary macro-policies aimed at increasing employment or wage levels' (Rupert, 2000, 46).

Once again, the economy comes to be seen as an unstoppable force of nature, now due to the international pressures of a market beyond any government intervention or control. In their larger discussion of the need for regulation of financial markets, John Eatwell and Lance Taylor comment on the impact of this shift on understandings of national economic management: 'There is now no such thing as domestic monetary policy divorced in form and content from monetary events outside national borders.' (Eatwell and Taylor, 2000, 96)

This shift has consequences for everyone, but, as is so often the case, it is the poor world that suffers the most. International financial institutions have encouraged a model of development based on participation in international trade – and when nations have needed help, co-operating with this model has been a condition of assistance. Inevitably, it seems, one of the outcomes has been to erode an economy's defences against external fluctuations. The campaign group ATTAC (Association pour la Taxe Tobin pour l'Aide aux Citoyens) argues that the influence of financial markets has distorted all attempts to create sustainable economies in the developing world:

> The dependence of nation-states on the financial markets results directly from the development model imposed by neoliberal policies: instead of concentrating on their internal savings and their markets, nation-states are constrained to orientate their productive and financial activities towards international trade, especially when they are indebted as a result of prior deficits. (ATTAC, 2002, 42)

The impact of such currency volatility is another key reason why the IMF has become such a hate figure for so many parts of the world. Opening a nation's financial markets may be good for speculators, but it is bad for ordinary people and their savings, as seen in the experience of Argentina. If a country is in trouble and the IMF encourage acceptance of the market rate for their currency, then savings lose their value. If, on the other hand, for some reason the IMF wish to intervene to prop up the value of currency, this is done with a combination of IMF and government funds – all debts that are passed back to the population sooner or later. Either way, the gains of international speculators are subsidised by ordinary individuals, often from the poorest parts of the world. This scandal, however, is not what has initiated recent calls for greater regulation of financial markets. Perhaps predictably, this debate has been in response to the scary realisation that speculators may be able to unravel any part of the international economy that they choose. Since George Soros proved this point in September 1992 by creating a run on sterling that heralded the beginning of the end for the European Monetary System (Martin and Schumann, 1997), everyone has known that powerful players can guide market response by their actions, and that in the process individual economies are vulnerable to destabilisation by such non-state actors. Of course, this is not how markets are supposed to work – they are supposed to be reassuringly beyond the control of any one player, magically registering the combined choices of all buyers and sellers. The concentration of economic power in some kinds of non-governmental hands, a concentration itself enabled by financial speculation, creates the possibility of such concerted campaigns – something that even the so-called winners in the global economy are not so willing to countenance.

As a result, there is a renewed enthusiasm for the suggestion that a new system of regulation is required for the well-being of the global economy. John Eatwell and Lance Taylor bring together some of the key arguments for such an initiative in their book, *Global Finance at Risk*, where they argue against the suggestion that financial markets can be automatically self-regulating. They identify four key areas that support their view. The first is that national regulatory capacities have been undermined by the spread of economic liberalisation: 'Consequences have included high and variable real interest rates, increased volatility of asset prices, poor national economic performances, and the contagious spread of market instabilities worldwide.' (2000, xi) Their second point is that such developments can cause great turbulence and upheaval 'even in the large and integrated financial markets of the industrialised economies' (2000, xi). Point three links the late 1990s wave of currency crises with rapid capital market liberalisation and absence of regulation. Point four complains of the absence of agreed principles for determining exchange rates – as a result changes in rates are driven by market speculation. Eatwell and Taylor suggest that 'exchange rate volatility exacerbates all the deficiencies of unregulated markets' (2000, xi).

Overall Eatwell and Taylor argue, as do others (Coyle, 2000; Stiglitz, 2002), that speculation on the financial markets makes it impossible to maintain order and stability in the world economy – the result is unacceptable human hardship and the threat of political turbulence. Just as the model of Keynesian management that grew in influence in the post-war period represented an accommodation to the demands of organised labour, now the international economy requires a form of regulation that can guard against the creation of failed states that may become power bases for the forces of organised crime and/or political extremism. Eatwell and Taylor agree that the train of events leading to current levels of speculation began with the ending of fixed exchange rates:

> For privatisation of foreign exchange risk in 1973 was followed necessarily by the liberalisation of international financial markets. The need for financial institutions to spread their risks over many assets and activities in turn led to the liberalisation of domestic markets. (2000, 23)

These stages of liberalisation represented a concerted campaign by those who had an ideological belief in the benefits of liberalised markets. The Washington Consensus has been only the most high-profile aspect of this grouping and, far from relying on coercion, such beliefs have been absorbed by elements of many national governments. However, the currency crises of the 1990s ushered in some dissent, and not only from those who believed that social justice should come before profit. This time dissent came from those who argued that a lack of regulation was destabilising capitalism, not by creating a new revolutionary subject but by enabling the empowerment of a host of rogue traders who had no respect for honest business.

The liberalisation of financial markets had a range of unforeseen consequences – many of which form the interlinking areas that this volume goes on to discuss. Opening the financial markets created new opportunities for new kinds of economic actors, actors who emerged as significant players as the world was remapped after the Cold War:

> Nor are Asian and other emerging markets the only new players in the game. We must also note the growing involvement since the mid-1980s of organised crime in international finance and the importance of money laundering as one of the many financial services offered by it. The contributing factor to this change has been the growth of the transnational trade in illegal drugs, providing a source of wealth to the Mafia far greater than even American prohibition. Organised crime, too, rose from the ashes of the Cold War. Russians, Chechens and Georgians have dealt not only in drugs but in arms, illegal immigrants and even nuclear materials. (Strange, 1998, 10)

Susan Strange offers an abbreviated summary of the new monsters that haunt the post-Cold War world, or, at least, the world as viewed by keepers of the global economy. Money-laundering becomes part of the growth and development of transnational financial services, and is transformed by the same processes of global integration that have been championed by international financial institutions. At the same time, the key players of the shadow economy – organised crime, those engaged in new forms of nationalist and territorial struggle, a new faceless, rootless breed of entrepreneurs who capitalise on the opportunities of a liberalised global economy – seem to understand the new rules of international economy only too well, and threaten to become the major players in such a transnational arena, at least as influential as many nations and corporations.

This is a key concern of this work, the suggestion that global integration actively favours the most shadowy elements of the shadow economy. What is being suggested is not only that criminals and illicit traders adapt in order to continue their business in these new circumstances, but, more importantly, that this new situation creates greater opportunities for such groups. Global integration serves to increase their power and influence:

> It would have hardly been possible to design a 'non-regime' that was better suited than the global banking system to the needs of drug dealers and other illicit traders who want to conceal from the police the origin of their large illegal profits. The business of money laundering could not have so prospered and grown without the facilities for swift and relatively invisible transnational movements of money. That much is common knowledge. (Strange, 1998, 123)

These ideas echo those of many other commentators, some of whom are discussed in this volume (Finckenhauer and Voronin, 2001; Viano, 1999). Both left and right agree that activities such as money-laundering have become more widespread and influential in recent years and that this is a bad thing for legitimate business (Stessens, 2000). The point of debate is in the suggested solutions to the problem – economic regulation or more policing, new international rules or more effective coercion from the rich world. Both sides tend to agree that we are entering a new era and that a new conception of international co-operation is required to rebuild our relations with each other. The implication is that existing international institutions are not equipped to meet these new challenges. Yet international financial institutions have proved to be remarkably supple in the interpretation of their role:

The IMF likes to present itself as an organisation set up with wise forethought in the 1940s and whose development since then has followed a consistent path. Continuity, it suggests, has marked its expanding importance in the world market economy. That is not exactly true. It is an institution that has happened to be there, available to do different things at different times. Its role today is not at all what it was supposed to be at Bretton Woods. (Strange, 1998, 164)

Strange argues that initially, for the first decade after 1947, the IMF was effectively inactive, waiting for European currencies to become convertible in 1958 so that the fixed exchange-rate system could be launched. This role collapsed when exchange rates became generally floated in 1973, because the particular IMF role of providing short-term finance for countries with balance of payments problems that endangered their fixed exchange rates no longer existed.

Strange suggests that the IMF reinvented itself as a body that worked with less developed and highly indebted countries in order to maintain the stability of the international system. Linked to this role was another incarnation as a source of financial aid to governments whose banking problems were in danger of spreading contagion to international stock markets:

Although this is the role that thrust the IMF more than ever into the international limelight in the late 1990s, it is one that dates back to the early 1960s. It was then that the ground rules were hammered out on when, and on what terms, the IMF could acquire the funds necessary for it to act as global lender of last resort. (Strange, 1998, 165)

There is no reason why the IMF and the World Bank should not become reformed institutions, not least because they have adapted their own roles in the past. The only question is what is seen to be in the interests of global capital.

UNRAVELLING GLOBAL INSTITUTIONS

There has been no shortage of disappointment with the failures and shortcomings of the Bretton Woods project. In recent times, highly vocal and well-publicised critiques of the international financial institutions have not only circulated among a global network of anti-globalisation activists, they have also entered popular debate (Adams, 1997; Danaher, 1994; Klein, 2002; Mertes, 2004). As more and more people gain a sense that the changes of global integration can impact on them, often in unwelcome ways, this literature and these ideas have found a receptive audience. Perhaps most of all, the suggestion that the assorted and nebulous processes of globalisation can be embodied and identified in the forms of the IMF and the World Bank gives dissenters a concrete enemy. These bodies become a shorthand code for a far wider set of economic processes and ideas – portmanteau terms for that set of global relations that were engineered in the aftermath of the Second World War. In fact, the use of these bogeymen collapses a number of debates – from earlier critiques of neo-colonialism and dependency cultures to more recent discussions of anti-capitalism and unequal trade – and the critiques of the Bretton Woods project span a number of viewpoints (Danaher, 1994; Holland, 1994). Yet all the disparate views are united in one thing – the sense of disappointment that the project has not worked. That the dream of global governance and co-operation, of universal peace and prosperity, has not been realised.

The other theme that seems to unite a number of critiques is a larger disappointment with the theory and practice of economics. There is a familiar anti-intellectual element in this – all this abstract theory that damages human lives but has no human face or feeling – but there is also a kind of correction of an earlier over-confidence in the business of economic analysis and management. This discussion has been conducted in terms that make some of the previously obscure debates of economic theory accessible, and has often been led by economists, in an apologetic self-criticism of the overblown claims of their discipline. Of course, these renunciations of past faith hold a particular power and satisfaction for a wider audience that blames the whole business of economics for our current ills. Among the most high-profile and celebrated of these converts from the orthodoxies of international financial institutions is Joseph Stiglitz, Nobel Prize winner for economics, former chief economist at the World Bank and advisor to President Clinton – a man whose disappointment with the IMF holds some weight:

> A half century after its founding, it is clear that the IMF has failed in its mission. It has not done what it was supposed to do – provide funds for countries facing an economic downturn, to enable the country to restore itself to close to full employment. ... The IMF failed in its original mission of promoting global stability; it has also been no more successful in the new

missions that it has undertaken, such as guiding the transition of countries from communism to a market economy. (Stiglitz, 2002, 15)

The outcome of all these variously expressed doubts is a widespread sense that this is not the only way. Whereas Bretton Woods represented a moment of broad consensus about the need for global co-operation and the pursuit of peace and security through a certain model of trade, now there are rumblings that suggest that this may no longer be the only game in town.

Admittedly, much of this iconoclasm comes from professed opponents of what is described here as liberal globalisation. The emergence of new levels of global inequality and a strongly felt sense that globalisation wipes out livelihoods without offering any replacement and that, despite all arguments to the contrary, living standards for the many are getting worse has led, unsurprisingly, to resistance. Much of this resistance has argued that globalisation is a terrible tide that must be turned back. Global integration has gone too far, there has been too much emphasis on trade, most of all, too many agreements have been framed solely to further the interests of the rich world. Better to refuse all that and return to protected and planned national economies, this time around informed by the values of egalitarianism and social justice.

In contrast to such a position, this work takes its cue from the Bretton Woods institutions themselves. For some time, there has been a quiet murmuring of doubt and disappointment. The most obvious dreams of universal affluence have not been achieved. And while some have argued that the absence of world war is an indication that this contract of international trade and economic co-operation has had the desired outcome, increasingly there is concern about the impact of new forms of war and destruction. Trade has not stopped the fighting – the fighting has just taken different forms and terrains.

However, when I suggest that even the global elite are losing faith with the Bretton Woods vision, I realise that I am stretching things a bit. It is more accurate to say that there are quiet adaptations going on, even within the confines of the World Bank and the IMF. None of which is to suggest that these institutions are no longer dominated by Western interests or that key players have been converted to the benefits of redistribution as an end in itself. Instead, what I am identifying is the assortment of voices in favour of some regulation of the market, with regulation here signifying a wide range of practices that adapt and contain free trade and open competition. Hazel Henderson summarises some common views about the downsides of a global economy fuelled by financial speculation:

> Ever since the collapse of the Bretton Woods system in 1971, the global financial non-system has been characterized by increasing turbulence, mounting debt, widening poverty gaps within and between countries and a de-coupling of finance and currency flows from the real world economies of production, trade, and consumption that money is supposed to facilitate and measure. (Henderson, 2001, 113)

The reality, as even the most die-hard proponents of planning have accepted, is that circumstances have changed. The component parts of the international economy are tied together in quite a different manner from that assumed in the terms of Bretton Woods. That sense of creeping anxiety emanating from among the guardians of the international economy betrays a recognition of these changes, and the varied calls for some means of effective regulation are also a symptom of this realisation. Diane Coyle discusses this call as itself an outcome of global changes and consciousness: 'The hunt is on for a structure, and a set of modernised institutions, that suit the conditions of today's global economy as well as the Bretton Woods system fitted in the post-war years.' (Coyle, 2000, 35)

However, calling for effective regulation of the international economy is a very different thing from finding ways of making it work. The Bretton Woods institutions reflected a certain way of understanding the workings of the economy. Similarly, the sea-change that occured with floating exchange rates was a reflection of neo-liberal conceptions of economic life. We have entered a phase of the global economy where, despite well-articulated fears about the consequences of carrying on as we are, there does not seem to be any fresh conception of economic relations that can combine a framework of regulation with the reliance on new technological communications that characterises contemporary economic life. Coyle connects this to the shift to an information economy and the increasing importance of forms of value that seem resistant to existing methods of regulation:

> The more complex and intangible economic value becomes in the increasingly weightless world, the steadily more impossible it will become to replace or bypass the market mechanism. For nothing transmits information more

effectively than the free market. Direct public sector participation in the economy proved problematic even in the relatively simple post-war decades. It has no place in the global transfer of ideas that makes up a growing proportion of modern industry. (Coyle, 2000, 41)

We are left feeling anxious, but without clear solutions – another theme that will reappear in later chapters.

A NEW EMPIRE?

All of this discussion about the global economy and its impact on everyday lives takes place alongside a slightly different but related debate about the concepts of empire and imperialism. After what seems like a long time, such terms are re-entering mainstream discussion, even in the West (Guyatt, 2000, 2003; Harvey, 2003; Kupchan, 2000, 2003; Mann; 2003; Wallerstein, 2003). While this new/old gathering storm is not the focus of this work, much of what is discussed here shapes the terrain onto which this new imperialism emerges. In particular, the suggestion that this multifaceted creature that we know as globalisation has created a new structure of power in the world, one that we could understand as empire, but only once we have rethought what empire means, sits behind the discussion in each subsequent chapter.

When Michael Hardt and Antonio Negri published their celebrated work *Empire*, the rumours of a new imperialism had hardly begun. I began this volume before 9/11 – and although the emerging doctrine of liberal interventionism was beginning to be heard in public debate, few believed that we were on the brink of a new set of battles for global domination. Hardt and Negri pick up some themes from globalisation-speak and argue that we are living through a dismantling of national sovereignty as a final defence against international forces and entering a time where a new structure of truly transnational power shapes global relations:

The passage to Empire emerges from the twilight of modern sovereignty. In contrast to imperialism, Empire establishes no territorial centre of power and does not rely on fixed boundaries or barriers. It is a *decentered and deterritorializing* apparatus of rule that progressively incorporates the entire global realm within its open, expanding frontiers. (Hardt and Negri, 2000, xii)

Hardt and Negri are proposing a new conception of world power, one that moves on from previous understandings of imperialism. At the time of the publication of *Empire*, few in the developed world were arguing openly that globalisation represented a new imperialism. Whereas the intellectual and political debates of the poor world of all regions continued to analyse the uneven and unequal relations between different parts of the world through the prism of imperial relations, before 9/11 much First World commentary on globalisation paid little attention to the earlier histories that have shaped such unequal interactions. In the circumstances, Hardt and Negri reveal a spooky prescience with their suggestion that the crisis of regulation in global relations is not only about economics: 'Empire is not born of its own will but rather it is *called* into being and constituted on the basis of its capacity to resolve conflicts.' (2000, 15)

The movements of global capital are not co-ordinated and, far from representing a carefully planned conspiracy, are all too haphazard. The collection of happenings that we recognise as globalisation does not constitute a new world order, or any kind of order. However, these economic movements contribute to a remapping of the world that uncovers old and new tensions. Hardt and Negri suggest that the abstract entity 'Empire' can be understood as the emerging machinery of informal global governance, an order that seems bound to consolidate the most unaccountable and cruel incarnations of global power: 'These techniques … indicate that what we are witnessing is a process of the material constitution of the new planetary order, the consolidation of its administrative machine, and the production of new hierarchies of command over global space.' (2000, 19)

However, despite this depiction of a newly emerging faceless, rootless monster of absolute and unquestionable authority, Hardt and Negri write with exuberance of the unfolding possibilities of a globalised world. Although it is an analysis of a new structure of domination that is emerging in response to the challenges of a more integrated world, this is described with a sense of anticipation. What Hardt and Negri describe as the global multitude is just waiting for its moment, almost at the point of mounting an unstoppable resistance.

The chapters that follow give little sense of this impending revolution – the discussion is more focused on the unhappy histories that lead us to this moment. However, the question of how global tensions can be solved and by whom remains an underlying mystery. Holding on to Hardt and Negri's vision of redemptive change may help to illuminate what follows.

3
Winning the Cold War: The Power of Organised Crime in the Global Economy

There is an established mythology of the gangster, one that has entered popular consciousness through endless movies, comics, novels, and TV shows. Among the most influential have been the films of Francis Ford Coppola and his presentation of the story of the Corleone family as a metaphor for both migrant experience and capitalist development. In the trilogy of *Godfather* films there is a suggestion that this family saga of migrant life could chart the move from crime to respectability, from the illicit support networks of immigrant life to the mainstream influence of business proper. Unfortunately, in the belated third episode it seems that the dynastic hopes of Michael Corleone (Al Pacino) must inevitably be crushed by the new pressures of the globalised economy. Old-style organised crime, we are led to believe, operated through a code of honour. The new world of global gang warfare cannot sustain such niceties, apparently.

The rising profile of organised crime is among the most media-covered aspects of the adventure of globalisation. Gangsters are romantic characters in the popular imagination of many cultures, and films from Hollywood to Bollywood to Hong Kong have taught us to believe that the fraternity of crime operates around its own code of honour. If anything, compared to the corrupt structures of official power, popular culture suggests that the moral code of organised crime is more coherent and reliable than the shifting shapes of, say, our political representatives.

Looking back at the period after the fall of the Berlin Wall, and the remarkably rapid demise of the Soviet Union, it is hard not to believe that this glamorised representation of organised crime had infected the economic and political analysis of the West. During this phase of too rapid marketisation, all friends of the market also came to be seen as friends of democracy, freedom and all things wholesome. In effect, this meant that all manner of unorthodox economic activity was regarded as legitimate, part of the new toolkit of the emerging science of transitional economies. Although no one ever quite said this, there was a sense that the ability to make money from the restructuring of the Eastern bloc, pretty much regardless of how that money was made, became its own legitimation. Gangsters, presumably with their Godfather-like code of honour, can become allies in the journey towards economic liberalisation and political freedom.

In the television series *The Sopranos*, Tony Soprano tries to manage his emotional turmoil while also negotiating the changing context of his business. For hard men of the West, things are changing all round. Now gangsters also need to be in touch with their feelings, reworking their masculinity and their relationships with their mothers. At the same time, gangsterism has to adapt to changes in the global economy. Transnational competitors are encroaching on formerly assured home territory. In particular, one background narrative in *The Sopranos* shows that business must be settled with Chechens – because they are now significant players who must be respected and dealt with.

The Sopranos is one of those recent television success stories – quality drama that pulls large audiences and inspires immense devotion, not to mention scholarly comment. The depiction of the shady Chechen rival is as indicative of the sense of threat to US business as the endless therapy is indicative of a sense of crisis in Western masculinity.

NEW THREATS FROM THE EAST

The shady but glamorous figure of the Russian mafia has seeped into the everyday media consciousness of the West. True – Russian here has returned to its Soviet inspecificity and might cover a variety of ethnic groups, including those such as the Chechens who are in conflict with the Russian military state. Whatever the failings of cultural and historical understanding involved in this new media type, the message of their presence is clear. Once we tried to destroy you with military might and direct confrontation, now we have learned the ways of the market and we plan to destroy you from within. For all the heady celebration of neo-liberalism, both explicit and implied, that pervades popular culture from pop-rap to *The Economist*, the figure of the East European gangster seems to reveal some widely held distrust of the law of the market.

The international policy debate, on the other hand, reveals far greater anxieties about the apparently burgeoning influence and reach of organised crime (Berdal and Serrano, 2002; Friman and Andreas, 1999). This sense of creeping corruption throughout the machinery of the global economy is not limited to a fear of Russian organised crime, but it does identify the break-up of the Soviet Union as a key moment in the global expansion of organised crime networks. Despite somewhat premature celebrations about the 'end of history' and the triumph of Western values, new enemies have emerged in the aftermath of the communist threat, enemies that are not motivated by their ideological mission but by that old-fashioned desire to make money. We now know all too well that both intelligence services and academics have been scrabbling about to identify the next great enemy of the West – whether this involves an estimation of Chinese military development or a larger discussion of the potential clashes between civilisations. But organised crime is, on the whole, an enemy of a different nature.

This is an enemy that does not seek to destroy the other side, or to impose its own total control and vision of the world. Quite the opposite: organised crime, even at its most ambitious, is a parasitic endeavour. It has a necessarily symbiotic relationship with the formal economy and makes its profits from providing an alternative route through the interstices of 'legitimate' transnational business. Instead of an identifiable enemy that stands in opposition to the values and existence of the West and/or the vision of the world put forward by international financial institutions, organised crime creates an unpredictable thread within the terms of the global economy, another set of rules hidden within the business of trade. This is the underbelly of globalisation, a shadow economy that feeds on the processes of global integration:

> The shadow economy has at least three characteristics: evasion of state regulation; use of force and intimidation; and the use of hard foreign currency as capital. Within the domain of the shadow economy, a variety of illicit activities continue to crush legitimate economic activity. (Webster, 1997, 38)

The shadow economy might make money and maybe even enable the further integration of the global economy – but it is not playing by the rulebook of international financial institutions. Or, at least, not quite. Of the three characteristics identified, evading state regulation is the most obvious business offence. Force and intimidation may be nasty, but they are not offences against economic management – and, sadly, respectable businesses may not be above employing such extra leverage given the right circumstances and the opportunity. Using currency as capital is flighty, but again, has entered the repertoire of legitimate practice, particularly in more speculative endeavours – as we shall see when we come to discuss the fantasy possibilities that have been linked to transitional economies. Overall, there is little here that distinguishes the shadow economy from more mainstream business practice – even the explicit evasion of state regulation has its place in legitimate business.

There is, then, little in the practice or business style of the shadow economy that sets it apart – in the end, it is the illicit nature of this activity that makes the difference. Otherwise, it is all too much like the usual processes of transnational and other business. When the suggestion is made that the shadow economy crushes legitimate economic activity, it is not clear whether the allegation is that other less lucrative trades are squeezed out or that the influence of the shadow economy comes to infect all areas of economic life. Either way, the fear is that there will be no clean economy left all: 'The problem is not the "mafia" as a separate entity; instead, it is the emergence of a situation in which separate organised crime groups are only one element of a larger phenomenon of the interpenetration of crime, business and government.' (Webster, 1997, 18)

Organised crime threatens to become indistinguishable from mainstream institutional power. As the infrastructure of government and business is remade in many places, transnational criminal organisations are able to infiltrate this process of restructuring and realignment. Before we know it, and as a byproduct of the process of fostering market-friendly restructuring, the world is peppered with national governments who may be indebted to organised crime. Some of these governments may be indebted and infiltrated without fully knowing it. As the media scare-stories about infiltration show, there is a fear that the West is engaging in less and less regulated trade with partners who are only thinly veiled proxies for organised crime (Gustafson, 1999). This is not what was intended in planning for affluence through economic liberalisation or promoting development through trade.

In response a whole new policy industry has sprung up to assess and guard against the assorted dangers raised by transnational organised crime (UN, 2000a). As we will go on to discuss, in many ways this loosely defined and shape-shifting spectre takes on the mantle of absolute enemy of the West, the new post-Cold War

monster that makes us all afraid. The policy debate makes this explicit
– transnational organised crime is a threat to international security,
and just as we used to guard against the communist threat, now we
must guard against organised crime.

A recent collection outlines the reasons for linking transnational
organised crime to security issues, and in the process argues for inter-
state co-operation in defence against this threatened incursion (Berdal
and Serrano, 2002). Four key areas are identified. The first is the scale
and scope of growth – different reports suggest that organised crime
has been a growth industry in recent years, with greatly increased
capacity and reach across far greater areas, including across national
borders. The second is the suggestion that the opening of the global
economy has changed the nature and speed of business – now
transactions are conducted in a manner that can provide cover for
all sorts of criminality. Third is the idea that borders have become
more open and therefore law enforcement attempts must be co-
ordinated, something that is hard to do and for which there are few
precedents. Fourth, and most explicitly linked to security as it has
been understood, is the link between organised crime and the new,
often civil, wars that cut open the world after the Cold War.

Organised crime threatens to colonise legitimate business practices
and to benefit from the moves towards more open borders (for business
if not for people) that have characterised the global economy. In the
process, organised crime becomes a serious global player, another
faceless transnational corporation that is growing in influence
through the opportunities of an unregulated global economy.
Criminal networks may become powerful enough to destroy national
economies through the perfectly legal route of financial speculation,
and, in a world of almost failing states, may come to replace legitimate
systems of government in some places. In an echo of the dreams of
the Godfather, the business opportunities of globalisation can allow
organised crime to become legitimate, while also becoming richer
and more influential than any single government. The demise of the
Soviet Union has played a central role in creating these opportunities.
To understand how, we need to review the hopes that were pinned
on the so-called transitional economies.

IN TRANSIT TO WHERE?

It has taken a relatively short period for transitional economies to
move from being the bright hope of capitalist renewal to being a

casebook example of intractable problems. In the process we have all learned new ways of thinking about the hurdles and pitfalls of marketisation. Nowadays, while there are not many people suggesting that there could be any kind of successful return to the centralised planning of the Soviet economy, there are also far fewer people celebrating liberalisation through racketeering. Most importantly for our purposes, the exciting entrepreneurial skills of organised crime in the former Eastern bloc are now seen to have dangerous repercussions for other regional economies. Whatever codes of honour may or may not be in play, gangsterism is seen to have a price for the West as well (Viano, 1999).

The outcome of this period of rapid reassessment has been some significant and sometimes contradictory policy thinking at an international level. We will go on to discuss the frenzied attempts to map, contain and curtail the business of organised crime, most especially in its ability to span national boundaries. However, an examination of some other international interventions shows that there is still a high level of tolerance towards local networks of organised crime if and when this is convenient. Certainly, the unexpected and often unacknowledged patronage of gangsters is recognised as a danger in aid and development circles (Duffield, 2001). So we are left with the dilemma – how much criminality can be tolerated in the quest to free markets?

DID WE WIN THE COLD WAR?

Most accounts of the Cold War remind us that this was a conflict fought on many fronts, a historically peculiar combination of military, economic and cultural strategies (see, for example, Levering, 1994). It is hard, then, in these circumstances, to judge an outright winner. Despite this, the dominant account has suggested that the market-driven and democratic consumer cultures of the West have been the victors of history. Here I want to examine both the suggestion that this victory has brought its own burdens and the view that the Cold War was brought to an end largely by non-military means.

The opening chapters recounted the events that signalled the beginning of the end for the Bretton Woods vision. Here it is enough to remind ourselves that the Nixon administration chose to abandon the dollar standard as an unacceptable drain and constraint on the US economy, and that the resulting floating exchange rates created the opportunity for accelerating levels of speculation through finance capital.

For the Soviet Union, the shift in exchange-rate mechanisms enabled the beginning of the creeping destabilisation that also allowed organised crime to flourish, although few knew this at the time. There remains a question of whether we trace this shift to so-called objective changes in the global economy, instigated by the oil crisis and the responses this crisis drew, or whether we view this shift as pre-emptively initiated through US actions.

The second view could, at a stretch, be folded into the account of the many who regard the demise of the Soviet Union as the outcome of a long and aggressive campaign by the United States, often undertaken by covert and non-military means (Bogle, 2001). This is a view held both by those nostalgic for the old regime and by those who celebrate the victory of the market. For our purposes, however, it is more helpful to view the matter as a combined process, with internal difficulties being exacerbated by shifts in the global economy, and with all signs of weakness adding leverage to an ongoing US offensive.

The Soviet Union relied on the myth that the state could, would and must be a more effective allocator of resources than any market mechanism. If individual entrepreneurs pursued their own gain with no regard for larger social consequences, and corporate interests could distort the process of economic development to suit themselves, only the state cared about the overall health of the economy and well-being of the people and only the state was in a position to make planning decisions with these concerns in mind (Winiecki, 1988).

For most of the Cold War years, these views were not regarded as particularly outlandish by either side. Most Western governments were themselves employing a Keynesian approach to economic management, mainly interpreted as a highly interventionist version of 'fine-tuning', carried out with a view to avoiding short-term electoral penalties. As discussed earlier, this included varieties of military Keynesianism, which the United States in particular deployed to useful effect. Planning, intervention in the domestic economy and state spending on military build-up were strategies employed by both superpowers and a number of other major economies. However, it is only the Soviet Union that is seen to have crumbled under the weight of military expenditure – in part, no doubt, as a result of facing the combined arms capabilities of the entire developed world: 'The tight nexus which bound the command economy to growth and growth to military production was to prove fatal for the regime, for it produced waste on a scale unimaginable under capitalism.' (Skidelsky, 1995, 102)

This view typifies the range of opinion that regards the Soviet demise as an inevitable consequence of that system's internal contradictions. Whereas in the West military spending could offer a welcome boost to sluggish economies, for the Soviet Union military expenditure became a drain and a diversion from more everyday forms of economic development. Instead of enabling other economic activity, the military became a state showpiece that sucked life out of other sectors: 'Although based on the principle of investing more of its national income than a capitalist society could achieve, the regime could not make enough from its investments to support itself. Eventually it drowned in a sea of debt.' (Skidelsky, 1995, 106)

Castells also argues that the Soviet empire imploded due to the excessive burden of maintaining its military might. In part, this was a straightforward problem of resource allocation. Castells argues that although the military-industrial complex created a forum for certain kinds of technological development, these innovations did not spread into civilian life. Soviet citizens did not benefit from a sense of everyday progress. In Castells' argument, the Soviet Union failed to keep up in the technological revolution because 'Soviet enterprises ... were engaged in a technological trajectory increasingly removed from the needs of society and from the processes of innovation of the rest of the world.' (Castells, 1998, 29)

Instead of providing the magical fix of military Keynesianism, Soviet military expenditure diverted resources away from more urgent and everyday needs. While Western economies used military spending as a handy method of pumping extra resources into the economy via a sector that did not compete with other industries – so that other firms were not hampered by this state subsidisation and there was little appreciable inflationary pressure on consumer markets – Soviet military spending prevented the necessary development of consumer industries (Aslund, 1991; Schroeder, 2001). For a Soviet Union attempting to earn foreign, and preferably Western, currencies by trading with Third World nations, the failure to develop more responsive consumer industries led not only to dissatisfaction on the part of the Soviet population, it also made Soviet industry vulnerable to more innovative competitors from both developed and developing economies (Aslund, 1991). At the same time, the Soviet Union continued to expend resources on maintaining an artificially high exchange rate – encouraging those who could to convert their savings into another safer currency and making it almost impossible for Soviet industry to participate in international trade (Copetas, 1991).

Whichever of these two accounts we choose to follow, it is likely that this demise was greatly facilitated by the new possibilities of a speculative market. What is less clear is whether the Soviet Union could have survived if fixed exchange rates had been maintained. Although it is impossible here to quantify the extra pressure on the Soviet economy brought about by the uncertainties in currency rates, it is important to recognise the role of such large economic changes. Even the vast Soviet empire needed to engage in international trade for some key resources – fluctuating currency rates made this harder (Smith, 1993).

TRYING TO REMEMBER A WORLD WITH TWO SUPERPOWERS

The world of two superpowers already seems long ago: a distant and mythical time that leaves us with a few well-rehearsed stories but little sense of connection. A large part of this work consists of an attempt to show how close we still are to this lost era – however much we try to pretend that it has nothing to do with us at all. Our world is deeply shaped by this all too recent past. However much we try to avoid this awkward history and its many ripples around the world, the events of today are a continuation of the many stealthy battles of that time and, usually, that continuation is another unforeseen consequence of past decisions. Who knew then that it would come to this?

This is not quite the same as blowback, although the provenance is similar. But where blowback has been tied to the unintended impact of secretly pursuing the most dubious of foreign policy goals, here we are looking at the unexpected outcomes of economic interventions. The imprint left by the manner of the demise of that previous world promises to reveal the barely hidden secrets of the present.

For a large part of the twentieth century, economic success was measured against the achievements and limitations of the Soviet Union (Hobsbawm, 1994). What could capitalism offer as compensation for its exploitative relations? To understand the strange demons we now face in the mysterious transactions of transnational finance, we have to remind ourselves of the machinations and extreme tensions of that covert battle. For us, the triumph of the West and the demise of the Eastern bloc can seem like a force of nature, an unstoppable course of events that was bound to happen: 'Nobody really understands what happened to the Soviet regime. With the benefit of hindsight we now think of the whole structure as a sort of ramshackle affair, doomed to eventual failure.' (Krugman, 1999, 3)

What can be harder to recall is the very real sense that the Soviet model represented a serious threat and perhaps even a credible alternative to the ways of the West. This was not a ramshackle kind of an enemy – at least, no one seemed to think so at the time. Quite the opposite, this was the Empire of evil, centrally planning its economy without any sops to the weaknesses of consumerism, and therefore able to devote untold resources to an ever-escalating arms race. That is what we seem to have forgotten. Despite all the jokes about the unbearable austerity of Soviet life, no one really believed that the Soviet economy was in danger of imploding. If anything, in relation to economic matters the West was racked with self-doubt. The Soviet Union crushed individuality and denied democratic freedoms, but those people knew how to plan an economy, or so we thought. How else could such a mighty arsenal be maintained?

Since then, there has been a revision of our understanding. Once the West believed that the Soviet Union had uncovered a route to endless economic growth – and a certain moment of Cold War hysteria was animated by this belief that the West could be outstripped by its ideological enemies. Various popularising accounts of recent international economics have talked of this period when the Soviet Union was heralded as its own kind of economic miracle (Krugman, 1999; Desai, 2002). This is apart from the earlier commentary that congratulated the revolution on taking a still feudal peasant economy into a rapid industrialisation that would rival the imperial powers of the West (Carr, 1970). The economic miracle that fixated and concerned the West was the sustained level of growth that the Soviet economy appeared to display in the 1950s and early 1960s. This was the age of Sputnik, a time when it seemed that the Soviet Union was winning the technological aspect of the Cold War and a period during which the USSR appeared to be greatly outstripping the economic growth of the USA.

It is for these reasons that for a large part of the twentieth century the Soviet Union was regarded as an example and inspiration to developing nations (Keller and Rothchild, 1996). Here was a country that had transformed itself from a backward feudal nation with a failing agrarian economy into one of the world's major superpowers. This was a living example that development through central planning could work. For countries who wished to improve their own levels of prosperity, the Soviet Union appeared to be one of the most effective and sustained models of how to achieve this. However, after the 'stagnation' of the Brezhnev years and the limits of military-led development became more apparent (Aslund, 1991), the Soviet Union ceased to be regarded as a role model for nations pursuing development. Mark Galeotti describes this decline in influence as a symptom of a larger decline in the global status of the Soviet Union. Whereas at one time the developing world had looked to the USSR as an inspiration and proof of what could be achieved:

> By the 1980s ... the opposite seemed true. Developing world nations were moving away from the crude collective approach to modernisation, realising that while it was an effective way of building a war-fighting economy in a hurry, it had little to offer in an age when the need was for food, not guns, and when national prosperity was to be found in microchips and motorcars, not yet more coal and pig iron to swell a glutted market. (Galeotti, 1995, 173)

In its later years, the Soviet Union could not serve as a model of prosperity for anyone. The heady and highly-crafted claims of earlier phases of Cold War propaganda were abandoned. The famous Soviet military machine was enmeshed in its own imperialist quagmire in Afghanistan, which both revealed how tightly military resources were stretched and how dissatisfied the Soviet public had become with the consequences of such adventures. With hindsight, it has become easy for us all to act as if the Soviet experiment was doomed to failure from the start.

According to Aslund, 'the fundamental problem that doomed communism was its institutions' (2002, 40). Although he is committed to arguing that the Soviet system was unsustainable for reasons intrinsic to its ideological and institutional basis, Aslund's explanation of what this failure means echoes that of many others (for example, Aganbegyan, 1998; Ellman and Kontorovich, 1992; Winiecki, 1988). The Soviet system was ill-prepared for new challenges and unable to foster innovation – information technology highlighted this weakness and anticipated new economic forms that could be encompassed in the careful plans of industrial development. Despite all the public bragging and relentless diversion of resources into arms build-up, the Soviet Union was not able to keep up with US levels of military investment. Although there were some attempts at economic reform, they did not deliver the expected and needed growth – instead this became another loss of credibility for the economic approaches of socialism. At the same time as these challenges to the economic miracle of Soviet planning were emerging, the pressure to democratise was calling into question the political legitimacy of the Soviet system. Given this range of factors, the ultimate demise of the Soviet Union and its satellite states across Eastern and Central Europe appears to have been inevitable and unstoppable, not least due to the impact of the international economy. 'In the end, most countries were hit by fiscal emergencies, such as severe shortages, excessive fiscal deficits, and excessive external debt service, and these crises were accompanied by external shocks.' (Aslund, 2002, 40)

Although a range of commentators have focused on the internal tensions of the Soviet system, both economic and political (see Blackburn, 1991), participation in the international economy brought a number of issues into crisis. The accusation that the Soviet Union was itself an imperial power, even while acting as patron and funder to a range of anti-imperialist struggles in other regions, appears unanswerable. While the communist bloc operated as its own trading region, it was the Soviet economy that benefited from the docile markets of the periphery. More recently, many have suggested that within the Soviet Union itself, the benefits and goods of the planned economy were enjoyed disproportionately by a Muscovite centre that revealed the geographical and ethnic hierarchies of actually existing socialism (Gerner and Hedlund, 1993).

The crises that brought down the Soviet economy are not dissimilar to those that have beset other developing nations. However, as a global superpower and example of the possibility of affluence through planned economy, there was a greater impetus for the Soviet Union to mask such difficulties. The failure to check and limit such internal tensions far earlier, and particularly the failure to review economic planning with an eye to the impact on everyday life, rendered the eventual fall far more extreme and unstoppable. Ultimately, the costs of keeping up the appearance of a world superpower – costs that were exceptionally high in both economic and political terms – continue to be borne by the people of the former Soviet Union.

THE RISE OF ORGANISED CRIME IN THE FORMER EASTERN BLOC

The above discussion has been informed by a range of well-known accounts suggesting that the Soviet Union collapsed through a combination of pressures. These included an unsustainable imposed economic model, the situation made more difficult by perpetual military overspend; increasingly organised political pressures to democratise; and the ongoing turbulence of US interventions through many means.

In all three strands of explanation, organised crime emerges as a key player in the process of change. Here is an alternative type of economic actor, at once created and nurtured by the strictures and unexpected opportunities of the hyper-planned system. Organised crime emerges as perhaps the only indigenous model of market maximisation. Here are a group of people who are not afraid to make money, who understand the drawbacks of the planned system and are well versed in overcoming its hurdles, who are willing to take risks and who can persuade the general population to participate.

It took some time for the spectre of the Russian mafia to become such a bogeyman. It is only relatively recently that this mythology has become such a standard figure in accounts of the need for greater financial regulation (Finckenauer and Waring, 2001). During the rapid restructuring of the Eastern bloc, there was a far greater tolerance of criminal connections and even criminal activity when fostering the transition to a market economy.

A significant factor in the debate about transitional economies and the most effective way to ensure their future prosperity is the implicit analysis of the Soviet economy that shapes different positions in the discussion. Although there has been room here only for the most cursory review of these debates, it is worth spending a little time reminding ourselves that this was not always such a one-sided discussion. Similarly, debates about the rise of organised crime in the former Soviet Union veer between different viewpoints, from those who view this as a covert continuation of Cold War tensions to those who view crime as a necessary tool in the quest to free markets. Phil Williams describes the range of opinion in the following terms:

> At one end of the spectrum are those who consider Russian organised crime a dangerous successor to the threat posed to western values and western societies by the Soviet Union. Adherents of this view provide what is, in effect, a worst-case estimate of the Russian organised crime threat. At the other end of the spectrum are those who not only believe that the threat from Russian organised crime is greatly exaggerated in many Russian and western commentaries, but also argued that, in present circumstances, organised crime has certain positive functions in Russian society and the economy. (Williams, 1997, 1)

Both positions rely on only thinly veiled Cold War mythologies. On the one hand, there is that old and versatile favourite – a threat to Western values that places Russian organised crime as the new unseen enemy, a kind of communist threat gone underground. On the other, a similar model of infiltration is simply reversed – organised crime plays a vanguardist and necessarily covert role in the world-historical mission to spread market values. In both accounts, the space of the former Soviet Union is seen to retain certain essentialised characteristics, regardless of political changes. The Cold War is never really over, because there is always the danger that 'they' will revert to type. Whether it is blood or history, it is always there, just below the surface.

What is at stake between these two viewpoints is both the role of organised crime and also its provenance. Is Russian organised crime a continuation of the corrupt shadow economy which developed under the Soviet system? Or are we witnessing new forms of organised crime that emerge in response to the opportunities of these transitional economies? In this sense, the debate about organised crime is a continuation of the earlier debate about the demise of the Soviet Union. Does the Soviet system collapse under the weight of its own unsustainable practices and systems, or does it fall victim to the multiple incursions of the West?

There is a strong and developed argument that suggests that the Soviet Union collapsed along its own internal fault lines – one aspect of this debate has been discussed above in relation to military spending and the shortcomings of the planned economy. Another argues that such an authoritarian regime was not sustainable – the lack of democracy also stymied economic and social development and this, combined with the imperial basis of the Union, demanded unsustainable levels of internal policing and repression (Kagarlitsky, 1988). Economies cannot run on guns alone, people need to feel free in order to thrive, the histories of a place will continue to shape social relations – the Soviet Union was trying to swim simultaneously against the lessons of economics, politics, history and culture. Although this analysis includes a range of approaches and viewpoints, the linking theme is the suggestion that the break-up of the Eastern bloc is an outcome of the particular histories and choices of that region, as opposed to being the culmination of a successful assault by the West (Aganbegyan, 1988). This is an account that views material circumstances and the alignment of political interests within a region as more significant than the more abstract notion of an ideological struggle with the West. Within this account the theme of corruption looms large. This idea of the corrosive parallel structure of corruption and nepotism can be seen in a range of commentaries, from an economic analysis of the failure of planning, to a political analysis of the crisis of legitimacy and the call for democracy, to a sociological analysis that speaks of the distrust that pervaded Soviet society.

A CORRUPT CULTURE?

The portrayal of Soviet society as a world consumed by internal corruption has become prevalent. In his account of global social change, Manuel Castells focuses on this inner tension and diversion of resources when he discusses the decline of the Soviet Union:

> The shadow economy, which grew considerably during the 1970s with the compliance of the party's Nomenklatura, deeply transformed Soviet social structure, disorganising and making more costly a planned economy that, by definition, was no longer allowed to plan, since the dominant interest of 'gatekeepers' throughout the administrative apparatus was to collect their shadow rents rather than to receive their bonuses from the fulfilment of planned targets. (Castells, 1998, 21)

The figure of the Nomenklatura embodies a number of tasty Cold War mythologies. The Nomenklatura are those privileged through party structures, who therefore have access to goods, services and sources of wealth that are denied to the ordinary citizen. As stock characters, partly phantasmic, partly rooted in reality, the Nomenklatura and the world that their image calls up does a large and mobile amount of ideological work. These are the figures who reveal the unthinking practice of everyday authoritarianism, each slotted into a faceless machine of party business. Yet somehow they are also emblematic traitors to the Soviet dream, selfishly corrupt instead of selfless servants of the people. This double legend makes the Nomenklatura both the evil archetype of the omniscient Soviet machine and the betrayers of the Soviet promise, carriers of a corrupt ideology and indications of the frail individual's susceptibility to corruption.

Is this fixation on the corruption of the Soviet system itself a continuation of the ideological warfare of the Cold War period (see Volkov, 2002)? There is a sense in which the characterisation of lawlessness and criminality has been presented as an almost ethnic trait, as yet another instance of our clashing civilisations.

In other chapters there will be further discussion of this ethnicised understanding of global events. Despite the apparently homogenising tendencies of globalisation, both popular and policy accounts of some significant episodes in global integration seem to fall back onto ethnic caricatures to explain the uncertainties of local events. The account of Russian organised crime builds on these kinds of ideas, but as behaviour passed down through culture, not an ethnos based on blood. In his examination of the role of organised violence in the transition to a market economy, Vadim Volkov argues that the mythology of the 'Russian mafia' has been used as an excuse for the failures of marketisation:

> The alliance between the corrupt ex-communist Nomenklatura and the Soviet criminal underworld, concluded for the purpose of appropriating former state property, has since been coined the 'Russian mafiya', and has been discussed in connection with the allegedly traditional Russian culture of lawlessness and informal relations. It is not difficult to see that the overdetermination of the Russian transition by various aspects of the legacy of 'communism' conveniently rescues the policy of 'shock therapy' and the underlying idea of liberal capitalism from responsibility for some major failures in the reforms. (Volkov, 2002, 18)

Few commentators would deny the existence of a long-standing co-operation between organised crime and some elements of the Soviet party machine – and others have placed this phenomenon in the context of wider debates about unaccountable state structures and their vulnerability to corruption. However, as Volkov explains, transforming this into an ethnic myth serves as cover for the turbulence and disappointments of economic reform. More than this, ethnicising the argument becomes a defence of the economic analysis – shock therapy would work were it not for the degenerate character of some nations. The ability to make this very particular and prescriptive form of economic restructuring work comes to be seen as a trait of the deserving poor, those who can accommodate themselves to the demands of the global economy, whatever the accompanying pain.

PARALLEL MARKET ECONOMIES

The frenzy to introduce the freedoms and benefits of the market in the former Soviet Union created a number of unforeseen side effects.

To some extent, these unfortunate unintended consequences are now being acknowledged and analysed, with a view to rethinking the received wisdom of international economic institutions. As Peter Andreas argues in his account of the growth of transnational organised crime: 'Regardless of their illegal status, the economic activities of transnational criminal organisations are in many ways the quintessential expression of the kind of private sector entrepreneurialism celebrated and encouraged by the neoliberal economic orthodoxy.' (2002, 37)

This is one of the central arguments of this volume – whatever fears may have arisen about the consequences of organised crime across national boundaries, transnational crime is a very effective response to the economic challenges of globalisation. For some groups of people, this may be the only effective response open to them. In a manner that is most obviously seen in relation to the former Eastern bloc, but which clearly applies to other regions of the world, the instructions and interventions of international financial institutions themselves can appear to give succour to organised crime:

> Economic liberalisation also creates a new opportunity structure for those involved in criminalised markets. Some of the very initiatives designed to encourage and facilitate legal economic exchange – trade and financial liberalisation, privatisation, deregulation of transportation – can also benefit illegal economic exchange. (Andreas, 2002, 40)

In fact economic liberalisation creates a whole range of opportunities for those who are involved in a whole range of business, including the business of crime. Organised crime operates through parasitic processes, latching on to the infrastructures of the formal economy when it can. Make legitimate business easier, less regulated, better supported by transport and communication, and organised crime will lap up the benefits as well. However, what is suggested here involves a little more than this. There is an implication that economic liberalisation not only facilitates criminalised markets, as it facilitates the freer working of markets more generally, but that it creates a business climate that is more attuned to the needs of organised crime and more in keeping with its practices.

In the case of the former Soviet Union, this suggestion tends to cast doubt on any business success achieved through the period of liberalisation:

A substantial part of the assets of new entrepreneurs in the post 1987 boom originated in the shadow economy of the late Soviet period, but those who responded to the new economic policies and who had no connections to the underworld were also regarded suspiciously by the public. After all, what the 'cooperators' and private traders were now doing openly had only yesterday been a criminal offense, speculation or illicit trade. (Volkov, 2002, 30)

GETTING RICH QUICK

The rapid restructuring of East European economies – under the most extreme pressures and with crumbling governments and little defence against speculation – has instituted a whole new area of academic and policy debate. The study of so-called transitional economies was, for a time, a fairly overt celebration of the benefits of the market. Since then, this same area of study has developed to examine the hurdles and difficulties facing economies that attempt the transition from planned to market economy and from protectionism to international trade (Blejer and Skreb, 2001; Hann, 2002; Pickles and Smith, 1998). In the process, debates about transitional economies have become part of the larger discussion of how less affluent and powerful nations and regions come to be integrated into the global economy.

Eastern Europe, and the former Soviet Union in particular, have served as the exemplars of such transition. Their experience has confirmed another aspect of interest in transitional economies – the belief that there are rich pickings here for those who know how to get them. As others have commented, the hurry to invest, engage and trade with transitional economies has become a new gold rush, and, in popular imagination, the former Eastern bloc has come to represent one of the best opportunities of our time to make a fast buck, not least for those unable or unwilling to engage in more mainstream business avenues.

In the wider literature about the growing and dangerous influence of transnational organised crime – and the particular threats that come from that increasingly lucrative and popular transnational service offered by organised criminals: money-laundering (see Beare, 2003) – two categories of economy crop up again and again. The first is the emerging market, the other the transitional economy – often the two terms refer to the same places, but there is a distinction in the manner in which the threat is formulated. Money-laundering is presented in policy analysis as the activity that brings organised crime into legitimate financial business, blurring the boundaries between legitimate and criminal economies. Charting the manner in which this worry is articulated offers some lessons in conceiving the global economy.

First let us consider the concept of the emerging market: those places that show potential and are picking up economic speed. Increasingly, the emerging market is a term that includes a wide variety of 'developing' nations – a recent article uses a sample of Argentina, Bolivia, Brazil, Chile, Colombia, Mexico, Peru, Indonesia, Malaysia, the Philippines, Thailand, Turkey, Hungary, Poland and South Africa, showing that emergence can span a range of continents, economic situations and historical circumstances (Burkart and Coudert, 2002). The increasing integration of the global economy demands participation, but it also creates new opportunities – for both development and exploitation. For some regions of the populous poor world, the flighty flexible capital of the globalised era represents a chance to accelerate development. As has been much commented upon, this hope has been built around the example of the so-called Asian miracle – an experience of rapid economic expansion and change that has lost much of its miraculous lustre in recent years.

Of course, new regions have always emerged – no economic process in history has been geographically static. However, the recent phase of accelerating global integration has given new status and attention to the emerging market. In part this signals an overhaul of development thinking. The very term 'emerging market' indicates that at least some segments of the poor world are being reconfigured as positive economic possibilities, opportunities to be taken rather than disasters to be managed. I want to focus on the significance of the emerging market for our understanding of globalisation and its points of vulnerability.

The most cursory scan of contemporary advice and information in the field of international business reveals the value accorded to good information about emerging markets – which locations are ripe for economic entry, points of engagement, developments that enable investment in particular states. Emerging markets represent some of the fastest bucks to be made in the global economy. These are the places that are just beginning to lift themselves out of being too poor to participate. They can be characterised as countries with low or middle per capita incomes, countries without developed capital markets, or countries which are not yet industrialised (Mobius, 1994). Of course, all three criteria may apply. The most immediately lucrative locations may also offer a supply of cheap labour, including a section with a certain level of education and just enough communications and financial infrastructure to allow suitable development.

These are the locations that have the potential to enter the formal networks of the global economy. Unlike the dispossessed regions of the Fourth World and its illicit parallel economies, these spaces can be infiltrated, marketised and drawn into formal transactions by and through transnational corporations and the intervention of international agencies.

The emergent market is closely related, but not identical, to the concept of the transitional economy. This debate arose with the disintegration of the Eastern bloc and the rapid and often unruly shift to market-led economies in places that had been planned and tightly controlled. Such an unprecedented degree of economic restructuring, unstructuring, fragmentation and all-round unpredictable change, across such a diverse and significant region, has led to a whole new branch and industry of economic thought and business advice (Anderson and Pine, 1995; Nelson, Tilly and Walker, 1997).

In this field, the transitional economy, struggling to make the transition to being market-led and therefore able to participate in the global marketplace, becomes the central question of economic management. At first, this was a debate about the triumph of the market, with its unstoppable and irresistible forces remaking human history despite the resistance of political doctrine or authoritarian states. In these early discussions, the transitional economy was depicted as a place of endless opportunity, the fresh terrain of which developed capitalism had been dreaming.

With hindsight, transition to a more market-led economy has come to be viewed less as an overnight spiritual transformation and far more as a varied process of institutional reform and old-style power struggle. Some have suggested that the outcomes of this struggle have been compromised by the role of the previous elite:

The extraordinary economic distortions had bred strong vested interest. State enterprise managers favored a market economy of sorts, but they wanted to reserve this privilege for themselves, favoring regulation for others. This was probably the most important precondition of the transition, but few understood it at the time, and all underestimated the might and tenacity of these vested interests. The winners became so rich that they could buy politics lock, stock, and barrel. (Aslund, 2002, 68)

There is a school of thought that views the problems faced by a number of Eastern European economies as being caused by incomplete and insufficient marketisation (see Copetas, 1991). This view alleges that political transition has not taken place effectively – the former elite has remained, albeit under cover, and it is they who have reaped the major rewards of privatisation and other policy changes. It is clearly the case that the sudden and massive fortunes that have been made from the liberalisation of former communist economies have become tied to new holders of political power (Sampson, 2002). However, opinions differ about the identity and allegiances of such groupings – with some alleging a continuance of the Nomenklatura (Copetas, 1991), some identifying a new breed of 'ethnic' entrepreneurs (Chua, 2003) and others arguing that we are witnessing a reinvigoration and strengthening of organised crime (Varese, 2001). More plausibly, other commentators suggest that a range of actors have benefited from the processes of transition, and that such processes have shaped the emergence of new actors as a particular product of the moment, not only as a continuation of past structures. The rapid changes that have reshaped former communist societies have thrown up a range of unexpected and sudden opportunities – and those who are able to remake themselves and their futures through such opportunities seem to straddle the worlds of legitimate business and organised crime, creating a new class of entrepreneurs who have learned their trade through this new process of transition.

'There is an enormous task of restructuring entirely apart from the problem of institutional reform. Related to the restructuring of the economy is the acquisition by the population of an entirely new set of skills.' (Clague, 1992, 6) Clague is writing here of the need to develop suitable human capital and to nurture the technical, managerial and professional skills required by contemporary market economies – but his remarks could apply to the parallel survival skills that develop in response to the turbulence of liberalisation. After the basic but universal safety-net provided by centrally planned societies, many find that the restructuring has left them free for nothing but all too rapid impoverishment (Milanovic, 1998). However, at the same time a new elite has emerged – Eastern Europe's new millionaires who are freed to patronise a new market in luxury goods, to become leading players in the political life of former Soviet republics, and to undertake high profile investments across Europe and beyond ('He won, Russia lost', *Guardian*, May 8, 2004). These local winners of the transition process quickly come to be regarded as threatening rivals to more established guardians of the free market.

A review of the first ten years of transition argues that most transition strategies, insofar as a strategy is discernible, consisted of three prongs – liberalisation, institution building and macroeconomic stabilisation (Blejer and Skreb, 2001). Unfortunately, liberalisation seems to have taken precedence, with the result that there has been little opportunity to stabilise economies or to build accountable institutions. Instead, in a process that has been analysed in many recent commentaries, liberalisation has enriched a dubious group of gangsters, speculators and corrupt officials from the previous regime (Guyatt, 2000, 2003; Stiglitz, 2002) – any new entrepreneurial class is indistinguishable from this company. The privatisation of state assets does not enable wider participation in a market activity that is purported to remake societies and build democratic institutions, and neither does it introduce the desired efficiency gains of competition. William Webster comments on this process:

> One of the most pernicious aspects of Russian organised crime activity for law enforcement is financial criminal activity. Russian organised crime groups have acquired former state enterprises through privatization at pre-arranged 'auctions' and at knock-down prices. (Webster, 1997, 19)

Instead, this process is derided as the formation of a kleptocracy – a straightforward handover of economic, and with it political, power to a small and unaccountable grouping which has been enriched by dishonest financial dealings (Guyatt, 2000, 2003). If there is any doubt that economic transition has not lived up to its promises, then the impact on standards of living should persuade anyone that this is an experiment that has proved unsuccessful: 'Along with the economic changes that have accompanied transition in central Europe and the former Soviet Union has come a major and often dramatic deterioration in the social conditions of the population.' (Linn, 2001, 31)

Across the former Eastern bloc, there has been a rapid rise in inequality and poverty, with the most extreme decline in living standards experienced in the former Soviet Union. The number of Russians living in poverty rose from 2 million in 1990 to 60 million in 1999. Key social indicators such as life expectancy show a sharp decline (Linn, 2001). The exultant hopes that the transition to a market economy would bring general affluence now seem very outdated indeed.

That heady optimism soon became tempered by the uncertainties and violence of the experience of transition. The lived turbulence of these changes demands new forms of understanding and advice – some addressing strategies for minimising turbulence within, others for managing business with these new entrants to globalisation. As with so many things, here opportunity is laced with danger; and while individual actors may have regarded Eastern Europe as the new gold rush where untold fortunes could be made, for those with an interest in the stability and management of the global economy, this uncontrolled rush to who knows what kinds of economic activity also represented new dangers. There is a larger and more accomplished literature that examines the particular threats that emerge with the restructuring of Eastern Europe (Keren and Ofer, 1992; Piirainen, 1994). For now, it is enough to note the place of the transitional economy in the development of the global economy.

In this work, the characters of the emerging market and the transitional economy make many appearances, and under a number of guises. I want to argue that these entities and the attention that they draw must be central to any attempt to comprehend the globalisation of economic life. This is due, in part, to the historical factors that shape the machine of globalisation. However, it is also due to the unexpected turbulences that emerge as the global economy becomes more integrated, more unstoppable, and increasingly develops into something unlike any previous version of world economy. It is in this context that the best opportunities come to represent the most intense dangers.

GLOBALISING FINANCIAL CRIME

One aspect of the global economy that has been much commented upon is the role played by the rapid development of an international financial market and systems. A well-known and highly theorised debate has taken place about the role of communications technologies in this process (see Castells, 1996; Harvey, 1989).

It is not the place here to revisit all aspects of this debate. There are huge differentials in access to information and communications technology and these differentials echo other disparities of access and power. However, I do want to argue that new technologies of communication significantly alter the conduct of economic life across distance – and that even those who never engage in this form of transaction directly will feel the impact of these larger trans-regional, transnational transactions. In relation to the growth of international financial crime, the emergence of this network of potentially instantaneous and anonymised transactions enables new levels and perhaps even new forms of crime.

'One of the most important factors in facilitating international money laundering is undoubtedly the globalisation of the world's economy, sometimes even referred to as a "speculative global economy."' (Stessens, 2000, 91) Stessens identifies a number of factors that allow this development. One factor is the often cited role of new technologies in enabling instantaneous communication and adapting the place of transport. Stessens links this to 'the creation of an instantaneous payment system'. With transactions enacted through the click of a button, and with many transactions crossing each other in short amounts of time, it becomes much harder to track the source and legitimacy of trading. Alongside these shifts, the liberalisation of exchange controls also makes money-laundering a more available and profitable endeavour. 'It is clear, however, that this evolution, while undoubtedly beneficial to the growth of the world economy, also creates considerable difficulties for law enforcement authorities who seek to monitor transnational financial flows.' (Stessen, 2000, 91)

Here Stessen pinpoints the essence of the problem. For all the concerns expressed, money-laundering and other illicit financial transactions still contribute to economic growth. The factors that enable these forms of crime are the same factors that have enabled the development and growth of the world economy as we know it. Curtailing this kind of activity threatens to impinge on the larger dynamic of the international financial world. Not everyone who benefits from the speed and anonymity of the international economy is engaged in criminality – but clamping down on criminality might impact upon these other non-criminal benefits. Or at least, this has been the fear, a fear that has militated against greater regulation in the past.

After September 11, 2001, and the appearance of international terrorism as the cipher that signifies all evil in the world, the regulation of international financial transactions has taken on fresh urgency. No longer the terrain of sad book-keepers and faceless mandarins, the world of financial regulation has come out of the shadows in this new climate of joined-up security. While others have taken the opportunity to strut around world stages, quickly relearning the double mission of diplomacy and militarism, the regulatory bodies of the international economy have risen to the challenge with another form of heroism. Now, in the face of this dehumanising threat against the amassed forces of democracy and the free market, we hear that regulation can make globalisation fair. With a belated acknowledgement that the unstoppable motor of globalisation, despite its many achievements, has not brought the good life to all, bodies such as the International Monetary and Financial Committee (IMFC) propose a better, more just and equitable version of globalisation:

> You can see that this has been an important meeting for the international financial system, that global financial cooperation is being strengthened in all these areas, that we accept and act upon the increasing interdependence of the world economy, and we recognize the responsibilities of the richest countries to the poorest countries around the world. We affirmed that it is not only right to focus on globalization, but that it has never been more important to get globalization right. (Gordon Brown, IMFC, November 17, 2001)

This is the statement that indicates the IMFC response to the crisis of international terrorism. This is a time to take stock and take responsibility. It is for others to call for revenge. The careful role of financial regulation is to maintain order and stability – this is part of what it means to get globalisation right:

> It is a recognition, particularly after the events of September 11, that our interdependence means that what happens in rich countries affects poor countries and what happens in poor countries affects rich countries, and there is, I believe, a new determination and political will to make the changes that are necessary to make the international economy work better, particularly in the interest of those people who are presently excluded. (Gordon Brown, IMFC, November 17, 2001)

Considerable criticism was levelled at journalists and other commentators who suggested that the attacks on the United States should be understood in a context of global inequalities. Yet here at the heart of the capitalist machine, among those who see freedom as the extension of one version of the market to all, the lesson of global terrorism is that we are unavoidably interdependent and that this interdependence places responsibilities on the rich. Here I want to argue that this kind of talk emerges at the turn of the twenty-first century as a result of two pressures – one the desire to find some ethical contract and commonality amongst the insistently economic relations of globalisation, the other the unwelcome realisation that the unfettered spread of the market brings its own economic devastation, and not only for the poor world. My point here is not that the expressions of concern from Gordon Brown and others are hypocritical veils for their own self-interest – although that also may be true. Instead I want to explore the interrelation between these ethical and economic concerns – and to suggest that these two trends shape and inform each other in unpredictable ways.

DEMOCRACY AND ORGANISED CRIME

The recent concern to combat organised crime and terrorist funders in fact continues and extends a longer debate about the terms of international trade of all kinds. In this respect, I want to argue that the move towards greater financial regulation is part of the cultural shift that questions the aims of development economics, that demands fair trade and debt relief on both ethical and economic grounds and that fears that the unchecked growth of the market threatens the terms of democracy (Soros, 1998). I am not suggesting that these disparate ideas and movements constitute any coherent whole or even that they acknowledge each other in any explicit sense. However, this does not mean that these developments are not shaped by similar historical forces, and my argument is that they all arise as responses to a sense of crisis in the process of globalisation.

To return to money-laundering as the symbolic shorthand for the rising influence of organised crime, the wish to introduce internationally agreed terms of regulation for financial transactions has arisen from the well-founded suspicion that the growth of global financial markets has produced greater opportunity for financial crime. However, as the dynamic of globalisation has developed and deepened, it has become increasingly apparent that this unregulated growth and unchecked speculation can itself cause instability and disruption. Whereas previously enabling criminality seemed like a small cost to pay when set against the opportunities of the anonymised market, increasingly this lack of regulation is seen to cause unforeseen economic consequences and costs. Organised crime becomes a concern for international policy makers at the point when it threatens to hamper the business of so-called legitimate trade. It is hard not to conclude that criminality is seen as a problem only if and when it impinges on the mainstream economy. When the reinvigorated and greatly enriched organised crime groupings of Eastern Europe begin to spread their interests into the institutions of international finance, that is when we begin to see the panic responses from the self-appointed guardians of the free world.

There is a longer-standing literature on organised crime that attempts to understand the nature and structure of these organisations and their impact on more democratically accountable structures of governance (Buckley, 1999; Gambetta, 1993; Jamieson, 2000). This is a discussion that focuses on the corrosion of democracy rather than the infiltration of economic life – corruption is a problem of power and that is why it matters to ordinary people. On the whole, this work is characterised by an honourable desire to separate moral judgment from the business of inquiry. What matters is learning how things work, not judging their ethical value. This is what is at stake in the idea that: 'The criminal organisation is much closer to that of a government establishing its own rules in the areas over which it extends its power.' (Fiorentini and Peltzman, 1995, 4)

Unfortunately, such similarities may enable organised crime to offer an alternative infrastructure when states fail. Part of the mythology of the state of transition is the idea that it represents the linear and unstoppable journey towards freedom and democracy. It is this absolute belief in the ultimate supremacy of the market and its accompanying social formations that opened the door to organised crime. Now those actors who were viewed as necessary and as enabling to the process of transition have ensured that the future also belongs to them. There is no quick transition out of this place. Louise Shelley argues that this infiltration represents a new and unstoppable authoritarianism, another threat to democracy and accountable government:

> The consequences of organised crime on the development of the state are particularly pernicious in the successor states of the former Soviet union that are presently in transition. Organised crime, by undermining the electoral process, is shaping the development of the future legal system and the norms that will govern daily life and the operation of the economy. (Shelley, 1999, 35)

If this is the case, it has significant and worrying consequences. The more celebratory accounts of globalisation often assume, albeit quietly, that there is a limit to the impact of these endless transnational transactions. The imagined idyll of global affluence through international trade relies on stable states to provide homes for these new populations of market-savvy consumer-speculators. Those stable states are the safety-net that allows the indulgence of speculation to be liveable – moderately effective state structures seek to maintain themselves through some level of law enforcement, some regulation of banking and financial business, some regard for social welfare, however flighty capital may become. Without at least this minimal attention to human well-being, the frenzied circuits of the global economy threaten to spiral away from everyone's control.

The disintegration of the Soviet Union represents not only an economic free fall; it is also a complete fracturing of previous structures of social order, governance and social relations. Despite Western excitement about perestroika, the process of rebuilding civil society was at the most embryonic of stages when the Soviet system fell. In the aftermath of an authoritarian and all-powerful party machine, people needed to learn new ways of recognising their responsibilities and bonds to each other and of creating a fabric of trust that could maintain some order in times of such rapid change. In another unhappy echo of the *Godfather* films, this is the space into which organised crime insinuated itself. Yuriy Voronin describes the creation of such alternative structures of authority:

> Social organisations which, in principle, should be contributing to the development of civil society have already been neutralised or co-opted by criminal organisations. Criminal networks are exploiting societies, associations, funds, and unions. This helps them in several ways: 'dirty' money becomes clean, necessary protection is created for criminal associations, symbolic actions create a more favourable climate of public opinion, Russian 'godfathers' are made to appear as saviours of the homeland, and political channels for promotion of representatives of criminal structures to organs of government power are secured. (Voronin, 1997, 60)

In societies which seem to have become overrun with lawlessness, organised crime offers protection, order, and some enforcement of social norms, but all at a price. Services that were previously the responsibility of the state can become part of useful business, a means of consolidating influence with and co-operation from the local population. The vacuum that is left by the crumbling of former state structures provides an opportunity for organised crime to become a, if not the, central player in an alternative system of government that is not a million miles away from feudalism. This suggestion seems to be at the heart of international concerns – organised crime has become so embedded in the rebuilding of some societies that it reaches into the institutions of government:

> It is also clear that organised crime has supplanted many of the functions of the state, and currently represents the only fully functioning social institution. For instance, organised crime provides many of the services that citizens expect from the state – protection of commercial businesses, employment to citizens, mediation disputes. (Voronin, 1997, 60)

Despite the virulent, and often justified, criticisms of the overblown Soviet state system, the aftermath of its dismantling has revealed the importance of state structures. Without order, the entry of the market appears truly frightening, an invitation to revert to the laws of the jungle. More than this, the unhappy plight of transitional economies has served as a stark reminder that capitalism requires a social infrastructure, but does not necessarily guarantee this through its own workings. The magical market does not spontaneously give birth to the orderly and accountable institutions of democracy. Instead, crime fulfils some of these requirements, but always for the most extreme of prices.

The unhappy possibility that has been raised by the post-Soviet experience is that key institutions of global economic integration may now be in the hands of organised criminals. The processes of liberalisation have given some people a chance to get rich quick, often at the expense of everyone else. In places where there has been little history of business and entrepreneurship, local organised crime may represent one of the few players in a position to capitalise on such opportunities. Certainly in the earliest days of 'transition', few other than the corrupt, the criminal and foreigners were able to take part in the rush to buy up former state assets. The fortunes that were made in this process transformed the status of key actors, so that those who did well could become major political forces and relatively small-time gangsters could extend their activity and reach to become international players. In the process, local difficulties with organised crime evolve into global problems. The dangerous underbelly of globalisation expands its power base through the unruly territory of failing states and starts to become a serious force in the global economy. The chapters that follow discuss some other aspects of this story.

4
Drugs, Territory and Transnational Networks

The novel *Twelve* catches public attention for a while. A portrait of the disjointed and empty lives of over-moneyed and under-loved white youth in Manhattan, the linking theme of the narrative is the magical and irresistible pull of the mystery drug 'twelve'. That is the holy grail of alienated urban living in this telling – the frenzied journey that makes the most dangerous of social relations. It is the use and trade in drugs that brings this moneyed youth into contact with the poor and criminal and dangerous – that sews together different layers of the city and, by implication, of the global economy. As with so many other explorations and exposés of drug use in the West, the journey across town and across racial boundaries comes to stand in for a whole host of other boundary transgressions.

White Mike, teen dealer and central character, provides a commentary on these transgressive interactions:

> Intellectually, White Mike knows everything. He knows that Lionel comes from a place where there actually was crack, even if there's not so much anymore. He knows that Lionel's neighbourhood can get really fucked up, manifest the spectre of the inner city he and all his friends heard about in history class but only White Mike ever came close to seeing. White Mike is *cognizant* of, even involved in, this other New York City. (McDonell, 2002, 63)

White Mike is young, privileged, uptown and, not to be too obvious, white. Lionel is frightening, violent, from a dangerous neighbourhood and black. Their parallel worlds are not geographically distant, but it is only their shared involvement in the drug trade that brings them into contact with each other. It is this illicit contact that enables White Mike to comprehend the barbarous underbelly on which his more privileged world is built. Unfortunately, such comprehension only seems to confirm the need for separation.

In the policy debates and public pronouncements that shape international understandings of the drug trade, illicit substances take on the status of 'twelve'. These are the much-desired substances that initiate a range of strange alliances and cross-border journeys, form the occasion for countless unexpected meetings, and still, it seems, constitute the trade that best sums up the unhappy interdependence of rich and poor worlds.

In the terms of international institutions, this is an unforeseen byproduct of globalisation. In the United Nations World Drug Report 2000, an overview of the production, distribution and use of illicit drugs, Kofi Annan introduced the report with the words 'Globalisation offers the human race unprecedented opportunities. Unfortunately, it also enables many anti-social activities to become "problems without passports".' (UN, 2000c, Foreword)

The central 'problem without a passport' to which he is referring is the trade in illicit drugs – signalled by those danger terms 'drug abuse' and 'drug trafficking'. The opening message of the report suggests that, with the concerted and co-operative efforts of the international community, 'we may at last be on our way to a world in which people can live their lives free from drug abuse, from drug trafficking, and from related crime and violence' (UN, 2000c, Foreword). However, despite this upbeat opening, the rest of the report goes on to outline the extent and influence of the drug trade – and indicates some of the reasons why this has become such a central concern for international institutions. What is described is a world in which the post-Cold War remapping of the globe, combined with the increasing integration of the global economy, has unleashed a truly transnational drugs industry, with production, distribution and consumption seeping across all borders:

[the] apparently neat division among producer, transit and consumer states has clearly broken down since the late 1980s. Over the last decade we have witnessed an increasing globalization of drugs markets, which has enveloped parts of the developing world, especially with regard to heroin and cocaine. At least 134 countries and territories were faced with a drug abuse problem in the 1990s. Three quarters of all countries report abuse of heroin and two thirds abuse of cocaine. (UN, 2000c, 4)

Although the trade in drugs is no new thing, the sense that drug abuse is a social policy problem for all regions is relatively recent. However, more even than the extent and geographical spread of drug abuse, the United Nations report reveals the widespread fear that the drug trade has become a powerful transnational player, able to capitalise on weaknesses of state and economy in a world where control of such vulnerable regions has become an increasingly important and fraught issue:

> It is after all no coincidence that as the geographical orientation of plant-based drug production contracts, it increasingly focuses either on the territory of failed states or geographically marginalized states. What one has to realize in this situation is not that such countries are somehow intrinsically wedded to the production of illegal drugs, but that drugs production has become a symptom of wider structural problems. It is from such areas, which display multiple associated problems, that drugs have become most difficult to eradicate. (UN, 2000c, 11)

The map of the drug trade reveals the failures and danger zones of a unipolar world order. Although the Cold War fostered many security emergencies and actual armed conflicts, there was also a form of stability in the bipolar arrangement. A later chapter will discuss this in more detail and outline recent debates about new forms of war and the disruptive influence that failing states can have on the wider international order. For now it is important to note that drug production is regarded as both a threat in itself and, perhaps more importantly, as an indication that the place of such production is beyond the reach of the norms of the international community. The geography of the transnational drug trade uncovers the uncomfortable fault-lines in our integrated world – some places may participate in international trade, but in a manner that makes trade seem dangerous, not happy, healthy, and the only route to freedom. This kind of industry and business is increasingly concentrated in places where formal and accountable state structures are not in operation and the process of such trade threatens to consolidate the power of drug traders and to further undermine the possibility of rebuilding formal government and social infrastructure – Michel Chossudovsky (1997) argues that Peru and Bolivia have fallen into this category. The transnational drug trade, as it is portrayed by the United Nations, represents the frightening possibility that the conduct of trade itself may destabilise the world. In his discussion of the opium trade through history, Martin Booth comments on the recent and burgeoning influence of drug traders: 'Drug traffickers are, save their illegality, no different from any other commodity entrepreneur operating in the best spirit of free trade and, because of the addictive nature of their wares, they will have no problem selling their product.' (Booth, 1997, 227)

The drug trade causes alarm because, despite its similarity to other forms of trade, it suggests that trade can be a destructive force. Contrary to the Bretton Woods vision of a world united in peaceful co-operation through a shared interest in international trade, the drug business represents the possibility that things may go another way. This chapter goes on to argue that the drug trade may be one of the formative networks of global integration and that the double process of linking and destabilising that it represents is a characteristic common to many other forms of trade in an unequal world.

Drugs have become an easy shorthand symbol for the everyday monstrosity of global trade. This is the horror that creeps into the metropolitan centres of the rich world, bringing the violence and instability of the poor world right up close. And a large part of this horror comes from the sense that it is somehow deserved. We know that much of this trade comes from the poor world, and our media demons tell us that this is a business peopled by shadowy migrants who move between the desperations of affluence and poverty. There is every indication that the drug trade is viewed as the return of a certain lightly repressed knowledge – that the sins of global capitalism haunt us through our susceptibility to pleasurable and addictive pathogens.

In fact, the various drug trades that have animated capitalist expansion in different eras have served to create unequal connections between different regions and this inequality has shaped, in turn, the development of the variously skewed geopolitics of different times. Throughout, prohibition has represented a fantasy solution to this dangerous interdependence – as if the contracts could be broken by magic. In recent times, this fantasy that history might be undone and its unpleasant consequences tidied away forever is represented most prominently in the US-led war on drugs (Gray, 2002). This chapter will go on to argue that this endless and ineffectual war is another attempt to renew neo-colonialism by force and to replace the dependency of one era with another that better fits the dynamics of a globalised world. In the process, the drug trade is not eradicated, merely redeployed for other ends.

IS ECONOMICS THE LANGUAGE OF GLOBALISATION?

One of the unexpected benefits of globalisation-speak has been the re-emergence of a popular debate about the role of the economy. For a long time, debates about social justice in developed nations were shaped by the concepts of identity and culture. Of course, class mattered – but class was manifested through cultures of deprivation. Now lots of people are concerned to learn about the terms of international trade and corporate power, and the impact of these international forces on their everyday lives. On the whole, populations in the West still look to their elected national governments to control and curtail ravenous capital and, in the process, to safeguard human welfare. Somehow most of the world has come to believe that economic imperatives shape our political and cultural lives. Understanding the world and its shifting shape really does come down to understanding economics.

The most accessible celebrations of globalisation, the narratives that form the public face of international institutions, also treat economic concerns as the central motor of the process. In this telling, economic integration is what globalisation is. Other forms of interchange – political, cultural, from below through new technologies or from above through media conglomerates – are seen as secondary byproducts of the economic forces.

What seems to have fallen out of our understanding is the sense that some political manoeuvres may not be tied immediately to economic imperatives. Not that there is no connection between these two spheres of life, only that the relation is complex. Sometimes the quest for power may seem to make little economic sense, and that is also something that requires understanding. David Harvey describes one pertinent incarnation of this duality in his discussion of what he calls 'capitalist imperialism' and 'the molecular processes of capital accumulation in space and time', or more succinctly, the 'territorial' and 'capitalist' logics of power (Harvey, 2003, 26). Territorial power or capitalist imperialism is a political endeavour in which power is accrued from territory and the ability to control such territory for political and economic ends. Capitalist power, on the other hand, has little interest in territorial control, operating instead through flows 'across and through continuous space' (26) in the pursuit of profit. Capitalist power can be regarded as shorthand for the behaviour of mobile and flexible capital, a rootless force that is not constrained by borders. Territorial power is invested in the authority that can be wielded through control of place, and therefore may be willing to invest resources in such expensive endeavours as state services or military occupations.

I am painfully aware that popular debate in this area has been changing very rapidly. The military excursions into Afghanistan and Iraq have caused a global debate about the world's remaining superpower and the unhappy prospect of a new American century – that euphemism for the enforcement of US interests through sheer might. This has been another of the strange and unexpected educations that have come along with globalisation. Suddenly, and after a long absence, 'anti-imperialism' has rejoined the lexicon of leftist slogans. The extensive publicity that has been given to the business and investment interests of key members of the (George W.) Bush administration ensures that many are aware of this master plan for global domination. Conspiracies have rarely felt so tangible (Klein, 2003). Against this background, it would be too easy to revisit the history of US foreign policy as a seamless precursor to the present, as if the will to global domination through military intervention is an inevitable and unchanging aspect of powerful states. I have tried to remain alert to this trap in what follows, but occasionally the connections seem too conspicuous to ignore.

What I intend to explore here is a model of global integration that does not take trade as its key determinant, although trade may play a central role in achieving other objectives. Frequently, the assorted processes that we group together as globalisation can be assigned straightforwardly to the ongoing project to maximise profit in the hands of those who already have. These processes and agreements are not secret and their intention is stated openly. What has less often been tied into these narratives of ever-increasing global integration is the parallel dance of global influence, the geopolitics that slides alongside international trade but which is not reducible to it.

The key story of this chapter is about how powerful states can shape the manner in which less powerful nations enter and participate in the global economy.

THE DRUG TRADE AS A SHARED GLOBAL ENEMY

Since the 1990s, the drug trade has come to be portrayed as a threat to the poor. Whereas an earlier phase of the war on drugs took its lead from the impact of drug use in developed economies, more recent discussion has stressed the economic damage that the drug trade causes to developing nations. A key part of the problem has been that the drug trade has proved to be a highly resilient and effective means of making money, and has become embedded in various poorer regions as their prime cash-crop in a reconfigured global economy, as can be seen in the so far unsuccessful attempts to diversify the economies of Afghanistan and Bolivia.

To counter this, the interventions of international institutions have argued that the drug trade hampers development by diverting resources away from legal economic activities:

> The opportunity costs of the drug trade include: (a) lost investment in legitimate enterprise as farmers and processors funnel their savings into illicit drug cultivation and production; (b) lost investment in human capital as drug-related employment provides a false sense of security to its 'workforce'; and (c) future costs to the quality of the workforce as children get caught up in the drug trade. (UN, 1994, 2)

While the US-led war on drugs has continued to favour punitive intervention against drug-producing states, or at least against unfriendly drug-producing states, the relatively recent attempts by international organisations to wage their own war on drugs have harnessed the language of development. The production and trade in drugs hampers 'proper' economic development. It creates economic cultures where the quick money of an illegal trade pushes out the incentive to engage in other activity – not least the painful activity demanded to qualify as an economically disciplined nation in the estimation of international institutions. State infrastructures that attempt to corral their populations into such disciplines cannot compete with the alternative development of the drug economy. In response, bodies such as the United Nations stress the social costs of this kind of economy, arguing hard against the apparent efficiency of easy money:

> Specifically, the welcome process of economic reform in the developing world will leave many economies vulnerable to an increase in drug-related activity. This vulnerability is fed by profound financial and economic needs and can be explained by a simple premise: drugs can bring in money, and a lot of it. (UN, 1994, 9)

Hidden in this statement is the admission that economic reform, although welcomed by international institutions, brings hardship to people on the ground. Despite all the much heralded benefits of creating financial discipline, reforming public institutions, and most of all, of rolling back state spending and opening nations to the efficiencies of the market, the immediate impact of such endeavours is to increase the economic uncertainty and poverty of those who are already poor. In these circumstances, the quick cash potential of the drug trade can find ready participants. Worse still, there is all too little to distinguish between these transnational entrepreneurs and the dynamic market players that economic reform is designed to encourage:

> Over the past five years, developing countries have led the world in reducing barriers to trade. And yet, despite significant benefits to the global economy, there are potentially negative side-effects insofar as higher trading volumes and fewer official constraints can facilitate the cross-border transactions of drug traffickers. (UN, 1994, 11)

This is a recurring theme in our discussion – the facilitation of transnational trade that we characterise as globalisation, and the form this facilitation has taken, has created new opportunities for criminal traders. Although much of the rhetoric celebrating the market argues that enabling such entrepreneurial initiative is a necessary component of building democracy, in practice marketisation has enhanced also the power of such unaccountable social forces as drug traders and organised crime. 'The ongoing transfer of allocative influence to the market has exposed a need to ensure that reliance on market forces is not exploited by actors involved in illegal activities.' (Keh, 1996)

The opportunities of transnational trade, combined with the constrained avenues of neo-colonial relations, have created a new economic actor – drug traffickers whose reach and power have been enhanced through the development of the global economy, and who now represent significant interests within some less developed regions, as seen starkly in the attempts at post-war reconstruction in Kosovo and Afghanistan. The particular manner in which the global market has been shaped has enabled some of yesterday's local gangsters to become serious global players. More than this, and beyond the dubious backgrounds and characters of particular individuals, the transnational drug trade itself becomes part of the infrastructure of the global economy. In the manner of other powerful transnational industries, there is a momentum of continuance and growth that goes beyond any single player:

> Another relevant factor working against international eradication is that some national economies are now almost overwhelmed by the drugs trade. This has coined a new noun – narco-economics. It is argued, with some

validity, that traffickers make up the world's most influential special interest group, their economic power such that many poorer countries could not survive without their financial presence. (Booth, 1996, 343)

Although Booth is speaking here of the often voiced concern that the drug trade has become the controlling force in some regions, this insight assumes a particular power for the non-state actor. For our purposes, this suggestion is important. Narco-economics, inasmuch as it is a developed concept at all, refers to the manner in which the destiny of some regions and nations is shaped by transnational traders, in this instance of drugs, who have no allegiance to any place. It is a conception of international economics that recognises the unaccountable powers of special interest groups – those shadowy figures who are able to safeguard their own economic interests through the influence they wield with national governments and international bodies, influence which itself stems from the magnitude of those economic interests. The discussion that follows tries to explain a little further how we come to such a situation where unaccountable and often unidentifiable groups play such a shaping role in international economics and politics – and why such a situation has become an opportunity for drug traders.

BINDING THE WORLD ECONOMY TOGETHER

If organised crime was once tolerated, albeit covertly, as an aid to the processes of global integration and has only lately come to be seen as dangerously corrosive and uncontrollable, the trade in drugs has been vilified consistently. The drugs trade is blamed for, at the very least, eroding local economies and institutions in the poor world and contaminating urban life in the rich. When the rhetoric of the war on drugs calls upon the shared interests of a global alliance, this is the connection that is made. Drugs damage us all, allegedly.

Against this, we shall here review the central and strategic role played by various incarnations of the drug trade in the creation of an integrated global economy. What is particular about the drug trade in this account is the combination of neo-colonialism via highly dependent one- or two-crop economies and the extra leverage and military opportunities that can be squeezed from a criminal trade. Despite the high levels of rhetorical weight extracted from the war on drugs, the drug trade has been a central mechanism for engaging key areas of the poor world in global trade on terms specified by the rich world. Whatever the social costs of the drug trade, there has also been a certain instrumental benefit for legitimate business.

To understand this process, we need to revisit some old debates, debates coming back into fashion through the force of events. Later chapters will consider some key aspects of the discussion and identification of a new imperialism – and what such an analysis implies for attempts to contain the scary underbelly of globalisation, especially as it bubbles up to threaten the inhabitants of the affluent world. However, for now our focus is on an earlier account of global domination and its repercussions.

Neo-colonialism emerged as a subject of hot debate in the era of Third World consciousness and activism, and predated discussion of globalisation by several decades (Amin, 1973; Nkrumah, 1965). However, the suggestion that former colonial structures of power are maintained through the terms and conduct of international trade has more than a little contemporary resonance.

At the heart of the neo-colonialism debate is the question of what constitutes power and influence. Colonialism proper showed itself openly – through military presence, a system of colonial administration tied explicitly to the occupying power, the creation of a settler society and the co-option of local collaborators (Hobsbawm, 1987). Independence consisted of ejecting and overthrowing these tangible symbols of another power – once they were gone, a newly independent nation could emerge triumphant. Neo-colonialism is the concept that seeks to explain why such hard-won independence fails to deliver its promised prizes. Kwame Nkrumah, president of independent Ghana, leading Pan-Africanist and proponent of co-operation between Third World nations, wrote a groundbreaking examination of the workings of neo-colonialism that identifies the challenges facing newly independent nations:

> The essence of neo-colonialism is that the State which is subject to it is, in theory, independent and has all the outward trappings of international sovereignty. In reality its economic system and its political policy is directed from outside. (Nkrumah, 1965, ix)

Wallerstein argues that the concept of sovereignty is a 'shibboleth of the interstate system', a claim and defence that is circulated for effect, but which is acknowledged to be partial and uneven, nothing like the absolute principle that has been claimed (Wallerstein, 2003, 181). Wallerstein is writing from the vantage point of the twenty-first century, and is informed by knowledge of how imperfect the experience of decolonisation and independence has been for much of the world. In this his view coincides with that of Nkrumah: the outward trappings of sovereignty are no guarantee of effective independence. Stronger states intervene in the affairs of weaker states through a variety of means and weaker states work to defend their sovereignty as best they can. In recent years, this question of the boundaries of state sovereignty has become more contentious, with some arguing that 'failing' states do not merit the privilege of sovereignty and that the international community has a responsibility to intervene against such potential threats to global order (Kaldor, 1999). However, Nkrumah was not speaking of this formal sovereignty – at the time of his writing, the rights of sovereignty were not in question – he was identifying structures of power that can bypass the boundaries of political sovereignty. Others have claimed that this is a direct substitution of a domestic ruling class for the previous occupying power. No new nation emerges, local rulers just slot into place and leave all else intact.

This criticism has been discussed in an earlier chapter. Once in government, nationalist movements in a range of locations have been described, and sometimes denounced, as strategies to create a national elite who can benefit from the exploitative relations that previously served a foreign occupying power. However, the account of neo-colonialism given by Nkrumah is not quite this. His is not another disappointed denunciation of the corrupt and self-interested national elite; it is a description of another structure of domination, one that disguises the forces of power and appears to defy resistance:

> Neo-colonialism is also the worst form of imperialism. For those who practise it, it means power without responsibility and for those who suffer it, it means exploitation without redress. In the old days of old-fashioned colonialism, the imperial power had at least to explain and justify at home the actions it was taking abroad. In the colony those who served the ruling imperial power could at least look to its protection against any violent move by their opponents. With neo-colonialism neither is the case. (Nkrumah, 1965, xi)

This is the essence of the analysis of neo-colonialism. By bypassing open intervention in the political arena, in favour of the indirect prizes of unequal trade and corporate occupation, neo-colonialism institutes a form of domination that can abdicate any responsibility towards those dominated. Nkrumah offered an early example of critiques of multilateral aid, something he described as 'another neo-colonialist trap', identifying international financial institutions as 'having US capital as their major backing':

> These agencies have the habit of forcing would-be borrowers to submit to various offensive conditions, such as supplying information about their economies, submitting their policy and plans to review by the World Bank and accepting agency supervision of their use of loans. (Nkrumah, 1965, 242)

This is a comment on the processes of international financial institutions during a period now regarded with some nostalgia, a time when there was far greater goodwill towards the project of development as it was imagined by both the World Bank and the IMF and by decolonised nations. Nkrumah's comments indicate that dissatisfaction has accompanied the Bretton Woods project since its formation – and that much of the world can never be content with a model of development that imposes a First World vision of economic management upon everyone.

UNINTENDED CONSEQUENCES

The theoretical conceptualisation of neo-colonialism focuses on the manner in which economic processes can continue previous structures of domination and control but at a distance. The messy and resource-heavy business of actual occupation is no longer necessary – neo-colonialism can deliver the same goodies with far less trouble. What needs to be added to this account is the hovering threat of coercion that hangs over such neo-colonial relations. If there is any hint that the clean distance of neo-colonial forms of domination may be resisted, more old-fashioned and hands-on styles of domination are waiting in the wings at all times. In a volume deeply influenced by the protest movement against the Vietnam War, Sidney Lens summarised the manner in which this constant threat and frequent use of force has lead to what he terms the forging of the American Empire:

> From the CIA coup in Guatemala to the invasion of Cambodia under President Nixon in 1970 – and beyond – the United States intervened on scores of fronts to defend and build its empire. It intervened through exaction of concessions for economic aid – for instance, through Point 4, the

Alliance for Progress, or the PL-480 food-assistance program. It intervened by supplying and training satellite armies in dozens of countries. It intervened through the CIA. It intervened through the Lovestone apparatus in the American federation of Labor, and AFL-CIO – in British Guiana, for instance. And on occasion, when other methods proved insufficient, it intervened by landing its own troops on foreign soil – for example, in Lebanon, Vietnam, the Dominican Republic. The imperial drive was never checked. (Lens, 1971, 2003, 391)

In practice, the era of neo-colonialism has been punctuated by a series of military interventions, overt, covert and by proxy. The arms-length exploitation of neo-colonial relations is backed up by an ever-present threat of force. In the course of the nineteenth century, the United States had established itself as key power of the Western hemisphere – in part through proclaiming itself an anti-imperialist patron empowered to intervene against improper European incursions in newly emerging Latin American republics. However, in the course of the twentieth century the United States became a truly global power, and eventually the pre-eminent economic and military force in the world. Through the Second World War, the United States was making preparations for this role, largely with an eye to establishing access to sufficiently large export markets and sources of key raw materials. Three areas were identified as central to US interests – the Western Hemisphere, the Far East and the British Empire – and this identification served to commit the United States to all kinds of coercion in its attempts to integrate these regions economically (Pearce, 1981, 25). However, such an attitude to the world was not motivated only by economic concerns. The Second World War changed the map of the world to such an extent that now it was the Soviet Union that appeared as the other great global power. As a result, US interests were reinterpreted to include defeating communism and the *threat* of communism anywhere in the world. The pattern of relations that had been established in Latin America continued to provide the preferred model for this flavour of neo-colonial endeavour, confirming that the United States favoured an arms-length approach to military intervention: 'A United States-trained army and a friendly dictator became the established and favoured means of maintaining order in the region and protecting American interests.' (Pearce, 1981, 21)

In fact, more traditional models of imperialism arguably employed similar tactics to these – exploiting local social divisions, creating local leaders who were dependent on the patronage of the occupying power, training a local military and police force who were identified as agents of the occupying power by both themselves and the local population. The more developed European imperial bureaucracies sought to limit the costs and dangers of empire by adopting an administrative role in relation to a machinery of domination powered by locals – an arrangement which also produced anti-imperialist leaders schooled in the language and culture of the occupiers (Hobsbawm, 1987). The distinction in the United States model, after the land grabs of Mexico and Puerto Rico, was that, on the whole, the dominated nations remained ostensibly independent. This allowed the United States to install chosen 'friendly dictators' under the pretence of defending democracy, usually against the alleged threat of communism. Under such dubious pretexts, various unpopular and repressive regimes have been supported, such as successive generations of the Somoza dynasty in Nicaragua; Batista in Cuba; Trujillo in the Dominican Republic – before he came to be seen as a threat to US corporate interests and was assassinated with CIA assistance; Françoise and Jean Claude Duvalier, Papa and Baby Doc of Haiti. Similarly, a series of elected leaders have been replaced, including Jacobo Arbenz of Guatemala and Salvador Allende of Chile. This interpretation of US interests allowed the Central Intelligence Service (formed in 1947 as another key institution in the global remapping that took place after the Second World War) to grow into a worldwide network of untold resources accountable to no one but, and this only theoretically, the President of the United States. Although the United States has been keen to promote and protect its trading interests and to create docile markets for US corporations, the logic of the Cold War also lead to interventions that made little immediate economic sense under the logics of capitalist or of territorial power.

Arguably, the strategies of intimidation and intervention employed to maintain United States' influence were an effective means of securing US access to key markets and materials, and of safeguarding the holdings of US corporations. However, this could be done only through the deployment of considerable resources. This will to territorial influence was animated by a desire for global dominance that is not quite reducible to an immediate economic imperative.

The infamous concept that summarised US practice in the post-war period was that of 'counter-insurgency'. The phrase itself is framed to imply legitimate defence, a response to the prior provocation of insurgency. Of course, insurgency here is code for communist leanings, overthrow of the natural order, potential satellite for the evil empire of the Soviet Union – but counter-insurgency was deployed as a suitable tactic in a host of situations where ordinary people voted for social welfare and some modest redistribution of wealth, from Guatemala in 1954 to Chile in 1973 to the 1980s backing of Contra forces in Nicaragua. The imagined spectre of communism was used to mobilise terrible violence at the slightest imagined sign of resistance to the US vision of the world – a violence that was suffered by ordinary people (Chomsky and Herman, 1979; McClintock; 1985).

> The paramilitary militia concept at the core of counter-insurgency doctrine, in practice, provided for the creation of an armed elite set apart from the bulk of the society, with in some cases life and death discretionary powers. (McClintock, 1985, 274)

The US-trained armies of friendly dictators provided the muscle for the police states of neo-colonialism. After all, these armies were mobilised against the improper conclusions of the popular will. As a result, lack of accountability was built into the logic of counter-insurgency. It was only a short step from this to institutionalised terror. Although the Pentagon defined counter-insurgency as 'a combination of military, paramilitary, political, economic, psychological and civic action carried on by a government in order to destroy any movement of subversive insurgency' (Pearce, 1981, 52), the term has become synonymous with US-backed repression. As a strategy, the doctrine of counter-insurgency committed the United States to aiding, training and sponsoring truly brutal regimes, all in the name of safeguarding US interests.

In *Blowback*, Chalmers Johnson suggests that the multiple crises that face the world at the beginning of the twenty-first century can often be traced back to earlier phases of US foreign policy. Johnson argues that the United States has been engaged in a long and often covert process of empire building, and that this has drawn a number of consequences, including violent and unorthodox forms of resistance to such imperial ambitions. He takes the term 'blowback' from CIA accounts of the unforeseen consequences of earlier actions. In intelligence usage, the term refers to the turbulence and further difficulty that follows covert interventions in other states. If anything, this is regarded as a necessary hazard and may even come to shape the terms and objectives of future missions. Johnson borrows the sense of secrecy only in that the general public remains unaware of the connection between past actions and present consequences, even when the initiating actions are not covert:

> I believe the profligate waste of our resources on irrelevant weapons systems and the Asian economic meltdown, as well as the continuous trail of military 'accidents' and of terrorist attacks on American installations and embassies, are all portents of a twenty-first-century crisis in America's informal empire, an empire based on the projection of military power to every corner of the world and on the use of American capital and markets to force global economic integration on our terms, at whatever costs to others. (Johnson, 2003, 7)

Although *Blowback* is written for the general reader, Johnson has a distinguished academic record and his broad-ranging discussion of US engagement with Southeast Asia is shaped by this scholarly background. It is also indicative of a larger conceptualisation of postwar US power. Johnson is proposing the idea of an informal empire in order to describe the close interdependence between military and economic strategy. As he says, this is an empire that at once occupies and trades, with each reinforcing the other. This is the double project that the present chapter seeks to explain – drug trades play a certain central role in some aspects of this process, but other commodities can just as easily wield this power. The leverage comes from the integration of corporate interests with superpower foreign policy; it is this seamless co-operation that characterises this particular structure of international intervention: 'There is a logic to empire that differs from the logic of a nation, and acts committed in service to an empire that is never acknowledged as such have a tendency to haunt the future.' (Johnson, 2003, 8)

National interests may benefit from a larger imperial project, but the national project and the project of empire are not the same. In fact, I think Johnson is wrong to suggest that there is any absolute distinction between these levels – the US imperial project could be seen to remake the terms of national interest for powerful nations. However, it is true to say that there has been some international agreement about the legitimacy of national interests and their pursuit. The machinery of the United Nations, an international institution that runs parallel to the financial infrastructure of Bretton Woods, formalised this understanding. Empire, on the other hand, in the covert twentieth-century incarnation described by Johnson, at the very least bends the rules of international law. 'Even an empire cannot control the long-term effects of its policies. That is the essence of blowback.' (Johnson, 2003, 13)

This unspoken project of US imperial expansion has become a highly debated issue in recent years. Since September 11, 2001 and the open articulation of possible US military aggression against a range of long-standing enemies, many voices all over the world have railed against the new American Empire and its endless hunger for oil (see for example Mann, 2003; Ali, 2003). But this whole clamour has sprung up relatively suddenly. Before this, the idea of imperialism had fallen away from popular debate in the West, even among the Western left. Johnson reminds us that the United States has a long history of covert and dubious forms of intervention in the business of other parts of the world, and that such activity has spawned its own sub-structure of the military-industrial complex, an intelligence service that requires an endless series of covert operations in order to justify its existence. If such interventions lead to blowback in the form of new threats, then this further confirms the analysis of the security services, a view of the world as a series of emerging dangers to be contained. Johnson argues that, as well as the unspeakable price paid by the populations subject to the effects of such actions, this cycle also has a considerable cost for the US public. Although the essence of blowback is that much of the activity is secret, the US population has to pay for the costs of these covert and not so covert operations and also suffer the fresh enemies and increased risks that such operations bring to America: 'In the long run, the people of the United States are neither militaristic enough nor rich enough to engage in the perpetual police actions, wars, and bailouts their government's hegemonic policies will require.' (Johnson, 2003, 230)

However, the people of the United States have been paying such a price for some time already. The impact of the drug trade – real and imagined, economic and political – is one aspect of this price. The drug trade has taken on an excessive significance within the imagination of western policy makers. A multiplicity of global anxieties, or anxieties about the global, have been folded into this one icon. Fix this and all of these other evils will be undone at the same time – this has been the hope. Most famously, the so-called war on drugs that shaped US foreign policy for a generation, and which continues to frame the legitimising discourses of US intervention, has presented the drug trade as the incarnation of one form of global evil.

The trade in drugs of various kinds has not always been regarded as a threat to global order. Arguably, drug trades have been at the centre of the development of international trade. At various points in world history certain illicit and yet highly prized goods have played a central role in remaking the boundaries between nations and markets. In one telling, international trade emerges as a result of the quest for these magical commodities. Whether this is the Silk Road, the spice trail or the search for some unnamed rejuvenating elixir, sensational foreign goods have animated the development of world trade: 'Europeans first went to Asia in their quest for spices. All of the subsequent empires that they built in Asia were simply modified versions of the initial venture.' (Trocki, 1999, 8) Trocki's argument is that this model of the spice trade reveals the centrality of drug traffic to colonial expansion: 'there was always one exotic chemical or another that became the object of European trading monopolies' (8) – from spices to coffee to sugar to tea to opium and beyond.

What follows attempts to chart the continuity between these earlier trades and the ambivalent role of the contemporary drug trade in international commerce. More particularly, I want to keep in mind the excessive interest and military response to the drug trade that has characterised a whole raft of recent US foreign policy. Although the war on drugs has concentrated largely on the unlucky region designated as America's backyard, it seems that the violent histories of Latin America are now being exported around the world. Although it is a little overstated to suggest that now everywhere has become America's backyard, there is something in the dynamic of a unipolar world that allows a replaying of superpower mistakes, perhaps with a view to doing it right this time around.

COMMODITIES WITH AN EXTRA AURA

There is confusion about the boundary between legitimate goods and trade and illicit goods and trade. Of course, there is a significant enhancement of profit from trading in illicit goods, but it is important to remember that this is not the only way to make obscene amounts of money. Much of what is discussed in this book spans the boundary between illicit and legitimate business, and although the drug trade appears to be more certainly criminal than some other case studies, I want to link the trade in drugs to more general ideas about highly profitable commodities.

It is not a startling insight to say that it is the money that makes the drug trade so dangerous. In terms of its damaging effect on producing regions, cocaine production, for example, could be replaced with diamond mining (Campbell, 2002). The mind-altering properties of the commodity itself have no particular relation to the dangers and dynamic of the trade. Given this, it is interesting to consider why some commodities take on this extra aura and capacity to embody all our dreams of getting rich quick. Most importantly for our concerns, I want to spend a little time considering how poor nations become enmeshed in drug economies. What is it about these overly lucrative and highly dangerous trades that cause such a shift in local economies? How is it that one such over-valued trade can reshape the trading space that surrounds it, shifting the rest of economic life? Trocki writes of opium as this kind of society-shaping commodity, endlessly valuable, better than money:

> From the late eighteenth century until the middle of the nineteenth, opium was the major commodity of the Asian trade. It was a single most valuable export from India for many of these years. It was the single most valuable commodity which China imported. Opium also flowed to all of the ports and states of Southeast Asia. Wherever people had cash to buy it, or wherever a valuable commodity could be offered in exchange, opium was sold. Opium pushed old commodities, such as Indian cloth, out of the market, and at the same time, brought new ones into the market. Opium seems to have supplied an irresistible incentive to produce, or at least to make others produce. In China, it was not long before others began to produce opium themselves.
>
> Opium became new money and thus a new form of exchange medium as well as a consumer commodity. As appears typical of newly established drug trades, the opium trade created massive transfers of wealth, new accumulations of capital and new owners of capital. (Trocki, 1999, 167)

Such a lucrative trade leads to rapid shifts in entrepreneurial choice and buying power. Much local industry will compare poorly with the returns available from this new magical trade, so those who can will shift their investment to where the money is. At the same time, sudden and new pockets of wealth create their own economic dynamic – new demands, new products, new circuits of exchange. As Trocki suggests, this process remakes the internal dynamics of an economy completely, throwing up new key players and displacing former sources of wealth. Before you know it, one trade has remade class formation across society and created a situation where increasingly the rich and powerful have investments in the drug trade. One key crop is controlled by a privileged elite who through this control come to shape the trajectory of a whole society – a set of social relations that evolves to form the basis of the neo-colonialism that haunts so much of our discussion.

The debate about neo-colonialism is not only a critique of Western power, it is also an attempt to understand a new mapping of the world. Despite the high hopes of national independence movements, decolonisation did not bring a quick route to freedom and affluence. Instead, newly independent nations found themselves operating within the constraints of an international economy with terms of trade that seemed all too familiar. Somehow, even without a actual occupying force, the relations of occupation continued. Central to this situation is the creation of one-crop economies and their legacy. However, in other circumstances the push towards a single valuable crop can be part of an economic ascendance, the kind of focus that enables a whole society to step up a gear:

> The trade in such drugs usually results in some form of monopoly which not only centralizes the drug traffic, but also restructures much of the affiliated social and economic terrain in the process. In particular two major effects are the creation of mass markets and the generation of enormous, in fact unprecedented, cash flows. The existence of monopoly results in the concentrated accumulation of vast pools of wealth. The accumulations of wealth created by a succession of historic drug trades have been among the primary foundations of global capitalism and the modern nation-state itself. Indeed, it may be argued that the entire rise of the west, from 1500 to 1900, depended on a series of drug trades. (Trocki, 1999, xii)

Alongside the various cultural pushes towards exploration and conversion, European expansion was driven by the quest to get rich quick. In the broad-brush accounts of European empire, it is the search for trade and wealth that creates the framework for the much later development of empire proper. In order to obtain and maintain these new sources of previously unseen wealth, it was necessary to monopolise the trade route. If you could provide sole access to magical commodities, then prices could be pushed to gratifying high levels. Super-profits.

Trocki argues that it is these hyper-profitable trades that enabled the accumulation required for capitalist development. This is a much suggested, but largely sketchy idea in a range of literature – Braudel's account of the ascendance of a Europe-centred world economy gives a similarly influential status to the outcomes of key trade routes, although these are not described as drug trades in his account. What is common to these discussions is the suggestion that traffick in rare and hard-to-get products expands the reach of European trade and provides an injection of cash into European economies that was so significant that it changed the wider economic culture. This was the remapping that sewed the world economy together at the beginning of European ascendance.

REMAPPING THE WORLD

The other underlying theme throughout this work has been the much more recent remapping of the world as a result of the Cold War. If the development and decline of the Soviet military machine triggered a series of unforeseen circumstances across Eastern and Central Europe, then the growth in power of the US military has also played its own role in shaping global relations and history. If we accept, for argument's sake, that the Soviet military build-up spawned a class of self-interested technocrats, then the US military machine too has had its own interested parties. In their book, *Cocaine Politics*, Peter Scott and Jonathan Marshall examine the manner in which the so-called war on drugs has enabled the further militarisation of US relations with Central America. In a series of highly detailed case studies, Scott and Marshall build an argument that shows the CIA capitalising on public concerns about drug-trafficking in order to provide cover for dubious military connections and interventions in other nations, while at the same time working with drug traffickers on this same interventionist project. At the heart of their analysis is the contention that the machine of US state security is a self-perpetuating entity, working tirelessly to keep itself in business:

> For half a century, starting with the challenge of fascism, America's national security establishment has enjoyed the most important guarantee of its influence, prestige, and claim on the national Treasury: a credible international threat. When Germany, Japan, and Italy became America's allies, international communism took their place as an enemy for almost four decades. (Scott and Marshall, 1991, 1)

The United States has built a superpower status around a combination of economic and military might. One of the arguments of this volume is that these two processes are interlinked. At a variety of points it is impossible to distinguish between security concerns and economic interests. Although I do not wish to suggest that there is any master plan co-ordinating these processes, I do want to suggest that linkages between different kinds of institutional power can operate to consolidate certain state influences. This is not a complex argument to make. All over the world people understand that the combination of guns and cash is hard to resist.

Although Scott and Marshall identify the challenge of fascism as the beginning of legitimised US militarisation, they later acknowledge that these processes of ongoing intervention have a far longer history. The particular and peculiar dynamic of the imperial relation between the United States and Latin America has been much discussed – in part this relation, where the imperial power does not occupy directly, becomes the model that illuminates our understanding of later neo-colonial relations (Galeano, 1973, 1977). The suggestion that US military might is created and sustained in response to a series of enemies, each of mythic monstrosity, also has become too banal – as much a block to understanding as an aid. Yet when we revisit the startling enormity of US military power and the manner of its ascendance, it seems important to remember that all those stories of reds under the beds and bogeymen in the cupboards also had a significant impact on a whole array of other decisions in the world. For the United States' economy, unlike that of the Soviet Union, there has not been such an obvious collapse through military overload. Yet the choice to pursue a certain conception of US interests through military means has had its own consequences for both the United States and the rest of the world (Kupchan, 2002, 2003).

US DOMINANCE AND BANANA REPUBLICS

If the quest for hyper-profitable commodities created the world market that shaped early capitalism, then the constrained choices of one- and two-crop economies provided the basis for unequal trade and neo-colonialism through the twentieth century:

> By the late nineteenth century, Honduras meant bananas. Soon much of the Honduran economy was controlled not from Tegucigalpa, but from New Orleans, the capital of the banana trade. And as the New Orleans banana market, in turn, came under the domination of organized criminal gangs, established banana trade routes also became drug routes. (Scott and Marshall, 1991, 51)

The strange and bloody systems of patronage that have characterised narcopolitics build on the structures and networks of older forms of neo-colonialism. Although there is a militarised aspect to this neo-colonial encounter, equally powerful has been the structure of economic dependency. This is the history by which large corporations become the colonising agents, a conduit for US expansionism. Unlike imperialism proper, this expansionist project has been pursued largely via indirect means – most typically the combination of US corporation and compliant local government. To understand the rich iconography of this structure, it is worth considering for a moment the histories that make the term 'banana republic' signify corrupt drug economy. That phrase, banana republic, combines the slur of economic and political underdevelopment with reliance on one cash-crop signifying resistance to social and technical change, the creation of an authoritarian political class that is owned by the company and, ultimately, a state that is open to colonisation by any criminal class sufficiently ruthless to take over company structures. It is the unfortunate history of banana production that lends itself to the signification of this compressed narrative.

In her groundbreaking feminist reading of international relations, Cynthia Enloe devotes a chapter to the place of the banana. She chooses the banana for its iconic status – key cash-crop, accessory to exotic performance and, in cartoon persona, the personification of US corporate presence. However, beyond the various symbolic associations of the banana itself, the larger argument is about the world that is created around the dangerous possibilities of such highly mobile crops.

> Between 1880 and 1930 the United States colonized or invaded Hawaii, the Philippines, Puerto Rico, the Dominican Republic, Cuba and Nicaragua. Each was strategically valuable for its plantation crops. The British, French and Dutch had their plantation colonies producing rubber, tea, coffee, palm oil, coconuts, tobacco, sisal, cotton, jute, rice and, of course, the monarch of plantation crops, sugar. Bananas, sugar, coffee, pineapples – each had become an international commodity that Americans, too, were willing to kill for. (Enloe, 1990, 124)

The single-crop economy is one of those enduring legacies of colonial relations. The export of the single crop, often a plantation crop, has been a standard route of incorporation into the world economy for colonised spaces. For the Caribbean, this crop has been sugar (Mintz, 1985, 1986). For much of Central America, economies have been tied to the production of coffee or bananas. This dependency on particular crops continues to hamper the development of these nations – still in thrall to fluctuations in particular markets, still tied to transnational corporations in an unequal relation of global feudalism. Sell to us or don't sell at all.

The concept of the banana republic stems from the activities of United Fruit, later United Brands, the US corporation that embodied an earlier phase of neo-colonialism in Central America. There is nothing about the banana itself that brings this corruption – no addictive qualities, no wrecked lives for banana junkies – it is the manner of corporate activity and the additional coercive pressure that lies just behind the company that creates the horrors of the banana republic. To really understand what this means, we need to consider the extent of United Fruit's influence and ownership:

> United Fruit's penetration of Central America began in the late nineteenth century with its construction of railroads and port facilities in the region. The company came to own, either directly or indirectly, nearly 900 miles of railroad in Guatemala and El Salvador, the major railroad network in Costa Rica and Honduras, and Guatemala's only Atlantic port. At the beginning of the twentieth century the company signed contracts with local banana producers to transport their produce to guaranteed markets in the United States, but gradually, through grants and purchases of land, it began to control production directly. United Fruit eventually owned half a million acres of the most fertile land in Guatemala and 400,000 acres in Honduras. (Pearce, 1981, 15)

The company literally owned the nation and its infrastructure. Moving on from the earlier example of colonisation via company set by the East India Company, United Fruit represented the workings of a more developed capitalism and a more explicit imperialism. Yet like the East India Company, there was little recognition that this was an intervention in the business of another nation – sovereignty was not considered to be an issue, either because these spaces were not recognised as sovereign nations or because the business of trade was regarded as of a different order to that of sovereignty. Whatever the reason, United Fruit invested heavily in the infrastructure that would enable their trade – a significant section of the local economy was built by the company – and through this became another form of occupying power. The most troubling and instructive aspect of the

United Fruit style of imperialism is the shaping impact this has had on the subsequent histories of the colonised nations. This is another parallel story to the displaced enmities of the Cold War and the never quite realised promises of decolonisation and independence – the struggle to achieve democratic and independent governments that are free from the reach of the company represents another kind of unfinished decolonisation. Again, the term 'banana republic' is a shorthand for that disappointment, an indication that independence is not easier just because colonisation is informal:

> A banana republic's sovereignty has been so thoroughly compromised that it is the butt of jokes, not respect. It has a government, but it is staffed by people who line their own pockets by doing the bidding of the overseas corporation and its political allies. Because it is impossible for such compromised rulers to win the support of their own citizens, many of whom are exploited on the corporation's plantations, the government depends on guns and jails, not ballots and national pride. (Enloe, 1990, 133)

The United Fruit mode of imperialism continues into the twenty-first century, and promises to offer exploitative opportunities for some time (Klein, 2000). Certainly, a major theme in the anti-globalisation debate has been the accusation that the poor world is shackled under the imperial yoke of transnational corporations, backed up by the coercive powers of international financial institutions. However, such plans can be derailed by the unexpected turbulence of blowback. At the time of writing, US corporations, many closely linked to key members of the Bush administration, have taken care to monopolise the pre-emptive privatisation deals of an occupied Iraq which has yet to be reconstructed. However, the escalating horror and instability on the ground in a supposedly liberated Iraq renders the future of these investments uncertain, to say the least, and reminds us that even the most mobile forms of capital require some underlying anchor of territorial power.

FIGHTING OUR OWN MONSTERS

Although much of this work may appear to be yet another tirade against the multiple evils of United States and all that it represents, the actual focus is the rise of a certain set of global power relations. Much of what is discussed here is an abbreviated review of the rise and demise of the two rival empires of the Cold War. The conduct of and fallout from that long rivalry played the central role in the construction of international institutions. More importantly still, the economic networks and political alliances that animate contemporary globalisation are the offspring of that history.

There is a strong trend in the literature that suggests that the US military also became a self-sustaining force during the Cold War period – in an echo of the monstrously overgrown Soviet military machine (Guyatt, 2000, 2003; Scott and Marshall, 1991). Once this organisation is constructed around the imperatives of continual threat, this is the model of national security that becomes hegemonic. Now the only way to feel safe is to build an endless fortification against some imagined enemy. The war on drugs offers some particular advantages to this project – by eschewing ideological antagonism in favour of a kind of moral crusade, there is much more leeway for the shifting alliances and targets of national security concerns. The threat of the drug trade is felt in the everyday lives of US population and that popular concern has developed its own momentum, so, even without the support of a propaganda machine, that sense that there is a threat from drugs already has an organic existence in popular consciousness (Gray, 2002).

Most of the literature on the US war on drugs predates the war on terrorism that utilises so many of the same tactics and structures (Lusane and Desmond, 1991; Wisotsky, 1986). With the advent of the war on terrorism, many of the half-spoken aims and assumptions of the war on drugs have come right out into the open. Instead of working through suggestion, the rhetoric of the war on terrorism openly tells us that we are fighting an endless battle against shadowy and shape-shifting enemies – and that is why this battle requires patience, resources and absolute support.

In fact, the basis for the war on terrorism is already laid in the war on drugs, and the monsters of the drug wars anticipate the mythic enemies of the twenty-first century:

> One answer was to invent a new threat, closely associated with communism and even more frightening to the public: narcoterrorism. The term, rarely well-defined by its users, encompasses a variety of phenomena: guerrilla movements that finance themselves by drugs or taxes on drug traffickers, drug syndicates that use terrorist methods to counter the state's law enforcement apparatus, and state-sponsored terrorism associated with drug crimes. (Scott and Marshall, 1991, 23)

Although this new enemy is presented as being closely associated with communism, somehow the child of the old monsters, in fact much of the growth of drug networks comes from the patronage associated with the war against communism. While it may sometimes be the case that previous allies become truly feared enemies, the US history of supporting criminality when it suits is too long and too well publicised to be accidental: 'far from considering drug networks their enemy, US intelligence organizations have made them an essential ally in the covert expansion of American influence abroad' (Scott and Marshall, 1991, 4).

CONTAINING THE MONSTERS OF NARCO-IMPERIALISM

The war on drugs is one of those highly ironic tragedies. The very particular kind of dependency economy that emerges from the combination of US intervention and patronage of warlords, subsistence living and the vagaries of the international market, may enable political leaderships agreeable to the aims of US policy for a time, but the cash and the violence that surrounds the key product has proved difficult to contain. Of particular concern is the extent to which this warfare spills over into the streets of America.

The war on drugs has been shaped in the main by a previous conception of spheres of influence. It has been the unlucky destiny of Latin America and Southeast Asia to have histories that are embroiled with that of the United States – and it is these regions which have been the focus of CIA activity and strategic intervention in the drug trade. However, in an echo of each of the new demons discussed, the circuits of the drug trade have been reshaped by the realignments of a post-Cold War world. In one sense, this may be another indirect indication of the extent of US influence. Most of the rest of the world has become enmeshed in the dynamics of neo-colonial dependency and the shadow economy, even old enemies:

Russia is today a country in which a variety of illegal drugs are produced, transmitted to final markets in western Europe and Japan, and are consumed by a growing number of young people. The former USSR did not participate significantly in the international narcotics markets as a consumer or a supplier of illicit substances. This pattern of relative self-sufficiency, however, drastically changed during the 1990s, at the same time as Russian drug demand consistently expanded and diversified. (Max Planck Institute, 2000, executive summary)

Cockburn and St Clair quote an Afghan opium farmer as saying 'We are cultivating this [that is, opium] and exporting this as an atom bomb' (1998, 272). If we accept that the drug trade is conceived as some kind of real threat to the interests of the United States, despite the various expedient alliances that have been struck in the pursuit of US interests, then this shift in the supply routes could be regarded as another aspect of the complex blowback from the end of the Cold War. This is a blowback experience for both superpowers, existing and former. For the United States, the concerted and underhand methods used to encourage the opening of market forces across the former USSR also create the basis of the region's burgeoning drug trade. For the former Soviet Union, narcotics use among its own population increased as an unforeseen consequence of the unhappy imperial adventure in Afghanistan (Volkov, 2002). The newfound dependencies and disillusionment of returning troops brought the war home for Soviet society, just as the returning addicts of the Vietnam War did for the United States (Volkov, 2002). The post-Cold War world reveals a latent memory of an earlier global integration, and old trade routes re-emerge to sew together the world through that old quest for magically hyper-profitable kinds of trade:

> Through Tajikistan and the other CIS states, heroin is also increasingly smuggled into eastern and Western Europe along the old 'Silk Road'. The international narcotics control board estimates that up to 65 percent of opiates intended for export from Afghanistan may pass through the porous Central Asian borders to Europe. (Max Planck Institute, 2000, executive summary)

The demise of the Cold War mapping of the world has uncovered the residue of earlier spheres of influence, with Central Asia, in particular, once again becoming a conduit between east and west. Alongside the exciting speculative potential of transitional economies, there is another level of integration into the global economy that cuts through this region, the level at which the flash-bang of high-tech globalisation relies upon old-fashioned methods of transportation along the trade routes of another era (Gustafson, 1999, 141). This is the manner of a global integration that touches a range of ordinary lives across non-technologised and barely developed localities and provides employment for some of those who have little access to other kinds of work in the global economy. The processes of globalisation are leading to a different polarisation, not of east and west, but of rich and poor worlds. Increasingly, even bodies that present IMF-style trade and development as a route to prosperity for all parts of the world accept that we are not yet at that point and that the outcomes of recent historical realignments have led to instability and impoverishment for much of the world.

Drug trades, among other illicit forms of trade, offer a much-needed cash injection for nations lacking the infrastructure to participate in the global economy. The aid packages offered by international institutions, when and if they are offered, come with a variety of often painful strings, as has been discussed in previous chapters. The alternative development route offered by drug money may bring dangers and pitfalls, but for some places may also prove to be more effective and accessible than mainstream routes to development.

For frightened Western societies, this raises some problems. The rhetoric, and in some cases the practices, of the US version of the war on drugs has been adopted by international bodies. Fears about a creeping invasion on our streets portray the drug trade as a dangerous criminal enemy, a threat to civilisation, a corrosion from within that has been introduced by a shady mobile minority who have no allegiance to anywhere. Any international co-operation against the drug trade relies on the assumption of some shared interests between rich and poor worlds, between receiving and producing nations. Attempts to curtail drug production and international distribution appeal to the drug-producing nations to stop hurting themselves. The problem in this appeal is that, in the manner of the legendary banana republic, the drug economy similarly infuses all areas of society:

> Research into the 'laundering' of drug money is revealing just how much the illegal and official economies have become intertwined; how the drug industry's tentacles have reached all sectors of society – from marginal-ised groups – such as peasant producers or street peddlers – to those well integrated such as business people, and state institutions. (William and Milani, 1999)

Drug economies may be scary and violent, creating societies that cannot guarantee the safety of ordinary people or the autonomy of state institutions, but they are resilient. And as we have discussed, for many, the horrors of drug economies may not be distinguishable from the horrors of supposedly legitimate economies. Dislodging the hold of the drug trade also threatens to undermine the livelihoods of a host of ordinary people who have few options other than to participate in the major economic activity at hand. Once drug money has seeped into all areas of life, hitting the trade in drugs hits everyone. Despite the rhetoric of global co-operation, international efforts to curtail the drug trade can appear to be another attempt to impose Western interests on the poor world:

> For them [the National Security Agency and Central Intelligence Agency], drug wars are interesting and terrorism is significant, but it is the struggle for political power in Third World countries that is the focus of LICs [low-intensity conflicts]. That is the real game, and the campaigns against drugs and terrorism, as well as their covert operations that spread drugs and terrorism, are all part of the contest for political power in the United States and in other states. (Hables Gray, 1997, 33)

Whether the demon enemy is characterised as communism, drugs or terrorism, the one constant is the legitimation of military intervention against the poor world. Although we are living through a time in which it seems impossible to imagine another world power that could challenge the United States, I want to stress here the focus on a more than national interest, another kind of coalition of the willing. The significant element is the creation of structures that make military intervention against the unruly poor world both legitimate and regarded as in the interests of those benefiting from global integration. The high emotion that surrounds the issue of drugs serves to legitimate all kinds of intervention in the name of drug eradication. Link drugs to terrorism and the argument that the international community has the right to intervene using force in any region deemed to be a threat to global security is won – for audiences across much of the developed world at least. The war against terror has been used to rehabilitate and even celebrate the tactics of counter-insurgency. Now such things are offered as part of America's gift to a world paranoid about security. For the poor world, there seem to be fewer defences than ever: 'The fight against drugs in one country is an attack on the well-being of another and is but a part of the eternal tussle between the developed and the under-developed nations which exists in everything from wild-life conservation strategies to trade.' (Booth, 1996, 340)

Unsurprisingly, the war on drugs continues to fail in its objective of eradicating the cultivation of drug crops. In the case of coca, other possible crops do not come close to the combination of hardiness and saleability. Although there have been periodic announcements of success – so many acres cleared, production decreased by so much – subsistence farmers who are cajoled, coerced and terrorised away from coca production appear to return to their previous crop as soon as they can (Gray, 2002).

In Bolivia, where the most organised defence of the right to grow coca has been taking place, protesters against the impact of the US war on drugs have been killed by members of an anti-drugs army on the payroll of the United States (Kunkel and Kunkel, 2002). The Expeditionary Task Force is an irregular group devoted to coca eradication, and although the force is under Bolivian command, they receive their salaries from the Narcotic Affairs Section of the local US Embassy. This has the effect of rendering such actions beyond the scope of Bolivian civilian law. Predictably, military tribunals have not found any soldier guilty of using excessive force or of taking part in torture, despite the report by Amnesty International in 2001 that the use of torture was widespread. The war against drugs offers an open and respectable cover to such paramilitary activity, this time explicitly under contract to the United States to perform precisely this service. Although the war against terror is set against the spectre of narcoterrorism, linking drugs and terrorism as an absolute enemy of the free world, Afghanistan has returned to pre-Taliban levels of opium production (RAWA, 2002). It seems that in the emerging techniques of twenty-first-century neo-colonialism/new imperialism, the drug trade provides both the dependent elites of a new kind of banana republic and a pretext for ongoing occupation via a private army. Either way, the old dream of independence seems to have escaped the poor world once more.

REMAKING GLOBAL DRUG WARS

After a long period during which it seemed impossible for poor nations not to jump to deny any role in the drug trade, there are signs that the global politics of drugs is changing. For the first time, farmers of the poor world are defending their right to supply crops for the drug trade, because this assertion of rights is part of the struggle against new forms of imperialism (see http://www.evomorales.net).

Even before this new phase of accelerating militarisation against terrorism, drugs and all threats to Western civilisation, there has been a well-developed argument against further militarising of drug economies. Scott and Marshall argue, as do others, that furthering the war on drugs by supporting more militarised policing of civilian society is doubly counterproductive – unlikely to curb the drug trade or to enable the development of democracy and a strong civil society. Any alternative to the violence and protection-rackets of drug economies must strengthen civil society, not weaken it further:

> … the strategy of further militarizing the societies of Latin America promises to be utterly counterproductive, not only for controlling drugs but also for fostering democracy. Surely the latter objective should stand higher in the priorities of both North and South America. It will be achieved not through wholesale destruction of peasant economies and drug wars but rather through strengthening civilian polities and economies. (Scott and Marshall, 1991, 192)

In any attempt to regulate the international economy, let alone develop new agreements and terms of trade, there must be some negotiation with developing nations, including a recognition that democracy in more than name is an essential prerequisite for any effective agreement. Admittedly, this is yet another highly skewed negotiation, not at all the implied conversation between equals – but neither is it a one-way imposition. As we have seen from the stalemate of the 2003 World Trade Organisation talks, with some organisation it is possible for the developing world to resist the game-plan of Western interests, although we have yet to see with what longer-term outcomes.

The continuing shadow of neo-colonial relations shapes the manner in which much of the world enters international trade. Whatever the drawbacks of dependency on key crops, particularly when the cultivation of such crops is deemed to be a part of the global criminal economy, these are the crops that ensure the productive capacities of these economies. Any possible accommodation about the terms of trade between rich and poor worlds must involve some compromise about the cultivation and trade of illicit crops. The only other alternative seems to be what we have now – an endlessly militarised policing of the terms of trade that creates occupations by proxy. Of course, this enforcement of trade interests through violence has its own unintended consequences. The following chapters will outline some of these.

5

Nuclear Holocaust or Drive-by Shooting? Arms in the New World Economy

The period of rapid and unpredictable change that we have been discussing unsettles established agreements about the relations between states and the possibility of global governance. Although there are various attempts to regulate international relations and to safeguard human dignity through the conduct of international law, a co-operative international community that can regulate through agreement seems more distant than ever. We are living through a time when even previous understandings of human rights and their desirability are under question – and this is before any discussion of actual conduct (Schulz, 2003). All of this accompanies a pervasive sense of threat that itself is used to legitimate an escalation in permitted cruelty (Scraton, 2002). What is allowable in the name of security and defence is, at the very least, up for debate – more pessimistically, some would say that affluent nations have decided that there is now no action so extreme that it is not acceptable as part of a defensive armoury. This chapter discusses the impact of these shifting ideas about the nature and conduct of conflict and examines the emergence of a post-Cold War global arms trade.

The conduct of war has been built around the pretence that it can be governed by laws. Most importantly, laws that can govern what is permissible, who can be killed and in what fashion, that can bring a sense of order to carnage:

> The laws of war have always answered two questions: When may one wage war? What is permissible in war?
>
> And international law has always given two completely different answers to these questions, depending on who the enemy is. The laws of war protect enemies of the same race, class, and culture. The laws of war leave the foreign and the alien without protection.
>
> When is one allowed to wage war against savages and barbarians? Answer: always. What is permissible in wars against savages and barbarians? Answer: anything. (Lindqvist, 2001, 5)

Sven Lindqvist summarises the underlying logic that has shaped modern warfare – that there is an etiquette of conflict, but that this etiquette applies only to some enemies. Arms must be controlled if they threaten people like us – otherwise, their circulation and stockpiling forms part of the legitimate business of defence. The parameters of the arms trade are marked by this conception of defence against some barbaric other.

Much of this work seeks to explain the stories behind new(ish) global demons – to find a way to understand some of the things that cause most fear to the West and to the navigators of international institutions. The fear of armed conflict also has its place in this array of contemporary nightmares, but this fear is hardly new or caused by global integration. If anything, there was a hope that some aspects of global integration would make the world a more secure and less conflict-ridden place (Cooper, 1999; Cornish, 1995). That hope passed all too quickly, and instead we now live with new fears about new forms of conflict. Any relief at the end of Cold War hostilities seems to have been short-lived. The more diffuse threat of violence from unseen and unknown enemies, or of instability that ripples out from the conflicts of other regions, or of forms of low-level informal warfare that creep into the spaces of civilian life even in the West, all rush forward to replace our previous fear of imminent nuclear holocaust. Some have suggested that we are experiencing a shift into two parallel concepts of war, each governed by their own code of conduct:

> One highly debated interpretation is that the global security and military order is undergoing a process of 'structural bifurcation'; that is, fragmentation into two largely separate systems each with different standards, rules of conduct and interstate behaviour. (Held et al, 1999, 101)

On the one hand, there are those who argue that military technology amongst advanced industrial states presents such overwhelming destructive power that major war can no longer be considered as a realistic strategic option between such states (Mueller, 1989). The objectives of war, such as resolving interstate conflict or changing the global balance of power, cannot be pursued effectively with such apocalyptic weaponry.

Against this, the developing world seems to be subject to increasingly irrational forms of warfare. In the so-called peripheral states, conflict continues to be conducted through small arms, informal fighting forces and intra-state rivalry (Kaldor, 1999). These conflicts are not motivated by the recognised objectives of inter-state war and the terms of resolution are far more elusive because of that. The two conceptions of war and conflict carry on alongside each other, with little indication of how their logics may meet or interact. 'Patterns of international military and security relations are radically diverging as the post-Cold War world order becomes increasingly bifurcated.' (Held et al, 1999, 101)

This chapter traces the recent trajectories of these two parallel tales. One is the relatively familiar narrative of big boys and their big toys, of powerful states and military build-up, of the ability to destroy the world many times over and to purchase this ability legitimately on the world market (Cooper, 1999; Roberts, 1995). This first tale is not strictly about traffick: the trade in advanced armaments has tended to be legitimate and state-sponsored and often that sponsorship has come from the most powerful and influential of states. The arms industry, unlike the forms of business discussed in other chapters, has been open and above board, a national asset to be promoted and protected. I hope that the discussion that follows will explain why this trade belongs in this book.

The other parallel tale is more often linked to the evils of the shadow economy. This is the more secretive and semi-legal end of the arms trade (Lumpe, 2000) – not the showpieces of up-to-the-minute technological development or the pet projects of regional regeneration through saved heavy industry. Instead this is the make-do-and-mend style of arms trade, a circuit in which everything can be recycled, where yesterday's technology can come into its own if you can only get it to the right region.

The prime nightmare of the Cold War was the possibility of nuclear holocaust. For those growing up through these years, the bomb represents both the horror and the security of modern life. Nuclear consciousness suffused everyday life during this time, popular culture threw up all kinds of strategies for living with the bomb, so we imagined the aftermath of nuclear meltdown in order to convince ourselves of how much there was to lose (Broderick, 1991). Children were taught risible survival tactics to utilise at the time of the much anticipated attack. People really believed that the end of the world was nigh. When the break-up of the Soviet Union made Cold War tensions obsolete, nuclear face-off slowly ceased to be the key fear of our time.

Instead, the new sources of armed disruption come from multiple locations and in unpredictable ways. For the rich world this can make war seem both endless and a long way away. Yet alongside this, there is the constant threat that the turbulence of the periphery will spill over into the developed world:

> In some senses the Cold War system acted as a kind of disciplinary mechanism which helped the order of political life in both the East and the West. This can be seen ... in the very way in which political life was represented as a titanic struggle between the political programmes of left and right (irrespective of how the labels were interpreted in specific national contexts). But in the post-Cold War era that 'discipline' has been removed. This, according to some, has contributed to the demise of the old left–right political alignments as well as to the emergence of a 'postmilitary' politics. (Held et al, 1999, 148)

Much of this volume has tried to uncover the violence and disarray which arose from the disciplinary mechanism of the Cold War. Despite this seeming tidiness of East and West, left and right, the rival powers of this era remapped the world as a patchwork of proxy wars (Keller and Rothchild, 1996; Vadney, 1987, 1992). With the loss of one key patron, many of these conflict zones lost their predictability. The discussion in earlier chapters shows that there was no lack of violence during the supposed long peace of the Cold War, so I am wary of arguing that the lack of discipline that followed the Cold War heralded an increase in violence. Instead, I will attempt to outline here some of the key changes in the arms trade and in the shape of conflict in recent years.

In order to understand these changes, it is necessary to register both stories, the high-tech developments of industrialised nations and the recycled weaponry of contested zones. However, it is equally important to understand how these two trades fit together, to see their relation and the interchanges between their different markets.

What follows takes the South Asian region as a case study of sorts, a space in which a number of useful examples can be identified. As with other chapters, this is in no way an exhaustive account. When possible, I point readers to more expert literature in the field, but inevitably this discussion can be no more than indicative, a sketchy outline of the fit between parallel arms trades as it plays out in a dangerous zone caught between old and new imperialisms. Aspects of what follows are very particular, possibly unique. Other parts, however, find echoes in many places, albeit with local variations.

To see what I mean, better to get on with the story. First, a quick glance backwards.

MILITARISATION AND THE BRITISH PRESENCE

The circulation of military personnel and hardware has formed one of the threads of imperial economic networks throughout the informal, formal and neo phases of imperialism. Although the occupation of India represents one archetype of European expansion and imperial success, debate amongst historians shows that British control was not maintained simply through military force, or at least not for most of the time. Although the army of the East India Company numbered 200,000 by the mid nineteenth century, no more than 5,000 of these were British – the colonisers were very much in a minority (Judd, 2004; Omissi, 1999). Instead, India came to be seen as an exemplar of successful imperialism precisely because the disciplinary mechanisms of empire became integrated into the occupied space through the participation of the occupied. Indians formed the majority in the armed forces of the East India Company, and continued to form the bulk of military personnel throughout British rule and up until Independence:

> In 1858, when India came under the direct control of the crown, the Armed Forces consisting of 60,000 British and 120,000 Indian troops, bequeathed by the East India Company, were reorganised. The Royal Navy was entrusted the task of the naval defence of India. Furthermore, the defence policy was formulated primarily for the local defence of the frontiers and to maintain internal security. (Mahajan, 1982, 39)

The militarisation of India under British rule followed the same uneven pattern as other aspects of empire. On the one hand, India remained under the rule of a foreign power. On the other, India itself made a major contribution to the military presence that maintained that rule, not least when it was threatened by the protests of the independence movement (Spear, 1965, 1990). In the manner of other occupations, India provided the resources that safeguarded the power of the occupier:

[in 1938] the Chatfield committee recommended that India should maintain units for security against external threats and to ensure internal order. The committee advocated the principle of 'joint responsibility'. During World War I India supplied 1,215,000 men for overseas service and gave supplies of equipment and stores amounting to $80 million. This was in addition to a gift of £113,500,000 to the British in 1917–18, which added 30 percent to India's national debt. (Mahajan, 1982, 40)

Unlike the military Keynesianism of the post-war era, this was a form of military build-up that further depleted this national economy, although the colonised periphery did not yet have such a status in any meaningful sense. India served as a pool of free resources, and the injection of this expenditure provided benefits for the British economy, not for Indians. In a precursor of the private armies of neo-colonialism, paying Indians to occupy themselves was a cheap and efficient method of policing this tame market, with the additional benefit that this military expenditure, including wages, had to be spent on British-made goods. The creation of a local military under the patronage of the occupier served as a means of siphoning still more value out of the colonised space.

At the time of decolonisation, India remained highly militarised and retained the infrastructure of occupation. In part this was a consequence of the timing and context of Independence, presented as a reward for loyal service and extensive sacrifice during the Second World War (Wolpert, 2000). As with so many other newly independent nations, when the colonisers finally left the new national elites inheried the institutions and paraphernalia of the previous rulers.

In the period of decolonisation, newly independent nations were faced with the challenge of remaking the terms of nationhood. Famously, the national liberation struggles in various locations revealed the aspirations and mythologies of these new nations. The Bandung Conference of 1955 indicated the linking themes of those wishing to retain a non-aligned status. This meeting, heralding the beginning of the non-aligned movement, outlined the philosophy of a number of newly-independent nations – a commitment to self-sufficient economic development, to independence from the geopolitical carve-up of the two superpowers and the militarisation of the world that this entailed, to fostering co-operation among non-aligned nations in order to create a counter-balance to superpower dominance of world affairs (Mason, 1997). Having thrown off the colonial yoke, the non-aligned movement represented the worthy desire to guard against any new imperial order.

However, despite the admirable attempts to bypass the national rivalries of imperial nations, newly independent nations came to be a prime market for the development of the post-war 'official' arms trade. Often, despite independence, it was this trade in arms that tied the poor world to its former colonisers (Arlinghaus, 1983, 1984).

For those nations regarded as of strategic importance, there have been a variety of inducements to militarisation. In the case of India and Pakistan, the case was made more persuasive by the tensions that arose during partition. Although other regions suffered more from the heat of Cold War tensions, the border dispute that was born with Independence (for some) ensured that South Asia remained an important nodal point in any global power struggle (Choudhury, 1975; McMahon, 1994).

The Cold War deployment of patronage, trade and intelligence solidified the strategic hot spots of geopolitics. Despite non-alignment, India developed a close cooperation with the Soviet Union. Equally, despite considerable internal political turbulence, Pakistan retained a relationship of political cooperation with the United States (McMahon, 1994). In relation to each other, both nations maintained their rhetoric of near war. It is not difficult to see how this might create the basis for a regional arms race.

FORMAL AND INFORMAL ARMS TRADES

In relation to the larger debates about the arms trade, there is an ongoing pretence that the formal arms trade – that arms trade that holds trade shows, develops cutting-edge technology and contributes to the economies of developed nations – safeguards international order and security. It is only the more anarchic and freelance trade in small arms that is seen to destabilise the global order. In part, this reflects a certain belief and confidence in the disciplinary powers of national economic interest. The formal arms trade inhabits the spaces of other formal trade systems. The trade in small arms is regarded as another unruly component of the hidden economy, that underground network that erodes the securities of the regulated economy.

The very different mythologies that surround the formal and informal arms trade are built around particular historical notions of legitimacy and responsibility. However transnational the arms trade has become, that trade that circulates the most up-to-date technology and methods of death is made legitimate as part of the project of national wealth creation. The arms industry has successfully exploited anxieties about the future of manufacturing industry in order to win particular and unusual protection and patronage from government. Much of the dubious sense of corruption and underhand dealing implicit in the following accounts of arms build-up comes from this unhealthy relation with the state. Yet it is precisely this idea of state ownership and patronage that is supposed to make the formal arms trade 'safe'. The attitude of government, when that government is legitimate, elected and recognised internationally, promises to pay proper respect to the norms of international behaviour – or so we hope. States are supposed to understand how high the dangers of inter-state conflict have become and to contain military responses accordingly. Against this the shadowy non-state actors who are part of the informal arms trade are regarded as dangerous and unpredictable – outside the constraining contract of mutual preservation that exists between nations.

Much of the mounting anxiety about the informal arms trade comes from this fear of the non-state actor. Despite the untold horror that has been unleashed by states in recent history, there is a widespread pretence that international agreements between recognised states can take the risk out of the trade in arms. States, apparently, build up their stockpiles of weapons with the understanding that they will not be used. Non-state actors, on the other hand, can only buy arms with use in mind. There is no parallel track of diplomacy for those not engaged in the business of running a state.

Of course, non-state actors may trade in all kinds of armaments, including the too-much-discussed weapons of mass destruction. However, it is small arms that fuel many, if not most, of the most entrenched and long-running conflicts of the post-Cold War period. This is the weaponry that has come to be readily available almost anywhere in the world. It is also the weaponry that flooded into all kinds of informal markets at the end of the Cold War, most especially in regions where the proxy wars of that era unravelled.

The continuing promotion of the arms trade, including explicit state patronage and special sales pitches by heads of state, reveals a lack of anxiety about weapons of mass destruction in some hands. However, despite this sense of security among allied states, there is also an increasing uncertainty about who the allies might be. Although Western states remain happy to maintain their own arms industries by selling to poorer nations, in particular those who are unable to sustain arms industries of their own, it is no longer clear which states are regarded as legitimate and safe owners of highly developed weaponry. In relation to South Asia, it is clear that the escalation of the regional arms race is regarded as a destabilising factor for the whole world – this despite the fact that the region remains a key market for Western arms. At the same time, a long-running and supposedly low-level conflict continues in parallel to the more formalised face-off between nuclear states, and this is fed by the trade in small arms. I hope to explain here that these are two strands in the same story, not two separate trades at all.

Plenty has been written about the arms trade in its many guises. This is not the place to rehearse that extensive literature (see for example Anthony, 1992; Emelyanov, 1983; Tirman, 1997). However, what follows has inevitably been shaped by these debates. So I assume that the trade in arms has played a central role in the development of certain economic infrastructures and that proliferation has its own logic and momentum. The arms industry that emerges from this process has been shaped by the imperatives of the Cold War. The more globalised trade in arms that forms the focus of this chapter is an outgrowth of this earlier history.

More recent writing in this field has remarked on the optimism that followed the fall of the Berlin Wall and the belief of many that this would finally herald an end to the arms race (Cooper, 1999; Cornish, 1995; Kaldor, 2000). For a time, there was some curbing of large state-sponsored arms programmes. In particular, former Cold War adversaries seemed committed to de-escalation. Unfortunately, one set of geopolitical goals appears to have been replaced by another, with equally destructive outcomes:

> It [the arms trade] no longer serves primarily to influence the international balance of power. Instead it helps to regulate the emergence of new states. Its most important role is not arming the forces of allies and regional powers as in the past, but as a lever for controlling or promoting ethnic violence and the outbreak of war in the near future. (Karp, 1995, 57)

What is not acknowledged is the extent to which controlling the emergence of new states and outbreaks of ethnic violence has become a key component of influence over the international balance of power. Instead of the previous territorial dance between two superpowers, now the world's hotspots show the outcomes of cumulative state failure, another part of the long aftermath of Cold War tensions. In a unipolar world, control over the emergence or non-emergence of new states is a key to global influence. Who is armed, and with what, is one of the deciding factors in this new tussle for ascendancy.

THE WORLD IS AWASH WITH SMALL ARMS

This section focuses on the more recent and unpredictable forms of arms proliferation. Most talked about is the trade in small arms, fast becoming identified as one of the new horrors of the global economy (see Makki, 2001; Pirseyedi, 2000): 'The world is awash with small arms. At least 614 million weapons are in circulation, and more than half a million people are killed each year as a result of their use.' (Muggah and Griffiths, 2002, 1)

Despite the various shifts in the arms race and agreements to contain weapons proliferation, small arms seem to circulate according to an alternative logic. This is the arms trade that is widely regarded as out of control – not because of escalating production so much as the numbers of weapons in circulation. The conception of the threat posed by the arms trade is reshaped by this differently imagined danger. Instead of nuclear holocaust, we have now learned to fear the instability caused by smaller scale conflicts. At a time when the blowback from global integration threatens the comfort and stability of the rich world, that fear is about more than immediate military threat, it is also a fear of the consequences of social disorder in the poor world: 'At the Millennium Summit in 2000, UN member states identified the poor as especially threatened by small arms. In their view, poverty alleviation and economic growth are undermined by the availability and misuse of illegal small arms and light weapons.' (Small Arms Survey, 2003, 126)

Once again there is a concern about the impact on development. Whatever the changes in ideas of development, and even if there is an acceptance of the need for sustainable development and an appreciation that quality of life cannot be measured through income alone, lack of economic growth remains a shorthand for a myriad of other social dangers. The combination of continuing low-level conflict and failure to develop economically forms the basis for that most globalised of fears – pockets of uncontrollable anarchy in the poor world that have the capacity to destabilise the rich:

The incidence of internal *armed conflict* and widespread social violence in developing countries intensifies the risk to civilians. In many developing countries, political armed violence is not clearly distinguished from the criminal variety, particularly after war. Small arms-related violence can be so prevalent that otherwise 'peaceful' states such as Brazil, Jamaica, and South Africa often exhibit warlike symptoms. (Small Arms Survey, 2003, 127)

This new era of diffuse conflict blurs the boundaries of the battle-zone – wars spill over into civilian life and civilian life may become so suffused with violence that it itself resembles a war-zone. The Small Arms Survey acts as a collator of international information, in recognition that the circulation of small arms represents a global threat. The suggestion contained here in the concern about the internal conflicts of the developing world is that criminal and political violence have become virtually indistinguishable – the recognisable and choreographed violence of warfare, which can be legitimate, has blurred into everyday criminality. The danger is that the fragile understanding that has existed, for some at least, about the place and manner of legitimate warfare is washed away in this tide of small arms.

Some would argue that this is no more than a continuation of movements that began during the Cold War. Since 1945 at least, the high formality and tidy boundaries of war as depicted (if not conducted) by the West have not reflected the experience of the rest of the world.

'More than 90 percent of the 218 wars that were counted in the period between 1945 and 2001 took place in Africa, Asia, Latin America and the Middle East.' (Jung, 2003, 1) The supposedly unprecedented long peace of the Cold War stand-off was a very geographically specific phenomenon. For most of the world, this much-celebrated peace never took place. Instead of arguing that the end of the Cold War has removed a disciplinary brake on world conflict, as if that order was preferable to this anarchy, others suggest that the post-Cold War remapping of the world has brought the unhappy experience of the periphery right up into the centre as well (Jung, 2003). The always fragile safe zones have been infiltrated.

In spite of all globalising forces, this bifurcation between democratic welfare and protracted warfare has suggested the emergence of a new global order divided in two worlds: on the one hand, into a zone of peace in which war has been ruled out as a means of conflict among democracies; on the other hand, into a zone of conflict in which political power is frequently contested by force and economic development does not make headway.

... In the US led war against terrorism, the two zones have been (re)united and western security forces have become embroiled in a kind of 'global civil war'. (Jung, 2003, 2)

In recent years the developed world has felt the threat of conflict in a more immediate sense, in its own cities and against its own population. Whereas there have been suggestions that developed nations have entered an era of postmodern war in which conflict is experienced as no more than simulation, a computer-game version of war (Baudrillard, 1995), a renewed consciousness of the threat of terrorism has shaken such complacency. Contemporary warfare remains hugely uneven, with inhabitants of the poor world suffering the excessive and high-tech violence of developed-world weaponry – while the extent and impact of such violence remains remote from the populations that it purports to protect. However, the developed world now feels that it too is under attack from the new monster of transnational terrorism. However overblown and unrealistic this fear of terrorism has become, the sense that such things are possible changes the dynamic of global conflict. Previously local and/or regional grievances may now have a global reach and, with devastating effect, migrant and diasporic populations may come to be regarded as potential terrorists that must be contained (CAMPACC, 2003).

In response, key parts of the developed world engage in a series of aggressive/defensive skirmishes in parts of the world only loosely integrated into the global economy or, more importantly, into global agreements. As we have discussed in previous chapters, these incursions may employ private armies of one kind or another, but, unlike some earlier neo-colonial interventions, such operations are not covert. The war on terror brings the tactics of counter-insurgency out of the closet and into the arena of legitimate national defence. In the process, the public becomes far more aware of the dirty wars fought in our name, but now these wars are presented as an unavoidable part of the never-ending battle for national defence. We will return to these points later in the chapter with the discussion of new wars.

GUNS AND MONEY

I have been very taken with the suggestion of Meghnad Desai that, in fact, the world economy de-globalised during the twentieth century and that we are now witnessing a return to more globalised transactions (Desai, 2002). This is not to say that there are not significant characteristics that mark out our current experience of globalisation as particular and historically specific. It is, however, to suggest that it has been national protectionism that is the unusual economic practice. The push towards the global is a far more natural logic for capitalist economies.

Desai also suggests that the rapid and influential take-up of Keynesian economic planning played a formative role in creating the arms trade as we know it. The desire to reinvigorate national economies through government expenditure looks for an avenue of spending that will not distort or limit the markets for other national products. Armaments fulfil this role very well it seems.

However, this Keynesian-style war economics has had its own geographical specificities. For nations without a developed industrial base, the trade in arms is more likely to destabilise than enhance the local economy. Another unhappy irony of attempts to restructure poor-world economies to enable participation in the global market is that this approach to development can become an avenue for new arms trades and new wars. 'The dynamics of commerce, the impact of aid, and the structures of capitalism can just as easily feed mafias, warlords and civil wars as they can support peace and state development.' (Jung, 2003, preface)

The coercive hard-sell of economic liberalisation says that moving towards a market economy will bring prosperity and democracy, and that these desirable experiences cannot be achieved through any other route. The various processes of shadow globalisation reveal that entering the global economy may be a far more mixed and uneven process, creating new elites of wealth and power who have no accountability to wider society.

The emergence of a new arms trade, that may perhaps span high-tech, conventional and small weaponry, but which is no longer shaped by the alliances of the Cold War, brings an added danger. The sudden wealth that can be gained through illicit trades creates a purchasing power that is not sanctioned by any state machinery. When such new elites buy arms, there is no pretence that their use will be governed by the supposed etiquette of inter-state conflict.

This realisation impacts on the possibility of arms control – another activity that has relied on the fictions of state authority and diplomatic understanding. For a number of states, neither the right to retain arms nor the agreement to disarm are real possibilities. These attempts at international agreement assume a certain level of state infrastructure and control over the flow of arms through territory. In the dialogue between North and South, only certain players can participate in this form of negotiation. In a discussion of the changing terrain of weapons proliferation and control through the 1990s, Brad Roberts argues that the debate about arms control itself has become an arena where nations struggle to assert their influence and power:

> In the developing world as well as the developed, important aspects of old thinking continue to shape the way arms control is understood and evaluated. Salient factors include the following. The first factor is the long-term dominance of the North–South security agenda by a few states whose views are unrepresentative of the rest. The near nuclear states such as India and others with major investments in weapons and military capability have co-opted many states of the developing world into a crusade for global equality and justice. But this crusade appears more oriented to the legitimisation of their own national choices than to the fact that most states of the developing world have no interest in unconventional weapons or in military solutions to problems of national development and security. (Roberts, 1995, 260)

This chapter takes the experience of India and Pakistan as a linking thread between the formal and informal arms trades because of this in-between status. While both India and Pakistan have vied for position as pre-eminent military power in the sub-continent and across the larger region, notwithstanding China's undeclared capacities, they have become receptacles for the trade in both large and small arms, from both state and non-state sources (Cordesman, 2002; Smith, 1993). This has lead to a situation where both states have argued vociferously on the international stage for their right to engage in arms build-up, including nuclear capacity, as a necessary component of maintaining stability in the region. At the same time, the flow of small arms continues to have a destabilising effect on the whole region. These two processes have had a strange complementarity.

The example of India and Pakistan provides an unusual but informative tale about the various phases of militarisation and arms proliferation that have reshaped the world since 1947. After the particular military presence of British rule, both nations fell quickly into mutual antagonism, an antagonism that has shaped the region ever since (see Dixit, 2002). This sense of being perpetually on the edge of conflict has impacted heavily on the particular flavour of development-speak that has suffused the sub-continent. However, for most of the post-war period, this ongoing face-off was not conducted through arms development. The build-up was in conventional force, through the numbers of military bearing conventional arms. Technical development came with the secondhand armoury offered by the international arms trade, a trade where until recently the developed world sold on not quite up-to-the-minute weaponry to everyone else.

All of this changed with India's nuclear tests – and Pakistan's quick response with some tests of their own. Suddenly, the international community began to show concern about the possibility of a regional nuclear arms race. For the world at large, 1998 was the beginning of a new phase of global nuclear tensions. Until India conducted its tests, world leaders in arms development could pretend that the dangers of nuclear weaponry were contained by the responsible gentleman's agreement that existed among the elite group of nations that had such arms.

Until this moment, the fiction that arms proliferation was a deterrent to military conflict retained some credibility, albeit only in certain highly interested circles. Nuclear capability was confined to the very wealthiest nations, and military and economic power were regarded as mutually reinforcing gifts from god – a sign that these are chosen nations who hold the future of the world in their hands. This sense of responsibility combined with a strong awareness of the possible consequences of any nuclear conflict that rendered such weapons beyond use: we may have them, but no one expects to use them – they are no more than a deterrent, the cement in the gentleman's agreement of non-aggression.

And, of course, no member of this exclusive group has engaged in war with another member during this period. Instead, as we have discussed, wars are fought elsewhere and through other means – although sometimes still on behalf of nuclear nations. The supposed lesson is that if the rich and powerful have weapons of mass destruction, then this can only encourage peace. Danger comes only if such weapons fall into less responsible hands.

MISSILES AND INFLUENCE

The Indian tests bring this whole uneasy arrangement into question. Part of the unspoken expectation of the nuclear club has been that less developed nations will be concerned with economic development before nuclear capability. Nuclear weaponry is another luxury that is allowable only to those nations whose populations enjoy a certain level of affluence and economic security. Criticism of the Indian testing echoed this idea – why would a nation with so many poor want to devote resources to useless methods of mass destruction?

Yet defenders of the tests also relied on such ideas of development to legitimate India's nuclear industries and, through this, its nuclear arms:

> ...the Indian tests in 1998 had a major effect within India. Up to May 1998 the Nehruvians had relied on diplomatic talk about international non-discriminatory arms control arrangements and about the importance of nuclear disarmament. But the Nehru line also kept India out of the nuclear club because of the Government's policy of unilateral self-restraint. The Nehru line had a deep negative impact on Indian interests because it exposed India to continuous international pressure to roll back its nuclear programme since it did not intend to exercise its nuclear option. (Kapur, 2000, 38)

The Nehruvian model of development was a product of a previous self-confidence among newly independent nations, celebrating self-reliance, non-alignment, and a belief that economic development could take place on a different more co-operative basis (Khilnani, 1997). However, the disappointments of a world colonised by other means have served to discredit such aspirations.

As a result we see accusations that continually fostering these attempts at co-operation amount to an abdication of India's status as a regional power. In fact, other nations may have felt that India has dominated the region in an unacceptable manner despite the rhetoric of co-operation between developing nations. However, the criticism stands – just as the United States must step up and accept its destiny as global superpower without shame, India must do the same in relation to South Asia. Across the world, the right has been working hard to rehabilitate the concepts of benign power and imperial duty (Mann, 2003).

The Nehruvian line was based on the belief that non-aligned nations must work together to curb and limit the excesses of world powers – not least because such neo-colonial activities threatened the newly-achieved independence of the non-aligned. However, for opponents of such a strategy, this call for a restraint on the powerful becomes a block to India itself ever achieving the status of a global power. Calling for restraint from the economically developed and politically influential nations becomes a constraint on the development of Indian power and influence.

The implied lesson is simple. There is only one route to global influence – that adopted by the existing global powers. Instead of seeking to develop a more inclusive alternative, Indian interests are best served by seeking power on the same terms:

> The Indian nuclear demonstration symbolised the demand for a legitimate space in the decision-making apparatus of this new world order. The Indian challenge was revisionist to the point that it rejected the older 'imperialistic' order and sought a participatory role in the management of world affairs. (Paranjpe, 2000, 50)

In an audacious reworking of the terms of decolonisation, nuclear capability is presented as a kick against the old imperialists, part of the struggle for freedom and dignity for formerly colonised nations. This twist in the telling elevates the everyday jingoism of building the national defences into a continuation of the struggle against imperialism, a far more honourable objective. Even better, in the renegotiating of international relations after the Cold War, nuclear weapons can be presented as the developing world's most persuasive argument for respect and inclusion:

> There is no denial that nuclear weapons accord a sort of prestige to the nation. What is meant by prestige is not the traditional role of a world policeman but a nation with a very high level of scientific and technological capability developed indigenously. (Pande, 2000, 87)

We are led to believe that the acquiring of nuclear weapons is not an indication of military plans and aspirations at all. Instead, supposedly, it is all about demonstrating the ability to develop such technology within the nation, independently of the patronage of recognised world powers. Although it does not seem credible to suggest that nuclear weapons are developed purely for the love of science, the concept of prestige suggests that there is more at play than brute force alone.

Since the end of the Cold War, we have been witnessing an unresolved series of negotiations about the shape of power and influence in the world. Whereas previously, and largely despite the aspirations to non-alignment, the world had been split between the competing spheres of influence of East and West, now the terms of geopolitical power became far less certain. For some, including those most invested in developing the nuclear capability of India, this uncertainty was regarded as an opportunity. Now there was a chance to rewrite the terms of regional, and perhaps global, influence. However, the question of what might determine such influence in this new terrain remained open.

The role of world policeman, able and willing to intervene in the affairs of others, has implied a number of capacities – military might, economic power, the ability and hardware to mount attacks, but also the wherewithal to maintain a disciplining occupation when necessary. In the early twenty-first century, we are beginning to learn how destabilising such a role can be to the world (Vidal, 2002). However, would-be regional powers such as India have not been vying for this particular privilege. No one seems to be rushing to take on such a policing role. The will to demonstrate status and prestige, on the other hand, is more apparent than ever, both as a message to neighbours and an indication to the international community that these new regional powers are an essential conduit for mediation in the new world order. Technological capacity appears to be the key to achieving such status as a regional power. Paul Bracken suggests that the growth of such technological capabilities represents a new focus of power for Asia and that this has implications for our understanding of political power across the world:

A new military-industrial complex is rising across Asia, built around missiles, weapons of mass destruction, and other technologies. It promises to be a significant bureaucratic and political force in the future. The army used to be the key actor in Asia, but a more technocratic arm offers to far surpass it in influence, mobilizing not the millions that armies did, but the scientific and engineering manpower of the nation for the use of the rulers. (Bracken, 1999, 82)

Whether or not this can qualify as a new military-industrial complex is debatable – in the era of liberalisation, in particular, it is not clear that such military spending can take the central role in domestic economic management that characterised one aspect of the power of earlier military-industrial complexes. However, the larger suggestion that a technocratic elite has emerged and is playing a disproportionate and largely unaccountable role in relation to government sadly fits the Indian and Pakistani experiences all too well (Chengappa, 2000).

None of this demands any wider modernisation of the armed forces. In terms of day-to-day military power, such changes make little difference. Instead, yet another two-tier system is instituted:

> The new technocratic forms are overlaid on a gargantuan, inefficient, and increasingly underfunded army. The composition of these two structures, one old and one new, is not simply a case of the modern replacing the old but rather typifies what is seen throughout Asia: modernized pieces of the armed forces linked to older, inefficient parts. (Bracken, 1999, 82)

These two very different segments of the military continue to operate according to different models of conflict. The overstretched and out-of-date conventional army must pursue conventional conflict – for an old-fashioned army warfare continues to be framed around lines of control, gains in territory and key points of influence, attempting to occupy space without losing people. This is the popular understanding of war, the one from the movies, and it is worth remembering that there continue to be disputes that are fought in this manner. The technologically advanced weaponry, on the other hand, creates a different arena and manner of conflict – one that can seem to confirm the sense of virtual conflict and computer-screen warfare. For India and Pakistan, this means that there is an ongoing and old-fashioned battle for territorial advantage along the border, while the grand gestures of technological capability continue elsewhere as if in relation to another conflict altogether:

> The Asian states have learned from the West. They have learned how to use nuclear weapons without actually detonating them in an attack, for political maneuvers, implicit threats, deterrence, signaling, drawing lines in the sand, and other forms of psychological advantage. (Bracken, 1999, 97)

This process has instituted a form of regional Cold War in South Asia – with that same sense of always impending doom, a fragile peace that is perpetually at breaking point, and a similar disturbing ripple through other parts of the region. In many ways, the outcomes of this process confirm the allegation that Western criticism has been imbued with imperial assumptions. The suggestion that nuclear arms are a useful and necessary bargaining tool in conflict situations is lifted straight out of superpower rhetoric from the Cold War. In a region that has undergone three major wars and untold skirmishes in the post-war period, the idea of arming to keep the peace can seem to embody a particular and effective Cold War logic. In these circumstances, it is unlikely that new nuclear states will be amenable to calls to disarm. At the same time, the attempts of the international community, under the somewhat compromised leadership of existing nuclear nations, to isolate and punish those nations developing their own nuclear capacity do not appear to be having the desired impact: 'The main response of North Korea and Pakistan to Western economic sanctions has been to step up their foreign sales of weapons.' (Bracken, 1999, 114)

At the beginning of this chapter we discussed the theory that we are living through a bifurcation of global security, splitting the formalities of the legitimate arms trade and diplomacy between recognised states from the haphazard networks of non-state actors involved in both conflicts and the trade in arms. One of the unexpected outcomes from the emergence of new nuclear states has been the greater diffusion in the global arms trade. Now states that were previously reliant on the patronage of self-styled great powers can themselves become distributors of scarce and dangerous technologies. If anything, the increasing use of sanctions by the international community serves to create ready clients in this alternative market, as can be seen in the emerging scandal surrounding the alleged sale of Pakistani nuclear technology to Libya and others identified as enemies of the West ('"Supermarket" Trade in Nuclear Technology Alarms UN Inspector', *Guardian*, February 6, 2004).

The other theme of First World warnings and veiled threats is, of course, the supposed impact of nuclearisation on economic development. New nuclear nations scupper their own economic development by threatening to become rogue states and forgetting the slow and steady business of building a strong economy:

> The possession of nuclear weapons does not level North/South disparities. Only economic development and reform of the international economic system can do that. The prospect of nuclear war also does little to inspire investor confidence in any region of the globe. Nor do such weapons automatically confer great-power status, enhanced national security, or electoral popularity. Nuclear weapons are not the proverbial 'great equalizer' – they are instead the 'great destabilizer.' That is the lesson for all nuclear weapon states – real, putative, or potential. (Dhanapala, 1999, 18)

Aspiring regional powers should concentrate their energies on building their economies, because this is the only way to challenge the hegemony of the North, but also because nations that develop a nuclear capacity will be punished by the market. Investor confidence will be damaged, more so than through any sanctions regime, with terrible consequences for errant nations.

It does not take much analysis to discern a distinct undertone of imperial concern in the commentary on the arms race in South Asia. The often-voiced worry is not so much that there are more such dangerous weapons in the world, but that such weapons are in dangerous hands. Dangerous here is taken to mean unlike us, the Western arbiters of world peace. Of course, such sentiments give more fuel to those eager to build up the nuclear and other military capacities of developing nations – the opprobrium of the rich world only shows how well the strategy works. For the militarising wing of Western opinion, these debates only prove once again that the arms race is never over:

> Hundreds of articles and speeches by Conservatives have used the South Asian tests and the Korean and Iranian missile launches as proof that future threats are inherently unpredictable, intelligence estimates are consistently unreliable, the proliferation of weapons of mass destruction is fundamentally unstoppable, and, thus, the only truly effective response is reliance on American defence technology. (Cirincione, 2000, 6)

Despite the endless rhetoric about non-proliferation, the emerging nuclear capacity of India and Pakistan adds weight to calls for greater investment in US defence capabilities. While nations such as India and Pakistan seek to co-operate with US visions of the world, as long as proper respect is given to their own regional importance, their own pitiful military capacities present little threat to US aspirations. If anything, such developments help to ratchet up the global trade in arms, with benefits for all major arms trading nations. At the same time, the reliance on US approval in order to evade international sanctions and to be recognised as legitimate partners in the international community may ensure that both India and Pakistan co-operate with the US vision of the world.

GUNS AND MONEY AGAIN

Alongside this much-discussed and high profile form of arms crisis, the region has continued to provide a conduit for the global trade in small arms. Unlike some other conflicts, there is little to suggest that the tension between India and Pakistan has been fuelled by the availability of small arms. This is a conflict between two states, both of which are heavily invested in showing that they as the powerful regional states retain control over their turf war – the role of the infamous non-state actors is underplayed, if not written out. In fact, various non-state actors in the region appear to be tied into a local version of Cold War patronage, with one or other state eager to claim ownership of any potentially independent players (Puri, 1993, 1995).

Yet at the same time, the region is also awash with small arms. This is a matter of tourist must-see – guns in the marketplace, including the leftovers of former Soviet presence. In this example, small arms are not a route into the global economy for either India or Pakistan. Although each nation has had a very different development trajectory, both have now succumbed to the pressures of economic liberalisation to some extent (Ahmad, 2000). Despite considerable economic difficulties, most starkly in the living standards of their poorest citizens, neither nation can be regarded as a failing state.

Unlike the drug economies that have developed in some Latin American nations, in their different ways India and Pakistan represent the development of postcolonial independence. Unlike the neo-colonial relations of some other regions, there is no clear colonial power that shapes the destiny of South Asia. India and Pakistan have achieved a level of economic autonomy.

In this region the trade in small arms comes into play as a knock-on from Afghanistan. Afghanistan has suffered from its pivotal geographic position in the geopolitics of the last two centuries, and continues to be ravaged by new versions of the great game (Coll, 2004). As a result, it has had little economic infrastructure for decades. Economic activity has been led by successive occupying powers, without even the rhetorical anchor of national development. In the aftermath of the Cold War, countless hand-held weapons remain in the region from the proxy wars in Afghanistan (Naik, 1999), and a host of regional cottage industries rely on the circulation of this Cold War debris. One major aspect of the new arms trade in the era of globalisation is the increasing availability of small arms. In part, this has been an outcome of earlier phases of attempted arms control: 'The 1970s and 1980s were not conducive to a spirit of multilateral transparency on conventional arms. In a strategic environment dominated by nuclear weapons, small arms were seen as more or less inconsequential, a marginal or "soft" issue.' (Muggah and Griffiths, 2002, 3)

Throughout the Cold War, the threat of nuclear holocaust, be it planned or accidental, saturated the debate on arms control. Few agreements were framed in relation to more conventional weaponry. However, since the fall of the Eastern bloc, the impact of increasingly available small arms has become an issue of global concern. Too late it has been realised that small arms constitute highly mobile and largely undocumented arsenals, that can change hands relatively easily, leaving little trace of the transaction. The real truth is that it is very hard to know how many small arms there are in the world, who owns them or where they are: 'In the post-Cold War international market, modern armaments are increasingly being traded like other "normal" commodities.' (Wattanayagorn and Ball, 1996, 147)

The more usual and well-known commentary on the spread of small arms has focused on zones of conflict where state infrastructure has been eroded and societies have been reshaped through the turmoil of long-term conflicts (Kaldor, 1999). This is the nightmare scenario that animates international concern and policy debate. Much of this concern has been expressed in terms of the threat posed to humanitarian practice. Small arms appear as a barrier to various forms of social intervention, not least the interventions of the international community. They also signify terrain where humanitarian workers may find themselves in grave danger:

> Three overlapping, but distinctly humanitarian, responses to the availability and misuse of small arms have emerged. The first is a supply-side approach, focusing on constraining the transfer of weapons to regimes that violate human rights and international humanitarian law. The second approach aims to mitigate the impact of small arms on civilians to the application of international humanitarian law and incentives to reduce the demand for weapons. The final approach, which takes an operational perspective, stresses the consequences of arms availability for relief workers and peacekeepers. (Muggah and Griffiths, 2002, 2)

These three approaches all typify the dilemmas of arms control in the post-Cold War period. In each instance there is a question mark over the ability of states to agree or enforce any workable agreements. Instead, there are attempts to police production and distribution, or to stabilise potential arms markets through other humanitarian means, or to appeal to the conscience of the international community by stressing the risks faced by humanitarian workers. None of these approaches requires an international agreement in the usual sense – there is little here that can be demanded of individual states. Instead, these are pleas for an agreement of international principles, because such agreements can be used to instigate arms control by other means. The role of individual states in such a process is relegated to the background. No one really believes that the circulation of small arms can be controlled through treaty; on this issue all states are failing.

INTERMEDIATE ZONES

Light weapons are particularly prone to recycling; they re-circulate time and time again from one conflict to the next. Stocks of weapons often surface in countries far removed from their original destination. As a result, it is very difficult to trace the provenance of weapons recovered or spotted in conflict zones. However, anecdotal evidence suggests that light weapons of Central and Eastern European origin are found in large numbers in many of today's warring countries. (Musah and Castle, 1998)

Some of the most long-running and horrific conflicts of recent times have been fuelled by the easy availability of small arms in zones where there is little state infrastructure or credible government. Quite rightly, these conflicts and their impact on global stability fill the pages of policy documents and the agendas of international meetings, although many would say with little impact on the lives that have been shattered by such conflicts. At the same time, older agreements that were designed to limit the proliferation of nuclear weapons seem to be crumbling. After so much concern about functioning states, the whole concept of state agreements about arms control seems to be in question:

Is nuclear proliferation a more serious worry after the Indian and Pakistani nuclear tests? Just prior to these tests, the conventional wisdom was that acquiring nuclear weapons was a mistake. Nuclear weapons, it was argued, lacked any true military utility. As for deterrence, a mere option to acquire them was considered superior to announcing possession of such weapons. (Sokolski and Ludes, 2001, xv)

Before the 1998 nuclear tests in India and Pakistan, there had been a quiet sense that the threat of nuclear conflict was abating. Everyone who mattered had come to realise that nuclear weapons were not a real military asset, were not ever meant for use, and hopefully could now be relegated to the ugly past. The India–Pakistan tests reopened the global debate about nuclear capability and confirmed that, whatever was suggested by the five nuclear powers who had been legitimated by the Non-Proliferation Treaty, who owned what kinds of weapons had a big impact on power and influence on the global stage. Whatever the public condemnation, the reality has been that open nuclear testing has admitted India and Pakistan into the nuclear club, and calculations about the future of the region must take this into account.

In the fictional divide between the formalised etiquette of state-sponsored arms build-up and the more diffuse circulation of small and other arms via non-state actors, the formal arms trade gains legitimacy by pretending to be part of the reasonable debate and agreement between rational states. However excessive the capacity for destruction, however great the build-up, however frightening the extent of the killing machine, the formal arms trade continues to sell itself as a force for peace. The informal circulation routes of second and third generation conventional arms and assorted small arms are portrayed as a threat to global order and stability. The state-sanctioned trade in high-tech armaments and new versions of conventional weapons, on the other hand, is represented as a legitimate component of inter-state diplomatic negotiation.

For this fiction to be maintained, states that are key buyers in the international arms market must be recognised as co-keepers of international agreements, actual or tacit. This is the case even when such states force their way into the nuclear club, because to acknowledge that such reliable arms buyers may not be bound by the honour codes of responsible agreements between states throws the whole business of selling arms into question.

The lukewarm sanctions that were mounted in the aftermath of the 1998 tests demonstrated the need to keep India and Pakistan in the club of polite inter-state behaviour, even when they have broken the rules.

> … the supposed need to ensure India and Pakistan act 'responsibly' in avoiding the further spread of nuclear technology gives the declared nuclear powers the rationale for doing away with the troublesome sanctions regime while appearing consistent with the non-proliferation 'regime'. (Gilinsky, 2001, 7)

If we accept that we are going through the process of structural bifurcation identified by Held et al. (1999), then states who are engaged in the arms trade, through both stockpiling and sales, have an investment in retaining a sense of legitimacy for the state-sponsored arms trade. This may entail reworking the terms of international norms in order to accommodate the new dynamics of a post-Cold War world. Former treaties may not be sustainable, but the central contention that legitimate states may obtain weapons of mass destruction legitimately, because their behaviour is bound by an understanding and acceptance of mutual responsibility between states, continues to justify the trade in arms.

The other side of the bifurcation makes other spaces into illegitimate states – places that are dangerous because they contain arms but are not bound by international convention. Small arms are regarded as an issue of global concern in part because of their impact in such illegitimate spaces. Small arms kill large numbers of ordinary people every day, in a drip drip drip of carnage that defies the theatrical promise of weapons of mass destruction. Sometimes these low-intensity conflicts use far older methods of violence – for example, knives and machetes, weapons that have remained unchanged through centuries of human conflict. Yet all these old-fashioned means of killing, unlike so-called weapons of mass destruction, have not been subject to weapons control. In much of the world, guns are legal and all too readily available. The only aspect which is considered open to legitimate control is criminality: 'efforts to cast the problem as one of "illicit" and "criminal" activity draw on traditional biases within the arms control and law enforcement communities' (Muggah and Griffiths, 2002, 7).

This splitting of the world into spaces of formalised and legitimate conflict and spaces of unregulated and dangerous conflict feeds into larger processes of international intervention. The organising assumption seems to be that we must strive towards an approximation of Cold War etiquette, so that, despite the escalating levels of armaments, states deal with each other in an understanding of their mutually assured destruction and interdependency. This is what meaningful participation in international agreements requires. Development means getting those other dangerous and unruly spaces to the point where they can participate in such agreements too. Whether we can make the agreements work, of course, is another question altogether.

NEW WARS AND NEW BUSINESS OPPORTUNITIES

> Policy schemes of reconstruction and punishment, which are implemented
> by international powers in order to foster the establishment of market
> structures and democracy, can lead to the opposite of what they pretend.
> Mafia style economies, warlordism and protracted internal warfare are often
> the unintended outcome of international interventions. (Jung, 2003, 2)

The ongoing theme of this work is the suggestion that interventions to
further global integration also yield other unexpected consequences,
often with effects that are destabilising to global integration. The
different phases of interventionist measures by international
institutions have all assumed a particular model of the functioning
and successful state. The various attempts at fostering economic and
political development, however clumsy, all hope to remake states as
this happily effective ideal. It is another unfortunate irony of our
time that such attempts to stabilise can become the income sources
that fuel another era of warlords and conflict:

> War entrepreneurs in the zone of conflict are at the same time local, national
> and global economic players, investing their financial assets in the zone of
> peace. The analytical distinction between formal and shadow economies
> thereby becomes blurred and offshore financial centers provide nodal points
> between war economies and liberal markets. (Jung, 2003, 3)

All wars have had their entrepreneurs – all of that accelerated
production and urgent need always presents a business opportunity
for somebody. However, what is being described here is a little more
particular to our time. The unruly spaces of the Fourth World throw
up people who can use this disarray to link into the global economy,
people who make money in the dubious business of trading arms or
exploiting the desperation of those whose lives are ravaged by conflict.
Sometimes such figures can achieve a temporary respectability, with
their ability to engage in the international economy elevating them
to the status of recognised representatives of their nation, called on
by the international community to help facilitate the processes of
peace and reconstruction:

> Contrary to their traditional predecessors, modern warlords act in a different
> context. Controlling local territories with their military power, they act
> both financially and politically in the international realm. While the local

conditions of insecurity serve them as a ground for economic extraction, global markets provide them with the secure environment for investment. The crucial linkage between protection and extraction is therefore severed, and parallel markets of violent expropriation and liberal accumulation coexist. (Jung, 2003, 20)

As we have noted above, despite the initial optimism about the endless peace that could be achieved with the end of the Cold War, unhappy experience has shown that there has been no lack of armed conflict in the post-Cold War period. Mary Kaldor has argued that the impact of global integration and the power vacuum left after the fall of the Soviet Union has led to new forms of conflict, what she terms 'new wars' (Kaldor, 1999). These new wars are described as distinct from traditional inter-state conflicts in three key regards: the politics of identity; the decentralisation of violence; and the globalised war economy.

The politics of identity refers to the mobilisation of ethnic, racial or religious identity as a means of winning state power – a concept that could be applied both to the battles in the former Yugoslavia and the genocidal conflict in Rwanda. This is in contrast to the politics of ideas, a politics which unites people around forward-looking and inclusive projects such as individual rights or democracy or a free nation for all. Kaldor acknowledges that such purportedly inclusive projects have spawned their own horrors, but argues that the wish to build better futures and to include all who support such a project is distinct from an identity politics that is racked with nostalgia for a fictional past and which excludes others because they are not believed to embody the celebrated but imagined essential identity.

The decentralisation of violence links a number of phenomena. The first is the shift from using battles to gain territory to borrowing the tactics of guerrilla warfare and counter-insurgency in order to avoid battle and gain territory through the political control of the population. This is seen as distinct from the practices of liberatory guerrilla warfare which work to win over the local population for support and co-operation. Instead, new wars employ the battle-avoidance tactics of counter-insurgency, with areas destabilised by widespread terror against the civilian population and territory gained by population expulsion, a phenomenon that can be seen in the experience of places as disparate as Kosovo and Darfur.

The second phenomenon is the decentralisation of military forces from vertically organised hierarchical armies to disparate alliances of a variety of fighting forces, spanning the divide between legitimate and illegal. Inevitably, this decentralisation changes the internal power dynamics of fighting forces, so that the lines of accountability that have been assumed in international law are much harder to trace and the supposed rules of war are less likely to be enforced, as demonstrated in a range of conflict zones, from Afghanistan to the Democratic Republic of Congo to Sierra Leone. The third is the spread of conflict zones into civilian life and the expansion of conflict into neighbouring areas. New wars are not contained by recognised battle-zones and civilians are not safe from falling victim to the conduct of such conflicts.

The globalised war economy refers to the opposite of the military-industrial complex, something like the war economy of the poor world. This is a situation where, unlike in a centralised war economy that fosters employment and growth, few people participate in war, unemployment is high, the economy is highly dependent on external resources and the infrastructure of the domestic economy is damaged by war. This leads to fighting units financing themselves through crime or external assistance, which itself may be criminal, with Kosovo and Afghanistan once again serving as well-known examples. Kaldor argues: 'All of these sources can only be sustained through continued violence so that a war logic is built into the functioning of the economy' (1999, 9). In this manner, regions become locked into a cycle of war that is hard to break. Inevitably, this has an impact on social and economic stability and pretty much annihilates any hope for our old friend, development.

Mark Duffield suggests that such changes in the practice and understanding of war must alter wider understandings of how societies operate:

> When the competence of nation states begins to change and they become qualified and enmeshed within non-territorial and networked relations of governance, one can assume that the nature of war has also changed. This relates not only to the way the new wars are fought, in this case beyond the regulatory regimes formally associated with nation states, but also to the manner in which societies are mobilised, structured and rewarded in order to address them. (Duffield, 2001, 13)

Duffield argues that our understanding of international security and its relationship with development has undergone a significant shift since the end of the Cold War. Increasingly these so-called new wars have been linked to a range of developmental issues, from the erosion of the local infrastructure, to food crises, to the failure of governance. This is what Duffield identifies as 'a new security framework within which the modalities of underdevelopment have become dangerous' (2001, 16). As he goes on to explain, this is a different way of thinking about security threats. Whereas the Cold War concentrated attention upon the possible actions of the largest states and the ongoing threat of high-level conflict between superpowers, it is now the unregulated and dispersed war machines of the poor world that threaten international security.

The central argument that Duffield puts forward is that the shift in ideas of global security has led to a rethinking of the role of development. Now security and development are seen as interrelated issues, as Duffield says: 'achieving one is now regarded as essential for securing the other' (2001, 16). The outcome of this shift in thinking has been an increasingly close relation between military and civilian organisations, between those concerned with security and those non-governmental organisations (NGOs) who work in the field of civil society. For Duffield this has led to some awkward compromises on the part of NGOs, until 'it has become difficult to separate their own development and humanitarian activities from the pervasive logic of the North's new security regime' (2001, 16); a suggestion sadly confirmed by the attacks against UN offices in Iraq in 2003 and the withdrawal of Médecins Sans Frontières from Afghanistan in 2004.

The increasing sense of insecurity that appears to be pervading Western consciousness impacts significantly on the contemporary conduct of international institutions. The trend that Duffield identifies has both escalated and altered in the light of an endless war on terror. Although economic development is prescribed as the cure for failing states, attempts to foster the building of suitable institutions may empower war entrepreneurs still further, and if NGOs become too intertwined with security endeavours they too may become targets of violence. In a climate where there is a growing crisis of trust in international agreements and their ability to offer protection, any organisation that appears to be linked to the military activity of the North may be greeted as another incarnation of foreign occupation. This is, in part, another indication that international agreements do not constrain the behaviour of non-state actors, but it is also a result of the actions of the North. Our escalating fear has allowed more openly militarised interventions in poorer regions, especially those deemed to be failing states; and the business of economic restructuring and humanitarian relief seems, increasingly, to be tied to such interventions. For developed nations, these multi-agency endeavours may seem a hopeful step towards a more regulated and inclusive world economy, a chance to rebuild failing states and smooth out zones of conflict. For the rest of the world, it seems that no international agreement can assure their right to sovereignty.

6
Circulating Bodies in
the Global Marketplace

So far this work has focused on the trade in highly profitable but often illicit goods. These are the magical objects that excite people to take great risks, face untold dangers and disregard the human costs of such trade. Some of these trades have benefited from attempts to liberalise the world economy, with the rhetoric of the free market making it harder to block or regulate some kinds of transaction. Although the fiction of the free market masks the extent to which developed economies cling to their protectionist privileges, international institutions have a great deal invested in such a fiction, not least as a means of legitimising their own role. However, as has been commented on many times before, the one market which is not presented as requiring liberalisation is the global labour market (Barry and Goodin, 1992). The movement of people is still something to be controlled, not facilitated – even in places that want to dismantle all other protectionist barriers. This chapter considers the debates that surround an earlier and very different phase of population movement in order to explore the role that migration flows, albeit forced, can play in wealth creation and the consolidation of international networks. This discussion is placed alongside a consideration of more recent events and the place of population movement in our larger narrative.

In fact, this whole volume takes the confused debate about migration as its conceptual framework. When does that beneficial activity of trade become the social danger of traffick? The definition and use of the term 'trafficking' has itself become part of the debate about migration. In its most precise usage, that favoured by international organisations and those researchers and NGOs who work against the trafficking of people, the term refers to the movement of people by force:

> Trafficking in persons shall mean the recruitment, transportation, transfer, harbouring or receipt of persons, by means of the threat or use of force or other forms of coercion, of abduction, of fraud, of deception, of the abuse

of power or of a position of vulnerability or of the giving or receiving of payments or benefits to achieve the consent of a person having control over another person, for the purpose of exploitation. (UN, 2000b)

Traffickers abduct their victims and transport them to other places against their will, usually for profit – they are a contemporary version of slave-traders. In contrast, a number of Western governments have expressed their concern in relation to a different interpretation of people-trafficking, where traffickers are those who are paid to assist would-be migrants to complete their journey to an illicit destination. Here those moving want to move, but are constrained by the anti-immigration policies of more developed nations. A new industry has arisen to exploit the desperation and vulnerability of would-be migrants – but although this is criminal and often ties migrants into a form of modern debt-bondage, the exploitation is of people who want to migrate.

This is the last segment of our story, the painful and desperate movement of people in this new era of globalisation. There is already a considerable literature about this so-called new migration, and the high levels of political anxiety around migration in the West. Whether or not there is a role for population movement in the project of global integration continues to be a fraught and contentious issue. Here I want to review some central themes in this still emerging debate. Are we, in fact, witnessing a new era of migration? In what ways, if any, can contemporary trends in migration be distinguished from the population movements of the past? Connected to this is the question of what migration adds to the global economy – what kind of things would not happen if people did not take the risk of moving?

However, this is also an attempt to approach these debates from another vantage point. Interested readers can access a wealth of valuable literature on policy, politics and migration, and these debates are well-rehearsed (Brettell and Hollifield, 2000; Castles and Miller, 1993, 2003; Cohen, 1987). Instead of repeating the plea for migrant rights in receiving countries, I have looked to the developing trend among countries of out-migration to create new categories of transnational citizenship that can mobilise and capitalise on migrant energies.

Throughout this work I have tried to pay attention to the phantasmic stories that swirl around such globalising events. My background is in the analysis and interpretation of stories, so I look to these everyday fictions in order to form a judgment about how people might understand the global. In relation to population movement, some well-worn themes keep returning: contamination and the fear of disease; the reduction of human beings into commodified pieces of meat and the horror that ensues from this; the disordering capacity of the foreign coupled with the sneaking suspicion that this is what the future looks like.

It is tempting to suggest that such mythologies which dehumanise the other have some kind of transhistorical status, as if hatred spews the same bile in all times and places. Historians of prejudice have outlined the extent to which certain themes recur in the articulated racisms of modern history (Gates, 1986; Memmi, 2000). More pertinently, the history of European racism shows a considerable degree of crossover between different strands of prejudice, so we see the myths of anti-Semitism reworked to demonise new groups (Gilman, 1985), or elaborate genealogies plotted to prove the common ancestry of Africa and Ireland. In contemporary life, the global upheaval that brings previously unfamiliar ethnic groups to the streets of Western cities also gives rise to an on-the-hoof reworking of old racist myths. Now it is this new 'they' who are the devil in every tale.

However, this suggestion of an endless continuity between forms of racism that never quite go away, just transmute into each other, does not quite ring true. If we really are experiencing a historic sea change in global structures of living, then there must be some impact on our understanding of national and ethnic boundaries. While it may be the case that people continue to fear the foreign, exactly how the foreign is perceived may change quite dramatically. Here I want to re-examine the old racist myths that continue to accompany the issue of migration, but I also want to look carefully at new narratives and beliefs that try to balance multiculturalism and self-interest. Attempts to 'manage' migration, whatever the weaknesses of such initiatives, are another kind of response to the demands and challenges of global integration (Veenkamp, Bentley and Buonfino, 2003).

This chapter echoes the arguments that have been developed throughout this volume, and brings together more popular debates about the dangers and tensions of everyday global integration. It presents an accessible version of the larger argument – that the most vilified and illicit forms of trade are quietly condoned and encouraged, as the only route to the global market for some. Migration represents a particularly apt example of this phenomenon, a process that both excites extreme emotions and enables the performance of absolutely necessary tasks in society. Unlike the examples of previous chapters, the issue of migration shows very starkly the disparity between public rhetoric and actual phenomena. The most prevalent representations of contemporary migration convey a fear of imminent crisis: Too many people chasing too few resources, dangerous social tensions, an all round sense of unfairness because some places receive more than their fair share of migrants, and a sense that things cannot go on like this. Allegedly.

Yet alongside this very public hysteria, it is apparent that migration fulfils a certain function. Without this pool of highly flexible and often desperate labour, there would need to be some serious adaptation in certain areas of work (TUC, 2003). Part of the discussion that follows considers the particular contribution of migrant labour. What is increasingly apparent is the aforementioned gap between public rhetoric and practical engagement – the first screams horror at the dangerous consequences of global integration, whereas the second happily exploits the inequalities that the global economy throws up.

MIGRATION IN A GLOBALISED ECONOMY

The sweep of global changes described in this volume also have an impact on population movement. Who moves, how they move and where they move to and from are all determined anew for the contemporary era. Of course, every era will have its own migratory histories, echoing other movements of the time. For our purposes, the point is not somehow to prove that there is something unique and unprecedented about the migrations of recent times, but to place the particularity of recent population movements in the context of other global shifts. Virginie Guiraudon and Christian Joppke summarise the wider debate in their suggestion that the key shifts of our time in the infrastructure of the international economy and the manner of conflict, changes that have been discussed earlier in this volume, have such an impact on migration that this should be regarded as a brand new world.

> The historical moments that ushered in the new migration world are well known, even though their impact and importance differs across regions: the European stop to new labor migration after the first oil crisis in 1973, which was notably not followed in North America and Australia; the onset of mass asylum seeking in the 1980s, which resulted from the dual factors of decolonization and civil wars in Asia and Africa and the closure of labor

migration in Europe; and the concern about illegal immigration, organized human smuggling, and crime that has come to dominate the post-Cold War era of the 1990s and beyond. (Guiraudon and Joppke, 2001, 2)

Although there may be disagreement about the interpretation of such events, the contours of this account are familiar from the earlier parts of our discussion. The sense of emergency in the global economy around the 1973 oil crisis and the ending of the dollar standard caused particular anxiety across Western Europe, as it turns out, in many cases with good reason. Others have suggested that these events served as an opportunity to consolidate the position of the United States as the pre-eminent economic power in the world (Harvey, 2003). It is certainly the case that from this time Western European welfare states were felt to require protection against outsiders and that the gains in social provision that had been made in the post-war period began to appear quite fragile. Immigration quickly came to be portrayed as another threat to societies which already seemed to be losing their bearings. Interestingly, this was not the case for all developed economies – as Guiraudon and Joppke point out, Australia, the United States and Canada did not succumb to this form of anti-immigrant hysteria at this time, whatever their later histories. Through the 1980s and beyond, the impact of new wars created more forced migrants, and other forms of desperation, economic, ecological and political, pushed people to move and claim sanctuary however they could. The tension between the need for population movement, as both a human desire and an economic pull, and state prohibitions against immigration led to where we are now, with the networks enabling illicit movement constituting another extensive underground industry.

THE FEAR OF FREE MOVEMENT

As has been noted, a central inconsistency in the celebration of economic liberalisation has been the attitude to migration. While all other forms of free movement have been championed, the free movement of people is hampered at every turn, often by those most vocal about the importance of dismantling barriers to trade. There are, though, a few who argue for the free movement of people as a necessary component of liberalisation:

From a global economic perspective, I take it that it is largely beyond dispute that open immigration is the optimal global strategy, with some well-

> defined qualifications. The argument for this is quite straightforward: open immigration encourages human resources to move to their most productive uses, whatever the localized distributional impact in countries of emigration or immigration. (Trebilcock, 1995)

This is the logical conclusion to be drawn from accounts of the benefits of economic liberalisation. Nothing can allocate resources as efficiently as market forces. Misguided attempts by individual governments to control the movement of labour in and out of their particular economy only serves to depress the capacity of the global economy. Free movement of labour might bring some turbulence to individual economies, but this is no more than another aspect of the shock treatment necessary for any transition to economic health. Such suggestions, however, draw disdain from most quarters:

> The model of the world economy that underpins all these developments asserts that openness increases efficiency, promotes growth and allows poorer regions to catch up with richer ones. It is based on a simplified version of economic life, focused on production and exchange, in which movements of people, like movements of capital, overcome local surpluses and scarcities in the supply of productive resources. (Jordan and Duvell, 2002, 2)

People are not like other commodities, and the social and political impact of their movement cannot be reduced to the theoretical tidiness of a self-regulating market. In fact, and as much of our discussion has indicated, no actual markets can ever live up to the perfection of a textbook equilibrium. Actual exchanges are complicated by the influence of particular histories and social contexts, by the strategies and beliefs and location of buyers and sellers, all of which confounds the promise that the market will offer the most efficient means of allocating resources.

However, the scorn shown towards the suggestion that an opening of the global labour market might benefit poorer regions may be misdirected. Enabling the free movement of people is unlikely to lead to a magical state where all local scarcities and surpluses can be evened out – and even if it did, it is not clear what this would mean in terms of human welfare – but it might aid the economic development of nations who send migrants to richer places. Despite the many barriers against movement to more developed economies, something like this process is already taking place, as demonstrated by the impact of remittance payments in Mexico, Bangladesh and the

Philippines among other places. This chapter will go on to consider what kind of opportunity this represents and for whom. For the time being, however, the movement that does take place in this supposedly new migration world is far from free and the hurdles that face would-be migrants can serve to create parallel labour markets. In a discussion of the remaking of gender divisions in a globalising world, Jan Jindy Pettman argues that barriers to the movement of people are another means of disempowering workers: 'Migration has become a global labour system, where borders that have been effectively dismantled for free movement of capital become ways of segmenting and exploiting labour.' (Pettman, 1996, 162)

Rendering some migrants 'illegal' makes them far more vulnerable to exploitation, far less able to claim basic labour rights or proper pay, and consequently far more attractive to employers in certain industries. Border controls do not stop people from moving, but they do ensure that they are disenfranchised when they arrive. Yet at the same time, immigration control seems to conjure up its own particular labour demand structure:

> Both the activity of international capitalist corporations and the adaptations of transnational networks offer economic opportunities and incentives for irregular migrants, arising from the differentials of advantage created by state boundaries. Although stemming from impoverishment and the decay of institutional structures in their countries of origin, individual decisions to migrate are prompted by demand for labour in First World economies, and especially for supplies of adaptable and mobile low-wage labour. (Jordan and Duvell, 2002, 7)

In the manner of other illicit trades, prohibition creates new business opportunities – attempts to safeguard the wage levels and benefits of more affluent states confirm their attraction as a destination; assistance in negotiating policed borders becomes a lucrative service industry; industries learn to covet the particular flexibilities of undocumented workers. In relation to the movement of people, in the right time and place, hampering market flows can be very good for some kinds of business.

FREE MOVEMENT AND FORCED LABOUR

Although this volume has concentrated on the formation of more recent versions of global integration, I am also interested in the suggestion that this is only the latest in a series of world economies that have animated human history. Nigel Harris (2002) reminds us that controls over the movement of people are a relatively recent development, another twentieth-century phenomenon that echoes Meghnad Desai's contention that the last century represented a short-lived experiment in de-globalising the world economy.

Most importantly for this section of the discussion, the trafficking of human beings formed the bloody and cruel basis of the previous era of globalised interaction. It is beyond the scope of this work to consider the extent to which different phases of the world economy have relied upon the forced movement of people. However, in order to understand some of the evasions and emotions that accompany the issue of human trafficking it may be instructive to think again about the consequences of the Atlantic slave trade.

IS SLAVERY THE SECRET BASIS OF INDUSTRIALISATION?

This is an old debate but one that has fallen out of favour. Somehow in this era of reclaimed imperial vision we have come to a point where we are encouraged to remember the positive contribution of empire. In these circumstances it is hard to make space for more long-running debates about the barbarism that enables prosperity for a few. That argument seems to have been consigned to the dustbin of history, along with a clutch of other careful debates now regarded as naive and tainted by Marxism. In relation to our hard to understand world, I would argue that Benjamin's aphorism about culture and barbarism remains an important lesson: 'There is no document of civilization which is not at the same time a document of barbarism.' (Benjamin, 1973, 1992, 248)

Benjamin argues that even the history written by the victors, the privileged documents of culture, cannot help but reveal the 'anonymous toil of their contemporaries' (248). Beneath the celebration of achievement, that other world of countless uncelebrated, undocumented and unrecognised lives is always there. All accounts of progress rest on some untold human cost – the sacrifices of those whose labour transforms society but who do not enjoy the benefits of this transformation. Benjamin is speaking of the successive class struggles that have made human history since the dawn of time, but clearly the forced contribution of African slaves to European wealth and ascendancy must be regarded as part of the ugly barbarism that underlies European civilisation.

The most influential scholarship in this area can be approached through two key ideas, ideas that I want to re-examine through two formative accounts of the legacy of the Atlantic slave trade. The first suggestion, which here I want to link to the debates outlined in and stemming from Eric Williams' *Capitalism and Slavery*, is that the industrialisation of the West is built on the surpluses extracted from the stolen labour of Africans. In this telling, slavery is not merely an incidental and barbaric aberration that occurs alongside the happy progress of the industrial age; rather, the economic advantages that are gained through different aspects of the slave trade in fact enabled the developmental leaps that we call the industrial revolution. Inevitably, there is some considerable debate about what this suggestion actually means, and how such advantages can be measured or their impact distinguished from other factors. In what follows, there will be a consideration of some of the more intriguing twists of this debate and a consideration of the role of the trafficking of people in an earlier phase of global integration.

The second suggestion concerns the impact of the slave trade on the development of Africa. Here I want to take Walter Rodney's *How Europe Underdeveloped Africa*, as the defining text. Rodney's groundbreaking argument is that the so-called underdevelopment of Africa, a problem that animates much debate in the twentieth century, is an outcome of colonial exploitation by Europe. This includes the extreme expropriations of the slave trade, a theft of human capital so drastic that its repercussions haunt Africa to the present day.

Williams lays out a complex account of the role of enslaved African labour in the development of the Caribbean and its relation with Europe. His argument, broadly, is that slave economies represented the most profitable option for colonial powers during a certain period of mercantilist development:

> With the limited population of Europe in the sixteenth century, the free laborers necessary to cultivate the staple crops of sugar, tobacco and cotton in the New World could not have been supplied in quantities adequate to permit large-scale production. Slavery was necessary for this, and to get slaves the Europeans turned first to the aborigines and then to Africa. (Williams, 1964, 6)

What forced-labour contributes here is a sufficient quantity of labour sufficiently quickly. The economic possibilities of the New

World required a large and pliant labour force who could adapt quickly to the arduous demands of the new wonder crops. Williams is building here on the suggestions of classical economics. From Adam Smith to John Stuart Mill to Karl Marx, there is a recognition that the enslavement of Africa provided the economic boost that enabled the creation and consolidation of European power. The conceptual, if not political, tradition that spawned neo-liberalism has acknowledged the role of this injection of labour.

Williams reminds us that there was no automatic turning to enslaved African labour. The labour needs of the Caribbean were a matter of debate. In fact, the transportation of servants and convicts from Europe was viewed, for a while, as a means of siphoning cheap and subjugated labour to plantations. There is little indication that the whiteness of these unlucky transportees improved their lot in any way. The racialised aspect of slavery, according to Williams, emerged to meet pragmatic requirements rather than to institutionalise white privilege:

> Racial differences made it easier to justify and rationalize Negro slavery, to exact the mechanical obedience of a plough-ox or cart-horse, to demand that resignation and that complete moral and intellectual subjection which alone make slave labour possible. Finally, and this was the decisive factor, the Negro slave was cheaper. The money which secured a white man's services for ten years could buy a Negro for life. (Williams, 1964, 19)

The European poor were vulnerable to the entrapment of bond labour, but even this lucrative exploitation of forced labour could not compete with the profits that could be extracted from African slaves. Herbert Klein argues that African slaves represented a uniquely malleable workforce – not only captive but 'kinless and totally mobile laborers ... from multiple linguistic groups and [who] had only the European languages in common and were therefore forced to adapt themselves to the European norms' (1999, 20). This was a group deprived not only of their freedom, but also of their language community and all other sources of support. Despite the biologised account of race that we inherit from the nineteenth century, this suggestion of biology as destiny was not yet apparent in the earlier phases of plantation economy. Although retrospectively the world has learned to internalise the racist mythologies that portray Africans as physically hardy, with physical power in inverse proportion to intellectual power, Williams encourages us to see the structural context of these economic choices:

> Negro slavery ... had nothing to do with climate. Its origin can be expressed in three words: in the Caribbean, sugar; on the mainland, tobacco and cotton. A change in the economic structure produced a corresponding change in the labour supply. ... Sugar, tobacco, and cotton require the large plantation and hordes of cheap labour, and the small farm of the ex-indentured white servant could not possibly survive. (Williams, 1964, 23)

Overall, Williams argues that the triangular trade between Europe, the Caribbean and the new colonies of North America relied upon the excessive brutality and profit of the slave trade only while colonial monopoly remained a profitable option. Some argue that this was always a complex calculation, with plantation economies always somewhat distanced from the development of the global capitalist economy: 'The plantation society that had begun as an appendage of British capitalism ended as a powerful largely autonomous civilization with aristocratic pretensions and possibilities, although it remained tied to the capitalist world by bonds of commodity production.' (Genovese, 1966, 15)

These slave economies enabled the integration of the world economy, yet were not themselves easily integrated into this process. The high profits that could be siphoned back into European economies from plantation holdings were one of the triggers that enabled wider social change and further economic development – but plantation societies themselves remained immune from such pressures. These enclaves provided the resources that allowed modernisation but were themselves frozen in a kind of faux-feudalism. Ultimately, this was an arrangement that could not last forever:

> In accounting for the destruction of British slavery it is necessary to emphasize how closely it was embedded in its social and economic world even when it chose to shift or change one element of that world. Without the context of a rising industrial order there would have been no social leverage available to destroy one of the original components of the old order. Yet linking the rise of anti-slavery to the evolution of capitalism alone leaves us far short of explaining the dynamic of abolitionism. (Drescher, 1986, 162)

Although slavery and the slave trade are identified as important components in the development of European capitalist economies and the creation of a world trading market, these same developments, it is argued, later outgrow any potential benefits of the plantation outpost. Drescher does warn against too deterministic a view of this process, arguing that abolitionism is not reducible to a symptom of changing economic interests and that it represented 'a power struggle rather than a display of hegemonic symbol manipulation' (1986, 162). However, after Williams, a range of commentators agree that the Atlantic slave trade and the plantation economies that it fed ended because they ceased to be profitable. Not everyone, however, has agreed with the view that the racist ideologies that surround slavery arose after the fact. Howard Winant summarises some of this alternative thinking by suggesting that: 'Modernity ... is a global racial formation project.' (2001, 20) Winant is concerned to reveal the central role of 'race' in the formation of the modern era. He explains: 'Imperialism's creation of modern nation-states, capitalism's construction of an international economy, and the Enlightenment's articulation of a unified world culture, I argue, were all deeply racialized processes.' (2001, 19)

Winant argues that the phenomena of racial consciousness and identification cannot be reduced to symptoms of economic processes. For our purposes, it is relatively unimportant which view we take – both agree that the Atlantic slave trade created the basis for European industrialisation and the formation of a capitalist world economy. The only consideration is the extent to which the manner of the slave trade is shaped by non-economic considerations.

Winant is arguing for the formative role of 'race' within this history. This would suggest that although the processes of slavery may have increased and exacerbated racial consciousness and the horrors that could be tolerated in its name, there is also a racial consciousness at work within the formation of the slave trade. This would suggest that, although the trade in forced labour answered an immediate instrumental need, responses to this need were already shaped by beliefs about the comparative worth of different human beings.

This kind of issue is notoriously difficult to resolve. Social determination is not a linear process and it is not possible to chart a clear sequence of events. There is no identifiable date at which racial consciousness takes hold, against which we can judge whether it is a cause or symptom. The question here for us is: how significant is the racial component in the identification of a suitably numerous and pliant labour force? In particular, what value is added through population movement and what through the dehumanisation of racism?

If we follow Williams' account, there is a sudden and urgent demand for a large labour force suitable for plantation work. The indigenous population is not sufficiently numerous and, for a variety of reasons including lack of immunity to Western disease forms, proves unsuitable for the work at hand. For Williams, this leads to a pragmatic choice of African labour. Europe cannot provide the numbers required, and, even at these levels of impoverishment, free white workers raise the awkward spectre of political and economic demands. Marked by physical difference, Africans were tied to the workplace – there was no escape that could allow them to pass as employers, traders or colonisers. The traffick in forced labour ensured the required numbers. The implication from Williams is that it was a historical accident that caused this trade to be in African people.

Against this, Winant and others imply that racial consciousness was one of the factors that overdetermined the choice of African peoples, because the horror of the trade was ameliorated by the belief that these people were of lesser worth anyway. Winant explains this process as another history of the longue durée; one of those extensively complex processes that builds and weaves across an extended period, where it is almost impossible to pin down any original cause and yet we can see that over time a significant change has occurred: 'We might usefully think of the racial longue durée in which the slow inscription of phenotypical signification took place upon the human body, in and through conquest and enslavement to be sure, but also as an enormous act of expression, of narration.' (Winant, 2001, 21)

The argument here is that this earlier phase of global integration required the lubricant of racial thinking. Without some more global conception of the terms of entitlement, there could be no rationale for the co-ordination of different mechanisms of division and hierarchy. I have been trying to understand the implications of this idea for contemporary forms of forced and/or hyper-exploited labour. Winant is making quite a large claim for the shaping power of racial consciousness, and in order to make it, he must paint 'race' in the broadest of terms. However, I have some sympathy with his project and the importance of treating 'race' in a manner that does not reduce its formation to a passing symptom in relation to the underlying and determining story of capital (see Bhattacharyya, Gabriel and Small, 2002). It seems much more plausible to consider that capital formation in certain significant periods has worked in conjunction with the ideologies of race:

The transition from an insular, regionally contained, and mechanically solidaristic social order to an integrated, global society with an increasingly complex division of labour demanded the creation of a worldwide racial division between Europe and the 'others.' To slavery and colonialism, through the extraction of immense quantities of natural resources, and most particularly through the institutionalization and elaboration of techniques for the exploitation of mass labour at a hitherto inconceivable level, the apparatus was synthesized for the accumulation of wealth on a grand scale. (Winant, 2001, 25)

In retrospect, it is clear that the concept of 'race' has had this central place in the formation of the modern era. What is determinant and what is symptom may remain undecided, but few would suggest that a racial logic had not played a role in this expansion. That modern creation of the 'other' continues to do considerable work in all sorts of social formations, and certainly continues to sift human worth into relative and unequal values. It is this notion of unequal worth that sews together the global integration of modernity.

Walter Rodney both echoes and compliments the work of Eric Williams. Rodney's project, however, is of a broader scope and seeks to explain the ways in which more than 400 years of contact between Europe and Africa has shaped the relations of the global economy. At the heart of his analysis is a critique of the concept of development. Rodney refutes the idea that the poor world is in a process of development that will allow it to catch up with the advantages of the rich world. Instead, he argues that underdevelopment has been an active outcome of contact with Europe. European intervention has interrupted the development process of some regions and replaced it with a set of exploitative relations that led to underdevelopment:

All other countries named as 'underdeveloped' in the world are exploited by others; and the underdevelopment with which the world is now preoccupied is a product of capitalist, imperialist, and colonialist exploitation. African and Asian societies were developing independently until they were taken over directly or indirectly by the capitalist powers. When that happened, exploitation increased and the export of surplus ensued, depriving the societies of the benefit of their natural resources and labour. That is an integral part of underdevelopment in the contemporary sense. (Rodney, 1973, 14)

There is little ambiguity in Rodney's account and he has no patience with accounts that try to argue that the colonial presence enabled Africa's transition to capitalism. Instead, Rodney reframes the whole idea of economic progress and development. There is not one path of economic development, with different regions placed at different points in the race, but with all travelling in the same direction and towards the same goals. In fact, Rodney argues that it is quite the opposite – the economic development of some is achieved at the expense of others. The West has developed through a set of exploitative relations with its colonies, and these relations have instituted a process of underdevelopment, an active and ongoing stripping away of resources and possibilities. This unequal relation shapes global interactions beyond the colonial moment, continuing into the present day.

> African economies are integrated into the very structure of the developed capitalist economies; and they are integrated in a manner that is unfavourable to Africa and ensures that Africa is dependent on the big capitalist countries. Indeed, structural dependence is one of the characteristics of underdevelopment. (Rodney, 1973, 25)

Of course, this is not an argument that is specific to Rodney – although his work does represent a particularly influential and formative example of this debate. The proposition that African and other underdeveloped nations are integrated into metropolitan economies in a manner that perpetuates the relations of empire springs from a certain moment of Third World consciousness (Amin, 1980; Nkrumah, 1965). This is an attempt to understand the limitations and failures of independence, as we have discussed in an earlier chapter. In relation to the economic advantages of slavery, what is good for one phase of European development ceases to be useful for another: 'Slavery is useful for early accumulation of capital, but it is too rigid for industrial development.' (Rodney, 1973, 87)

Rodney, in an echo of other commentators, argues that capitalist interests ended the slave trade and slavery, because despite the excessive profits that could be made by a few, slavery impeded the process of industrialisation. Rodney is putting forward a complex argument about the consistency through change of exploitative relations in different phases of European contact with Africa. Overall, his suggestion is that, despite the illusory sovereignty of national boundaries, Africa has continued to serve as a hyper-exploited extension of first European, and then Western, economies. In relation to the possible impacts of population movement, this suggestion is very important. In effect, the work of Rodney and others implies that the underdeveloped world is already an integral component of the economic circuits of the West – the labour of the poor world is not an injection from an external source, it is a redeployment within an unequal system.

The kind of long view that is proposed by Rodney and others helps us to understand how global relations have been formed, but it offers few suggestions as to how things might be changed. If these events have shaped the world for so long, what hope can there be of beginning afresh now?

The most influential responses to this dilemma also belong to the tradition of Third World consciousness – and, in the main, they recommend a refusal of the global economy (Amin, 1980). Starting afresh here means cutting away from this rigged set of interactions and refocusing on a development that is not defined in the terms of the West. Most of this work has assumed that this is no longer considered to be a viable option for most nations – North Korea aside, it is hard to think of anywhere that is actively eschewing international trade or not engaging in some version of development. We are left with the question of what manner of engagement in the global economy might address the wrongs of underdevelopment.

WHAT CANNOT HAPPEN WITHOUT POPULATION MOVEMENT?

The debates about the slave trade concentrate, quite rightly, on the horrors of forced labour. As we have discussed above, the stolen wealth created by forced labour is a central aspect of any understanding of the contemporary legacies of slave economies. However, for the purposes of this work, the issue of population movement is equally relevant even though it is less often discussed.

If previous phases of global integration have required the input of transportable labour, then what are the implications for contemporary battles over immigration control and profit maximisation? Can economic integration occur without population movement? While I don't mean to imply that these components of economic activity are abstract and interchangeable across time and place, there must be something to be learned from revisiting the impact of people-trafficking in another time. When celebrating the achievements and possibilities of movement, it is always the capacity of capital to travel that receives the acclaim. The role of labour is, at the very least, secondary in this story, and more often is not considered at all.

The literature on the Atlantic slave trade offers some suggestions about the role of mobile labour. One is the idea that new forms of economic enterprise emerge in places such as the Caribbean and North America with, arguably, no or insufficient local labour. Second, in an explanation that can follow from the first, local labour is unsuited to the required activity or unwilling to carry it out. Third, and most popular, the circumstances of movement make mobile labour more cost-effective. All three accounts can be transferred to other circumstances where labour is mobile.

Of all the very dubious get rich quick schemes known to mankind, the slave trade has been one of the most successful. Unlike other commodities, human beings once enslaved can continue to produce more and more value – the transformative capacity of their labour really is the trading equivalent of the goose that lays the golden eggs.

I want to argue here that remnants of forced labour have continued from the time of the Atlantic slave trade right up until the present day (Bales, 1999). The point here is not to suggest that human beings are so weak and susceptible to temptation that such evils are inevitable; rather I want to suggest that forced labour has continued to play a lubricating role in a certain form of global capitalist development. This is not an argument about the necessity of stealing people's labour and freedom, but it is to suggest that some spaces continue to offer relatively unregulated routes into the global economy and that this lack of regulation might be tied to the possibility of making a great deal of money. A number of modern-day slave trades live in the crevices of the global economy, not as unhappy anachronisms that will disappear when the enlightening force of free trade strikes, but as integral components of the complex and multi-layered sewing together of the world (Van Den Anker, 2004).

THE MYTH OF FINITE RESOURCES

There is an exceptional level of anxiety around the issue of migration in developed economies. Talk of this being a new era of migration has seeped into popular consciousness – often, it seems, as a way of articulating a displaced fear of globalisation. If borders become open to the movement of people, then we of the rich world will surely lose the privileges that some forms of border control can bring. Antimigration campaigns are the anti-globalisation movement of the rich and powerful.

Among the many trade barriers erected by the West, the barriers against the movement of people are the most publicly policed and the most frequently updated. These are the barriers that receive most publicity and elicit the highest levels of political investment. Political parties compete in their claims to be the most ruthless opponents of the movement of people, and even among developing countries there are indications that nations that have become regional centres in the poor world, such as India and South Africa, are entering the realm of immigration scares.

This brand of anti-immigrant feeling almost always points to finitude of resources as a justification for excluding some in order to protect others. Of course it stands to reason that those to be protected should be those identified as your own. Most often the boundaries are determined by an idea of nation, although in the context of recent border disputes this may also become a region or locality. The longer debate about migration in the West has tended to link fears about scarcity to these beliefs about the inevitable selfishness of the racial group. It almost goes without saying that this link in itself serves to naturalise the concept of 'race', as if we all instinctively know the difference between them and us and organise our interests around this boundary.

Unfortunately for proponents of such common-sense racism, demographic changes mean that a number of Western nations require migrants in order to renew their workforce. This is an aspect of the debate that signals a shift – it is no longer a question of enhancement; migrants are needed just to make sure that things do not get worse. This is already apparent in the rich world's rush to attract health-workers and teachers from other parts of the world, not least from their former colonies. Without this emergency injection of migration, key services would crumble still further. Of course, this argument is most simple to make in relation to essential services – everyone accepts that societies must keep their schools and hospitals running. Less straightforward is the role of migrant labour in times of wider social stagnation. If migrants will slot into the least desirable jobs in an economy in decline, is that a help or a hindrance in the larger quest for economic well-being?

Although this volume takes traffick and the unruly fear that this illicit form of movement brings as its focus, the assorted talk about people-trafficking cannot be separated from the larger debate about the movement of people. So it is worth for a moment considering again the contention that we are entering some new era of migration.

Nigel Harris reminds us that migration is no new thing and that, at least until the later twentieth century, economic growth in Europe and the Americas 'would lead to labour demand exceeding local supply' (Harris, 1996, 3). If anything, it is immigration control that is the recent phenomenon, a set of processes unknown before the twentieth century. Yet attitudes to migration remain heated and contradictory, and few wish to remember that many nationals of the developed world are themselves the descendents of migrants, or how recent this experience of migration has been. This wilful forgetfulness shapes the various non-debates that emerge in relation to the issue of migration – as if this is a new event and therefore a crisis, as if migrants are a species apart from settled populations. There is a widespread pretence that human history holds no lessons in coping with population movement.

Much of this volume has explored the more hidden aspects of international trade and has suggested that the political alignments of certain moments have shaped trading choices and opportunities. This account has largely accepted the contention that there is no alternative to participation in the global economy, and that the justness or otherwise of outcomes will be determined by the manner of this participation. In keeping with this theme, this section is based on the view that transnational migration is an inevitable and irresistible component of global integration. Once again, the question for those concerned about questions of social justice is not whether it will occur, but how and on what terms.

Harris points out an earlier relationship between economic growth – that magical development that we are all striving for – and the need for labour. Much of the most contentious debate about contemporary immigration focuses on the question of whether economic growth requires or is enhanced by such access to migrant labour. What follows is a consideration of the extent to which what has happened in the past can help us to understand the future, even if it cannot tell us what the future holds.

The myth of finite resources seems to assume a model of the nation where there is no international trade. The economic resources of the nation here seem to take on the aspect of natural resources, something that is inherently part of the landscape and once it's gone it's gone. There is no space in this telling for a more dynamic concept of the economy. No room to argue that the resources we have come from the things that people do, so that more and different people can bring more and different resources.

If anything, there is a scarily widespread confusion about what is a symptom of economic change and what causes these changes. Even when the particular market position of migrant labour has been established – at the dangerous, flexible end of the market – there is a suggestion that migrants themselves create this unhappy erosion of labour rights:

> The evolution of the labour market has tended to push the native born closer to the conditions of insecurity experienced by the immigrant. Indeed, immigrant workers – leaving aside the issue of skills – are in fact the most flexible of all, and thus best suited to the new pattern of labour demand. (Harris, 1996, 18)

Harris alludes to the well-developed accounts of the increasing flexibility of labour markets in developed economies, and the consequent erosion in working conditions suffered by all workers (Felstead and Jewson, 1999). He also outlines the extent to which migrant labour has smoothed and enabled economic restructuring in the developed world. Migrant labour has often filled demand for unskilled work, in periods where so-called native labour has moved into more desirable forms of employment. However, changes in working practices, changes which have been linked to the processes of global integration, have extended the uncertainties of migrant existence to others.

Harris is keen to remind us that not all this unskilled migrant labour is employed in declining sectors. Immigrants are willing to do work and maintain sectors that might otherwise fall into terminal decline, with a knock-on effect on other sections of the economy. In summary, 'in performing these roles, immigrants provide a margin of "flexible labour" where regulation has rendered the labour supply particularly rigid' (Harris, 1996, 175).

This is a tricky set of arguments. According to some market fetishists, the flexibility of migrant labour indicates that it stands in the way of necessary innovation. Industries and practices that would not survive in a situation of more open competition can sometimes muddle through with the cushion of a hyper-exploited labour force. When employers from some sectors argue that they cannot survive without migrant workers, there can be a suspicion that they are masking their own bad practice and failure to innovate – why else would employers prefer employees who are forced to be more flexible because of a lack of social status and entitlement?

HELPING THE TRAFFICKERS

The traffick in human beings has become an international scandal, eliciting countless policy papers, statements and legislative developments in different parts of the world (Skrobanek, Boonpakdi and Janthakeero, 1997). Although only a small proportion of these people represent forced labour, I would still like to argue that this is the abolitionist argument for our time. The traffick in human beings reveals the hunger of the global economy for human labour and disrespect for human dignity.

Unfortunately, the response of much of the rich world has been to view the traffick in human beings as yet another immigration problem. Although much has been made of the abuses suffered by desperate would-be migrants, policy has tended to focus on how to keep these people out. The underlying message is that trafficking is bad because it enables migrants to enter the rich world. In this, the traffick in people is linked to anxieties about other forms of illicit trade – like small arms, or drugs, people-trafficking is an unhappy reminder that global integration is unstoppable and that enabling transnational movement in difficult circumstances is itself a new form of big business. Attempts to curtail such movement create greater danger and suffering for would-be migrants, without any discernible impact on migration trends: 'It is from the denial of people's rights to travel to and settle in the place of their choice that some of the worst abuses of human rights in Western liberal democracies have sprung.' (Hayter, 2000, 152)

It is somewhat ironic that governments and parties who have worked hard to whip up anti-immigrant feelings, now protest loudly about victims of human trafficking. Trafficking has become one of the recognised monsters of our time, with international agreements phrased to condemn such barbaric practice and to commit states to co-operate in its eradication (UN, 2000b). Trafficking is presented as another global threat, something that brings no benefit to anyone apart from the traffickers – how could anyone not want to wipe it out?

However, as discussed at the beginning of this chapter, the outcry about human trafficking could be regarded as another incarnation of anti-immigration campaigning. Trafficking properly refers to the forced movement of people, yet in the West this is often merged into other forms of population movement. Anyone who enables people to migrate, especially those whose business is to make money by helping people navigate the highly policed barriers against migration to the West, is tainted by this accusation of people-trafficking. In this account, combating trafficking is another method of protecting the comparatively privileged against the encroachment of the rest of the world. Stephen Castles argues that this process can contribute to a wider anti-immigrant politics: 'The campaign against smugglers and traffickers can lead to criminalization of all migrants, and may serve to legitimate failures in official policies.' (Castles, 2004, 209)

Of course, even when people choose to move of their own volition, those who enable the journey may be exploitative, violent and ruthless. Those who smuggle illicit migrants may be careless or worse about the welfare of their clients, sealing people into airless containers or tipping them out into the sea. They may exploit people's desperation to move and coerce them into contracts of tied labour that consign them to debt bondage. They may have business arrangements with the most unscrupulous of employers, squeezing extra profits from people whose undocumented status leaves them hopelessly vulnerable to such exploitation. They are clearly people who are content to make money out of other people's misery. Yet all these dubious business options become available only as a result of the nature of immigration controls. The combination of politically motivated border control and continuing demand for migrant labour creates this entrepreneurial opportunity. Creating a new folk devil by rewriting the concept of trafficker looks suspiciously like a continuation of this same hypocrisy.

WOMEN AND CHILDREN

The aspect of the demon trafficker that has most attracted popular attention is, predictably, sex – the forced transportation of women and children for the most degrading forms of exploitation. All too often there is a sexual aspect to this trade, an aspect that confirms the less than human status of the trafficked (Brown, 2001; Hughes, 2001; Oppermann, 1998).

It is this gruesome intersection between the sex trade and forced labour that has most excited policy attention. Perhaps for this reason,

I have tried to keep this discussion out of previous chapters. This, after all, is the traffick that fuels the pornographic moral crusades of our time, our very own incarnation of the white slave trade. Once these images enter the debate, it is hard to make space for the more abstract arguments that I wish to make. In order to place the trafficking of people in the larger context of other forms of illicit movement, the reader must put aside their emotional response, at least momentarily.

But the horror stories cannot be excised altogether. The events of the later twentieth century have created too many desperate and displaced people. The excessive profits to be gained from stealing the labour and freedom of other human beings have continued to tempt barbarism, and the manner in which the global economy has become interconnected, combined with the misfortune that has befallen certain regions – from economic free-fall in Eastern Europe to the ravages of wars in Africa to the dismantling of small-scale agriculture across Asia – have all created new opportunities for this cruel trade. This is nothing new, except this very old trade has taken new inflections in new circumstances.

There are some unfortunate elements in the idea that trafficking is something suffered by women and children alone. Much of the anti-immigration hysteria of the rich world is directed against the movement of young men. Or, as the argument goes, healthy young men, those whose youth and masculinity renders them threatening not pitiful. Although these hapless young men may be tricked by traffickers, may lose money or even be forced to perform tied labour, they know what they are doing. They come of their own volition, they want to work. And although the work of young men may be far from pleasant, it is not regarded as an actual assault. Women and children are placed differently within these mythologies of unwanted migration. They most definitely do not know what they are doing.

Once again, relegating the businesses surrounding migration to the realm of criminality – another part of that shadowy underworld economy that is controlled by gangsters and drug dealers – greatly increases the risks to migrants. Sexual exploitation forms part of the repertoire of the criminal economy, as both the provision of a potentially lucrative and illicit service and as a terror-tactic to discipline captive workers. Anti-immigration policies make it harder for migrants to defend themselves against this abuse.

SEXUALISING HUMAN CAPITAL

Alongside this sexual abuse of those deemed to be without rights all over the world, there is a parallel story to be told about the use of sexual capital as a resource in the global economy. The most troubling element in this tale is the idea that nations may use their populations as this form of resource, so that this becomes more than an individual and desperate choice and instead becomes a part of the national development strategy. There is a small and honourable body of work that outlines the pressures and semi-articulated choices which lead to the inclusion of sex work in the official roster of national industries (Moon, 1997; Sturdevant and Stoltzfus, 1992).

One of the most well-known examples is the development of the sex trade in Thailand – and the research that examines this phenomenon serves as a template for understanding the place of the international sex trade in the painful turbulence that characterises the integration of the world economy. Thailand began its career as an infamous destination for sex tourism at that same moment in the 1970s that marked the beginning of other strands of our story. The combination of imperial crisis and changes in the terms of the international economy forced a new development agenda for strategically significant regions of the world:

> It was in 1971, at the height of the Vietnam conflict, that Robert McNamara, then head of the World Bank, visited Bangkok and arranged to send the bank's tourism experts to plan the development of Thailand's tourist industry. The rationale for this move was, in fact, the 'unstable geo-political situation in Indochina' and the consequent unreliability of the R&R supply. (Bishop and Robinson, 1998, 98)

With the self-interested intervention of the United States via the World Bank, Thailand embarked on a tourism-led model of development. Although the R&R market became sidelined, as the US retreated from the region in the mid 1970s, tourism retained its attraction. Bishop and Robinson suggest that the tourism industry, with a tacit acceptance of its sexual aspect, has become so lucrative and so powerful that this industry's need for a constant supply of fresh labour has shaped planning policies for the nation. Bishop and Robinson argue that the systematic move away from agriculture and fishing, and failure to support the regions where such work took place, created a stream of displaced young female workers to the city (1998, 99). Of course, the decline of rural economies and the subsequent movement to cities is a wider trend across the world, and it is beyond the scope of this work to assess the particular movements in the Thai economy. However, it is the case that the revenue gained from (only thinly disguised) sex tourism has allowed Thailand to gain the approval of international financial institutions:

> From the perspective of national and international policy, 'Lek' and her thousands of sisters make it possible for Thailand to be an exemplary client of the World Bank. Although the country's rate of borrowing is very high – yielding a deficit in yen, as well as in dollars – Thailand has not been reduced to the debt peonage characteristic of so many other oil-importing nations that have no stable source of foreign exchange. Thailand has been able to meet the interest if not the principal on its deficit, so that economic growth has not been slowed, even as the proportion of foreign debt to GNP (gross national product) has more than trebled. (Bishop and Robinson, 1998, 99)

In the manner of other trades discussed in other chapters, this has been an outcome of the intersection of US military expansion and participation in the global market. A US military presence could, over time, render a nation's women into another neo-colonial cash crop. Once enough of the local economy has come to rotate around this particular trade in flesh, this can create its own incarnation of dependency. Sex work can skew local economic relations in a manner very similar to other illicit but lucrative forms of business (Clift and Carter, 2000; Oppermann, 1998).

In the manner of other largely agricultural economies Thailand has not been well-equipped to compete in the international market. It is the income from tourism that prevents it from joining the ranks of the other 'basket cases' that have no option but to submit to the shocking interventions of international financial institutions. Sex tourism may be a byproduct of an imperial presence and the transnational purchase of sex may be animated by the most old-fashioned and unpleasant of imperial fantasies, but the revenue gained from this industry can serve to safeguard a version of sovereignty for vulnerable nations. For nations desperate for sources of foreign currency, promoting their populations as providers of personal services, however exploitative and unsavoury, emerges as another strategy of development:

> The international impacts upon the everyday life of people everywhere. Those caught up in different forms of international traffic in women are

especially vulnerable to rationalisation and eroticisation of their bodies and labour. While gender relations are part of international relations, so is sexuality. Women's bodies become quite literally a part of making 'the international'. (Pettman, 1996, 207)

This process of eroticisation is not limited to women, although women and children may be more vulnerable to this form of exploitation. However, I would argue that this is an eroticisation of global power imbalances. The fantasy is of poor and desperate people who will do anything for a little foreign currency. In the face of the turbulent uncertainty of global changes, playing out such imperial scenarios may offer reassurance for a Western subject in decline. The next section considers some survival strategies for the non-Western subject.

MOBILISING DIASPORA AND SURVIVING GLOBALISATION

In an era where the aspirations of the numerous but resource-poor populations of the developing world are hampered by the various measures taken by the rich world to defend their borders and trading privileges, it can be difficult to remember that, for many parts of the world, migrants remain an important economic asset. For some parts of the developing world, the willingness of their populations to uproot themselves in the search for economic opportunities elsewhere represents a central component of their engagement with the global economy. As a result, nations are beginning to develop methods of extending and adapting the terms of citizenship, in an attempt to retain the ties and benefits that come from an industrious and mobile migrant population abroad. This could be seen as a response to rich-world anxieties about traffick, as the poor world tries to find ways to make the untidy business of movement respectable. Once again, the example discussed here is India; but similar trends can be seen in Mexico and the Philippines among other places: 'India – for the first time, is officially engaging with its 20 million strong diaspora across 110 countries to rejuvenate its bonds with them.' (Government of India press release, November 12, 2002)

Some places can come to represent a much larger set of experiences – perhaps to represent the consciousness of a particular historical moment. The high market value of South Asian writers in English could be seen as an indication of this representative function – the world reads these stories in order to learn a narrative of postcolonial subjectivity. The point here is not some old-fashioned exoticism. Rather, this is a much more ambitious consumer project, the re-imagining of a universalist subjecthood, but this time through the lens of a life lived in the shadowy aftermath of empire proper. India is one of those locations that stands in as a sign of the assorted tensions of the postcolonial subject in the era of the new imperialism. Who isn't part of this story now? The point is not that all locations are the same, but rather that the contact with empire allows only a certain range of responses.

This, then, is my excuse for using India and her actions as a case study of the (relatively) poor nation re-imagining its networks and boundaries in response to the threatening advent of globalisation. India has already assumed a kind of synechdocal status, as one exemplar of the move from imperial occupation to nation-statehood. It is for this reason that India's cultural life, particularly in the form of literature in English, has shaped the discussion of postcoloniality. This is not, however, a discussion of cultural production. Here I want to make another kind of argument about the audacious innovations of the Indian state, and the circumstances that create these new strategies for surviving the global economy.

Of course, India is not the only location that has begun to employ new tactics to use transnational populations to navigate transnational economies. In fact, in its own discussion papers, India acknowledges the lessons learned from other nations, and looks to the institutional frameworks that other nations develop to administer their relation to their diasporic population. India is by no means the first nation to go through this process.

However, for our purposes, India offers one of the most developed commentaries on the resilient connection between nation and diaspora. At the same time, India runs ahead in another global-labour supply game – that of disembodied service work in the international system of call-centres and administrative services. Studying India's deployment of her best asset, her people, offers a larger insight into the challenges of globalisation and how they might be met.

On January 9, 2003, India hosted its first international conference exploring the role of the non-resident population in the business of the nation. The Indian diaspora is said to be second largest in the world with an estimated purchasing power of around US$300 billion. The conference was one result of the Report of the High Level Committee on the Indian Diaspora 2002 – a committee formed to examine the relationship between India and its diaspora, with a view to creating institutional structures and new legislation that might formalise these emotional links and transform the loose allegiance of the ex-patriot into a positive resource for the nation. This is a continuation of a much longer debate about the place of the non-resident Indian (the NRI); that diasporic population outside India that is seeking to articulate its relation to the homeland. The report reviews the experience of the Indian diaspora in a number of locations, examines the formal structures that other nations have instituted in relation to their own diasporic populations and discusses arenas of national life where non-residents may contribute. From this research and discussion, some key proposals were made. Most importantly, it is suggested that an annual conference should celebrate the achievements of the diaspora, a government department should be created with particular responsibility for diaspora affairs and there should be an extension of the Person of Indian Origin card to create a system approaching dual nationality.

This is another aspect of our turbulent times. In the light of recent events – not only the beginning of a new phase of globalisation but also a time in which the West has become unhinged by the impact of the attacks of September 11 and the world is hurtling into an endless spiral of conflict as we wage war on terror – migrant populations must once again reconsider the terms of their allegiance and identity.

Of course, we have all been talking about diaspora forever, and this discussion has spawned its own industry of academic publishing and activity. However, much of the analysis of diaspora has focused exclusively on cultural aspects, with little indication that these networks must negotiate with the actions of states. Here I want to offer a small corrective to this lack, and to suggest that one unexpected outcome of recent events, including the growth of a global economy and a concern to protect legitimate transactions from misuse by the bogeymen of international terrorism, has been the transformation of diasporic populations into a new extended infrastructure of the nation-state.

NON-RESIDENTS AS ECONOMIC AND POLITICAL PLAYERS

One of the characteristics that has bestowed a special analytic status on India is the particular history of that space. The foreword of the Report of the High Level Committee on the Indian Diaspora joshes about the outcomes of this history: 'The Indian Diaspora spans the globe and stretches across all the oceans and continents.

It is so widespread that the sun never sets on the Indian Diaspora.'
(2002, v) Perhaps one small consolation of the new empire facing
us is that, in the shadow of these new dangers, the old monsters of
the British empire become figures of fun, no more than posturing
from another age. Now, as the world trembles in the wake of the US
military machine, the Indian diaspora forms one of the most visible
remnants of the British empire on which, in one era, the sun never
set. The international networks of that empire survive only in our
scattered population; so now, instead, the sun never sets on us.

The Indian diaspora spans many generations and several continents.
It also links forced and bonded migrations to the relatively free
movements of wage-labourers. Most peculiarly, the self-conception
of being ethnically Indian continues to hail these disparate and
scattered populations. The committee describes the diaspora as being
made up of three distinct elements – those for whom the journey
commenced during the colonial period, those who have migrated to
the Gulf region in recent times and the current third wave of educated
elite migration to advanced economies.

This new claiming of all of these persons of Indian origin is an
active strategy of mythologisation. Despite considerable population
shift over different periods, the diaspora has not formed a central
theme in the self-narrative of the Indian nation. Some would argue
that the scattered populations of the earlier migrations have until
recently not been recognised as Indian at all. The sudden wish to
formalise the status of Indians abroad – and more significantly, to
include in this formalisation all those who appear to be 'ethnically'
Indians, regardless of how long ago their forebears moved from India
– is indicative of a particular moment. I want to argue that this is a
sign of new strategies for surviving globalisation, strategies primarily
being developed by poor nations, as a method of riding and surviving
the inequities of the global economy. It is into this space that the
non-resident population becomes the new superhero, rushing in to
'unleash the true power of the Indian diaspora' (Government of India
press release, November 12, 2002)

The Diaspora Committee report shows some familiarity with
academic debates on the contribution of cultural capital to the
growth of global networks. In an echo of Castells, we are encouraged
to abandon older models of centre and periphery or nation and ex-
patriots, and to welcome the more multiple dynamics of the network
society: 'Today, instead of the earlier "hub and spoke relationship"
between India and her Diaspora, we have begun to move towards

a network design of a "web relationship".' (Report of the High Committee on the Indian Diaspora, 2002, vi – hereafter Diaspora Committee)

There is a growing recognition of the role of the remittance economy in many parts of the poor world. For nations whose major contribution to the global economy continues to be their desperately flexible and mobile population, the many small transfers of money that trickle back from migrant workers abroad can become a substantial component of national income. The IMF estimates that remittances constitute a flow of more than US$70 billion worldwide and that these remittance payments account for more than 10 per cent of the GDP of a number of nations. India already benefits from these personal transfers and hopes that the formalisation of non-resident status will enable more public forms of investment. The proposal for formalised status comes as part of a wider rethinking of the role of migrants in the global economy.

Previous debate about the relation between migration and development portrayed migration from the poor world as a form of betrayal. Instead of staying to build the nation, migrants jump ship in search of a better life. They might continue to send money home in order to assuage their guilt at having escaped, but even this served to hamper the process of development:

> Beyond fostering dependency and being unstable, remittances destroy the process of economic development. The litany of complaints includes that remittances are infrequently (at best) invested in capital generating activities or even in job creating enterprises. Rather, they are spent on consumer goods with high import content; consumer goods which increase unproductive personal investment like housing or land. At the social level, remittances are accused of creating envy and eroding work habits. (Keely and Tran, 1989, 66)

Remittance flows do not fit easily with earlier dreams of development – they corrupt the aspiration to national self-sufficiency by introducing a flow of money that is not linked to economic productivity. Remittances contribute to no economic plan, apart from the plan of individual families to better their standard of living. At worst, the flow of remittances can create new social divisions, with privilege stemming from access to foreign currency and income from abroad.

However, as we have discussed, the aspiration to self-sufficient economic development has been under some attack in recent years, both from events and from ideological opponents. In these circumstances, there has been a reappraisal of the potential benefits of remittance flows. In a world driven, however turbulently, by the movements of finance capital, remittances can represent another source of foreign currency for hard-pushed economies:

> Remittances are the result of hard work by relatively poor people. Many of these migrants work under harsh conditions, and are often paid marginal wages. It is therefore crucial to maximise their benefits, and to reduce outside interference in the use of these funds. When planning to enhance their productive use, incentive-based initiatives, rather than regulatory and heavy-handed approaches appear most promising. Migrants and their families should be encouraged to allocate these funds in a way that enhances local development, as well as their individual needs. (Judith Van Doorn, 2002, 52)

How nations accommodate the remittance flows of migrant workers will shape their role in economic development. There is no reason to believe that the small-scale investments of ordinary people cannot contribute to development, and enabling better use of these resources can be of benefit to both migrants and to those who stay home. Most significantly, remittances have come to be viewed as a positive benefit to the receiving economy, something to be encouraged not regulated out of existence. This is the school of thought that influences Indian attempts to reclaim the diasporic population as an economic asset:

> NRIs [non-resident Indians] and PIOs [persons of Indian origin] need to become mechanisms that allow a transfer of their skills, leveraging of contacts, attracting investments, enhancing trade, and providing networking and insights into the American and Canadian market and psyche. (Diaspora Committee, 2002, 419)

The non-resident population is portrayed as an ambassadorial outpost of nation, so that the homeland is never really left behind. Transnational corporations have long understood that cultural competency is a key component of contemporary business – cutting deals across many boundaries requires the additional lubrication of culture. Now nations come to recognise that the half-way-house position of migrants may serve as contact points for these lucrative translations. In a global economy that privileges the business and activity of the rich to the exclusion of the poor world, diasporic populations can offer a legitimate entry into global networks.

TRANSNATIONAL CITIZENSHIP AS SURVIVAL STRATEGY

The poor world has learned to inhabit the informal networks of the global economy – largely through lack of choice and also through the unacknowledged asset of their scattered populations. When commentators remark on the formation of global financial institutions, they are not speaking of the ad hoc innovations that have enabled remittance economies to thrive. If anything, these are the arenas of non-regulated transactions that are now seen to threaten the rich world. It is this chain of middle-men and no-questions-asked opportunities for money transfer that causes alarm.

There have already been signs that the regulative clampdown in financial networks threaten the remittance economies of the poor world. However, I am not suggesting here that attempts to formalise the cash flows between non-residents and their homelands are a response to recent restrictions in transnational money flows. The Indian discussion predates these events by many years – although it is possible that the precise contours of the Pravasi Bharatiya Divas (Indian Diaspora Day) reflect these more recent concerns. More to the point, attempts to formalise the terms of some transnational version of citizenship reveal the pressure to find new ways to inhabit global networks while sustaining national interests.

Earlier I noted that discussion of diasporic communities had tended to focus on the cultural, as opposed to the political proper. This trend in the literature is mirrored in the arguments for formalising the status of non-residents. Whatever the economic gains and political imperatives, it is the sticky uncertainties of culture, supposedly, that link the network of diaspora. When India refers to the demands of the non-resident population, the demand is framed as one of cultural aspiration: 'the common aspiration of all members of the Diaspora is to maintain their cultural identity and civilisational ethos' (Diaspora Committee, 2002, 505).

It is no accident that these long discussions came to fruition under a bellicose BJP-led government of India. Although the conception of diaspora is largely inclusive, familiar barbs slip into the Committee's account. So we hear that Indians abroad are economically and educationally successful and regarded as a law-abiding model minority

– unlike Pakistanis, supposedly. More perniciously, the Indian culture that is seen to link the diaspora across generations and locations is celebrated as adaptable, peace-loving and encompassing of difference – all attributes that would seem highly desirable, were it not the case that this is also the account of Indian culture propagated by those who wish to reinvigorate the Indian nation through a militant and militarised Hinduism. Squashing difference and dissent under a more powerful narrative of national culture is a standard tactic of nation-building. My concern here is that this hailing of diaspora may become part of the larger project of remaking Indian culture on a model of a fictional Hindu culture that swallows all minorities while denying legitimacy to non-Hindu Indianness.

Interesting, then, to dig out a slightly more multi-faceted account of the cultural ties between diaspora and homeland: 'Driven by a combustible mixture of nostalgia, guilt, altruism, ambition, and profit motive, they seek to interact with India in a meaningful way through business, philanthropy, politics, culture, and trade.' (Diaspora Committee, 2002, 419) I am very taken by this slightly snide account of diasporic feeling, with its mixture of the emotional and the instrumental. There is no suggestion here that the longing of the diaspora is anything but a complex fiction, no hint in this account of the deep and essential cultural bonds that link scattered people across centuries. Instead, these are bonds motivated by a combination of delusion and self-interest – and their confused roots signal a potential danger. Despite the desire for mutual enrichment, there is always a chance of combustion. This volatility can be seen in the choice of figureheads. The centuries old traditions of Indian culture are represented in the Committee report by pictures of Ravi Shankar, V.S. Naipaul and Vivien Leigh – an odd trio who may give a better insight into the project of formalising cultural networks than any number of platitudes about the spiritual essence of Indian culture. If I caricature the three roles suggested by the pictures as (i) the commodification of the East; (ii) the theatricalisation of the place of the outsider; and (iii) covert exoticism passing as whiteness, then perhaps this is the model of transnational citizenship that is being created. This is a role that advocates flexibility on the part of the non-resident citizen – because success depends on a proper reading of location and audience. The flexible non-resident dual citizen must know when to inhabit the performances of ethnic culture and when to adopt the critical distance of the migrant outsider. Most of all, this is a role that depends on the actor knowing when to pass. The war on terrorism has reminded us all forcefully of the failures of multiculturalism. There is no longer much pretence that migrant minorities can become part of their adopted nations; better to rebuild the relationship with the nation left behind. A corollary of this is that even in our world of difference, niche-marketing and ethnic display, the place of the other can become uncomfortable and dangerous. Sometimes Vivien Leigh may be as Indian as it is safe to be.

MULTIPLE BELONGING IN THE ERA OF TERRORISM

We appear to be entering yet another era when safety is marked by allegiance and belonging, whatever the discomfort of these contracts. There is a new sense of danger surrounding the cultural differences that were so recently the material of civic regeneration and corporate multiculturalism.

Of course, it is far too late to go back to any pristine form of cultural identity – diaspora may call, but there is no easy and automatic communication between the nodes of the network. Being ethnically Indian might not amount to anything shared at all, except, perhaps, the aspiration to belong. In this context, the transnational citizenship of the non-resident is no more than another strategic identity, an attractive alternative to an increasingly closed and dangerous 'West'. Unlike the assimilatory strategies of previous moments, in this hailing non-residents assume multiple disguises – moving between exotic otherness and Westernised civility, hiding foreignness when necessary, ready to retreat to the protection of homeland if that is what circumstances demand. Although there is a reassurance that we will always be Indian, however long we have been away, there is also the parallel implication that we will never be settled in the new location. Of course, the South Asian diaspora has faced these dangers before, and in this light the fear of expulsion and of becoming a non-citizen are understandable. Perhaps an unspoken fear in the war against terrorism is that we migrant populations are once again becoming more vulnerable to the vagaries of national security in the West. Developing structures to transform non-resident populations into emissaries for the economies back home may become a useful survival strategy for both the poor world and its migrants.

UNSTOPPABLE MOVEMENTS

Much of this work has focused on the unfortunate and largely unforeseen outcomes of plans for integrating the global economy in the aftermath of the Second World War. Although I have tried to make space to acknowledge earlier phases of global integration, overall this has been a story about the second half of the twentieth century and the world that emerges in the twenty-first. The movement of people, however – the illicit movement that seems to cause the most intense emotions – is not a phenomena limited to this recent phase of global integration. Although some have argued that we have entered a new era of migration, in fact the very notion that population movement is something that should be subject to barriers and control is relatively recent. What is particular about this phase of global integration is that the failures and human costs of attempted immigration control have resurrected arguments against any barriers to the free movement of people: 'It is time also to question the assumption that governments and their citizens have the right to exercise control in their own interest over particular bits of land, any more than they have the right to appropriate the air and the sea.' (Hayter, 2000, 151)

In an era when states do not seem able to police their own borders in relation to the movement of finance capital or illicit goods, it seems unlikely that the pretence of immigration control can be sustained. However unpalatable this may be in political terms, developed nations are beginning to move towards a rhetoric of 'managed migration' – an admission both that migration is a necessary component of their economies and that prohibition is ineffective:

> European governments and their officials are beginning to recognise that immigration controls will never be made to work. They are engaged in a last-ditch defence of what remains of national sovereignty, in a period of growing power of international private capital. The attempt to maintain freedom of movement for capital and prevent the movement of labour will not indefinitely resist the pressures of so-called 'globalisation'. (Hayter, 2000, 152)

There is an increasing sense that national governments must accommodate the pressures of the global. As well as the recognition that developed economies rely on the contribution of migrant labour, there is also a concern that global inequalities may have dangerous repercussions for the West. In part, this can be seen as the slightly more benign aspect of war-on-terror rhetoric – such grotesque inequalities will catch up with the rich world sooner or later. Protect your privilege too intently, and other kinds of blowback may unsettle your world. Immigration or development – one way or another there must be some appeasement of the poor:

> If the rich countries do not want to let foreigners in, then the very least they must do is send much more money to compensate them for their being kept out. Those capital transfers really must be understood as compensation rather than as charity. They are merely the fair recompense for their being blocked from doing something (that is, moving to a richer country) that could, and quite probably would, have resulted in their earning that much more for themselves. (Goodin, 1992, 9)

This is not to suggest that attitudes to migration have been reshaped by some new global altruism. Very few people suggest that the rich world *owes* less affluent countries anything – this is not understood as a matter of duty. Instead, we are living through a shift in understanding of what seems possible, what seems good sense, what is the most effective means of safeguarding security and well-being. All round, sovereignty seems recognised to be an increasingly permeable affair: 'Now governments, most of them unwillingly, are being nudged along the way of accepting a decline in sovereignty and thus facilitating movement and the generation of incomes which protect those who do not move.' (Harris, 2002, 131)

Surviving global integration requires us all to accommodate ourselves to such transnational bargains. However intense the desire to block these movements, this just isn't happening. For all the talk about greater regulation of all sorts of illicit movement, of people and of things, such regulating is easier said than done. For now, we will have to live with the turbulence of all this movement.

Conclusion:
Violent Endings and New Beginnings

The world has changed a great deal since I began work on this book. When I started to assemble material for it, the machinery of globalisation appeared triumphant and immovable. There was an increasing awareness of the terms of resistance and protest, and a recognition that alliances were being formed across disparate interest groups, spanning old and new forms of organisation, from well-established trade unions and non-governmental organisations to the new breed of protesters who saw globalisation itself as the enemy and developed their campaigning techniques accordingly. However, there was little sense that global institutions were dented by these protests. Although NGOs and the representatives of poor nations have welcomed the impact that anti-globalisation protests have had on the formal negotiations about the terms of international trade, no one seemed to expect much more than concessions within the terms of the existing system. However much we all wished and believed that another world was possible, few had anything to say about how change on such a dramatic scale could be achieved. In short, although many people were developing a convincing and thoughtful critique of the inequalities and injustice of global processes, no corresponding global agent of change appeared. It was and is hard to identify what and where the levers of change might be.

However, more recently, there have been whispers that, in the manner of other empires before it, globalisation may destroy itself. Or, at least, adapt dramatically in the quest to survive. Some of this has emanated from the international institutions charged with management of the global economy – murmurs about poverty reduction not economic growth, attempts to work with governments and civil organisations. Some has come in response to the fear that the dispossessed of the world cannot be contained indefinitely, and that somewhere, somehow, something has to give.

This volume has looked at forms of trade and global movement that have become a cause of international anxiety. This creeping underbelly has been taken to signify the dangers of unregulated global integration, a warning of what an uncontrolled globalisation could become. In fairness, such trades have been portrayed as aberrations, a distortion of the wholesome benefits of international trade. Yet there is always a lingering concern – what if this is a sign of things to come?

DIFFERENT ACCOUNTS OF THE END OF THE WORLD AS WE KNOW IT

The forms of transnational transaction and movement discussed in this work have been the cause of intense concern amongst the self-appointed leaders of the world. As a result, international institutions have developed policy documents and drafted agreements, all designed to contain the corrosive influence of such undisciplined forms of business. Drugs, guns, illegal immigrants and organised crime – these form a nightmare vision of how the poor world becomes integrated into the global economy, in ways that endanger individuals and disrupt societies. In these instances, the reckless pursuit of profit is seen to run counter to human well-being and steps must be taken to curb excessive entrepreneurial enthusiasm. There is nothing much new about this arbitrary division between respectable and illicit business, and every Robin Hood-style mythology about stealing from the rich to give to the poor confirms the popular belief that the respectable business of the very wealthy is far from honest. The small but significant shift in our time is that many are now suggesting that the conduct of legal transnational business creates social costs that are similar to criminal activity: 'Financial instability alone is not always undesirable. Sometimes it is even a necessary indicator of changing market conditions. Rather I believe the current financial crisis that we so often speak about is actually a grave *social* calamity.' (Kapstein, 2001, 352)

For all the whining about exchange rates and the uncertainties of a speculative market, these things matter only in the impact they have on everyday life. Fictional transactions are not a problem if their impact is fictional also. When a range of commentators seems to suggest that we stand at the brink of an abyss, what is suggested is not so much that the (also fictional) machine of the world economy will stop working somehow, but rather that the human costs of this endeavour are not sustainable. The small consolations that have encouraged ordinary people to tolerate the inequalities and exploitation of the capitalist economy in previous crises now no longer seem to be available. If the bargains that have secured a version of social stability – the compromise of Keynesian economic management, some guarantee of living standards, safeguarding of savings and pensions – disappear or become ineffective, how can the co-operation of ordinary people be bought?

In this vein, a number of commentators have argued that we are living through an unprecedented crisis, one which must lead to dramatic social change. Without recourse to the small social reforms and benefits that have characterised liberal democracies, with these including a moderate sense of security, what will bind together societies which are being split apart constantly by the processes of capital accumulation? Here I want to consider three influential and quite optimistic accounts of this potential crisis as a prelude to revisiting the larger argument about the place of illicit forms of trade in global integration and re-evaluating the multiple calls for effective regulation of the global economy.

Immanuel Wallerstein argues that the capitalist world-economy, which has been in existence since what he refers to as 'the long sixteenth century', is at a moment of crisis. Wallerstein presents this as an inevitable systemic outcome, something that must have been coming all along:

> Like all systems, the linear projections of its trends reach certain limits, whereupon the system finds itself far from equilibrium and begins to bifurcate. At this point, we can say the system is in crisis and passes through a chaotic period in which it seeks to stabilize a new and different order, that is, make the transition from one system to another. What this new order is and when it will stabilize is impossible to predict, but the choices are strongly affected by the actions of all actors during the transition. And that is where we are today. (Wallerstein, 2003, 185)

To his credit, Wallerstein does not suggest that the outcome of this crisis is decided, only that systems reach such moments of crisis through the development of an internal logic. It is the processes of capital accumulation that spawn these tensions. Wallerstein identifies three key trends that indicate this crisis: deruralisation of the world; the externalisation of costs and the resulting ecological exhaustion; and the impact of democratisation. All three are a threat to the endless accumulation of capital, because they represent an unavoidable squeeze on profits.

By deruralisation, Wallerstein is referring to the escalating rate at which the rural population of the world is declining. This is important because wage levels have been kept down by exploiting workers who have relatively less bargaining power – most often by pulling rural residents into urban work. Over time, these workers change their economic expectations and come to demand higher wages, at which point a new rural enclave is sought. With fewer rural communities to exploit, the overall impact is that the average price of labour worldwide is increasing (Wallerstein, 1999, 80).

The externalisation of costs refers to the manner in which capitalists seek to avoid some of their costs by passing them on to someone else, most often the wider community. This can be done by dodging responsibility for disposing of their own waste; by paying the price for inputs but not enough to replenish these inputs; and by using infrastructure that has been built at a cost to wider society. The first two instances are understood increasingly to lead to unsustainable ecological costs – we are running out of places to dump dangerous waste and also of sources of raw materials. The third example of free-riding on social projects leads over time to an upward pressure on taxation, not least as the price of maintaining political stability, which adds to the squeeze on profits.

Democratisation is used here to mean that as more people all over the world are able to make demands on their governments, the demand has been for varieties of welfare and service from the state. Although people may not get the things they want, the pressure of their demands does increase state expenditure and, once again, this increases overall tax costs for everyone, including those chasing profits.

Wallerstein argues that this combined squeeze on profits is leading to a situation in which the accumulation of capital is under question. Each trend indicates that previous methods of ensuring the continuation of capital accumulation cannot be sustained – and without continual accumulation, capitalism cannot go on:

> We do indeed stand at a moment of transformation. But this is not that of an already established newly globalized world with clear rules. Rather we are located in an age of transition, transition not merely of a few backward countries who need to catch up with the spirit of globalization, but a transition in which the entire capitalist world-system will be transformed into something else. The future, far from being inevitable, one to which there is no alternative, is being determined in this transition, which has an extremely uncertain outcome. (Wallerstein, 2003, 45)

This is not an account of the inevitable and imminent triumph of the proletariat – although the pressure on profit is depicted as an outcome of the more mundane day-to-day forms of class struggle. Instead, the suggestion is that the world capitalist system is in crisis due to internal function failures, and that the powerful may find an alternative to this structure that enables them to maintain their position and privilege. This is not a crisis that proves that the underdog has won. What it is, in Wallerstein's account, is an opportunity to shape the future that emerges from these changes:

> ... we need to be debating the possible structures of the historical social system we want to construct as the present system collapses. And we ought to be trying to construct the alternative structures now, and in the next half-century, during the period of transition. We need to pursue this issue forcefully, if not dogmatically. We need to try out alternatives, as mental experiments and as real experiments. What we cannot do is ignore this issue. For if we do, the world right will come up itself with new noncapitalist alternatives that will involve us in a new, hierarchical, inegalitarian world order. And then it will be too late, for a long while thereafter, to change things. (Wallerstein, 2003, 245)

In times of crisis, rulers of the world become willing to adapt the rules of the game, to give a little to maintain their power and privilege. The intense revolutionary potential of the earlier twentieth century led to the concessions of Keynesian economic management and state welfare provision. The crisis facing capitalism in the early twenty-first century may lead to calls for regulation, rethinking, and a curbing of the excesses of capitalist accumulation. Anything to buy a little time while a new inegalitarian order can be built. The task is to find some alternative, while the possibilities of transition are open. For Wallerstein, there does not seem to be a privileged subject whose historic destiny it is to carve this new world project – so perhaps that is a duty for all of us.

We have already discussed the impact of Michael Hardt and Antonio Negri's work, *Empire*. This is at the euphoric end of prophecies of global cataclysm – Hardt and Negri describe a reworking of the machinery of global power that gives rise to a newly reinvigorated revolutionary subject:

> Here is the strong novelty of militancy today: it repeats the virtues of insurrectional action of two hundred years of subversive experience, but at the same time it is linked to a new world, a world that knows no outside. It knows only an inside, a vital and ineluctable participation in the set of

social structures, with no possibility of transcending them. This inside is the productive cooperation of mass intellectuality and affective networks, the productivity of postmodern biopolitics. This militancy makes resistance into counterpower and makes rebellion into a project of love. (Hardt and Negri, 2000, 413)

For Hardt and Negri, the expansionary tentacles of Empire have brought all resistance struggles into one – against the abstract power of Empire. Now the histories of all progressive movements have become folded into this new militancy, a militancy that does not privilege any one struggle or grant special agency to any one location, but which links them all. This vision of the new political activist is heavily influenced by the excitement of the early anti-globalisation movement and the energies that this new alliance unleashed, a movement that really believes that global capitalism can be dismantled through sheer force of will. However, there are few clues about how such leverage might be exercised – the new militant is not the proletariat formed as revolutionary agent through the contradictions of accumulation, and therefore has no particular structural advantage in campaigns for change. The fear is that, without this, we are hoping that protest alone will make a new and better world.

David Harvey, although also writing of the new imperialism and the fragility of US hegemony, is sceptical about the poetic vision of social change described by Hardt and Negri. Harvey is concerned that failing to differentiate between different struggles leaves us unable to identify potential progressive moments. Refusing globalisation, for example, can be a backward and reactionary business as well, and can spawn movements that are exclusionary and inegalitarian. Building a new world requires us to 'recognize the positive gains to be had from the transfers of assets that can be achieved through limited forms of dispossession' (Harvey, 2003, 178). Sometimes capital accumulation through dispossession – what Wallerstein explains as the externalisation of costs – creates positive possibilities for social justice, not least because the periphery gains some negotiating leverage through this process.

Overall, Harvey also believes that there is some cataclysmic change on its way, due to the overstretch of the US economy:

...if the US is no longer in itself sufficiently large and resourceful to manage the considerably expanded world economy of the twenty-first century, then what kind of accumulation of political power under what kind of political arrangement will be capable of taking its place, given that the world is heavily committed still to capital accumulation without limit? (Harvey, 2003, 35)

Despite all the talk about a New American Century, the United States is a debtor nation that relies on large amounts of credit from the rest of the world. At the same time, the escalating costs of the war on terror bring new pressures to an already costly military machine. Even such famous celebrants of empire as Niall Ferguson have questioned the sustainability of an empire based on borrowed cash (Ferguson, 2004). Harvey suggests that the US has been in danger of imperial overstretch for some time: 'Even before the events of 9/11, it was clear that neo-liberal imperialism was weakening on the inside, that even the asset values on Wall Street could not be protected, and that the days of neo-liberalism and its specific forms of imperialism were numbered.' (Harvey, 2003, 190)

This sense that neo-liberalism, despite its not quite hidden encouragement of global inequalities, cannot safeguard the privileges of the developed world frames the discussion of this work. The instabilities unleashed by the emergence of a speculative financial market have come to be regarded as threats to the global economy as a whole – not only an opportunity for a few to make some quick money, but also something that endangers everyone's assets, whether they are rich or poor. Harvey argues that the only available alternative to global conflict over scarce resources, as rival powers seek to safeguard their ability to accumulate at each other's expense, is what he calls a 'New Deal' imperialism. In an echo of the Keynesian interventions of the twentieth century, this international new deal would require greater intervention from states, or a coalition of states, into the workings of the global economy, primarily to curb the excesses of inequality, uncertainty and unaccountability that have plagued recent global experience. In fact, what is called for is a system of greater regulation – not unlike the calls we have heard from a variety of influential voices in world economic affairs.

ADAPT AND SURVIVE

This volume has sought to examine the fear that global integration may have given rise to an untameable underbelly, a kind of bastardised free trade that threatens to unravel the terms of respectable business. I have tried to explain that each new demon – gangsters, drugs, guns, migrants – establishes a global reach only by hitching a ride on the formal processes of globalisation. Illicit trade is enabled by some of the same structures as respectable trade; and while opening markets may encourage transnational transactions, it can also lock some regions into a dependency on such illicit trades. Economic liberalisation can allow organised crime to extend its ambition and reach – and the disarray after the demise of the Soviet Union has increased this opportunity. Drug economies have become embedded in certain regions as a direct outcome of the long and gruesome histories of neo-colonialism and global inequality. In the era of globalisation, the drug trade has also become a more powerful transnational player. Despite the hope that the end of the Cold War might end global arms build-up, new wars and battles over sovereignty and status fire new forms of arms race, now with far less predictable patterns. The movement of people has proved to be unstoppable, despite the harshest efforts of the developed world. Accepting and mobilising the benefits of migration may turn out to be the best option for rich and poor worlds.

Alongside all of this, the accusation that these dangers are harboured by failing states has accelerated the debate about the right to sovereignty. In response to all these real and imagined dangers, the international community has returned to the idea of regulation and global governance – some kind of institutional structure that can hold in all that free movement. Although little has been specified about what such a structure would be and how it might work, the multiple calls in relation to a variety of movements illustrate a shift in our way of life. No one believes that things can go on as they are. After all the painful and turbulent stories related in this book, in the end each one suggests that some kind of change is almost upon us. These seemingly solid structures are melting into air again. The only question is – what comes next?

Bibliography

Adams, Patricia (1997) 'The World Bank's Finances: An International Debt Crisis' in Caroline Thomas and Peter Wilkin, *Globalization and the South*, Houndsmills, Basingstoke, Palgrave.

Adepoju, Aderanti (1993) *The Impact of Structural Adjustment on the Population of Africa*, London, UNFPA.

Aganbegyan, Abel (1988) *The Challenge: Economics of Perestroika*, London, Hutchinson.

Ahmad, Aijaz (2000) *Lineages of the Present, Ideology and Politics in Contemporary South Asia*, London, Verso.

Ali, Tariq (2003) *Bush in Babylon, The Recolonisation of Iraq*, London, Verso.

Amin, Samir (1973) *Neo-Colonialism in West Africa*, Harmondsworth, Middlesex, Penguin.

—— (1980) *Delinking, Towards a Polycentric World*, London, Zed Books.

—— (1988) *Eurocentrism*, London, Zed Books.

—— (1997) *Capitalism and the Age of Globalization, The Management of Contemporary Society*, Delhi, Madhyam Books.

—— (2003) *Obsolescent Capitalism, Contemporary Capitalism and Global Disorder*, London, Zed Books.

'An interview with Chalmers Johnson', *Z Magazine*, November 2003.

Anderson, David G.; Pine, Frances (1995) *Surviving the Transition: Development Concerns in the Postsocialist World*, special issue of *Cambridge Anthropology*, 18(2).

Andreas, Peter (2002) 'Transnational Crime and Economic Globalization' in Mats Berdal and Monica Serrano, *Transnational Organized Crime and International Security*, Boulder, Colo., Lynne Rienner Publishers Inc.

Anthony, Ian (1992) *The Arms Trade and Medium Powers, Case Studies of India and Pakistan 1947–90*, London, Harvester Wheatsheaf.

Appadurai, Arjun (1996) *Modernity at Large, Cultural Dimensions of Globalization*, Minneapolis, University of Minnesota Press.

Arrighi, Giovanni (2003) 'The Social and Political Economy of Global Turbulence', *New Left Review* 20, March/April 2003.

Aslund, Anders (1989, 1991) *Gorbachev's Struggle for Economic Reform*, London, Pinter.

—— (2002) *Building Capitalism, The Transformation of the Former Soviet Bloc*, Cambridge, Cambridge University Press.

ATTAC (2003) 'Financial Capital, Controls on Finance Capital' in William F. Fisher and Thomas Ponniah, *Another World is Possible, Popular Alternatives to Globalization at the World Social Forum*, London, Zed Books.

Bales, Kevin (1999) *Disposable People, New Slavery in the Global Economy*, Berkeley, University of California Press.

Ball, Desmond (1996) *The Transformation of Security in the Asia/Pacific Region*, London, Frank Cass.

Bamyeh, Mohammed A. (2000) *The Ends of Globalization*, Minneapolis, University of Minnesota Press.

Barnet, R.; Cavanagh, J. (1994) *Global Dreams: Imperial Corporations and the New World Order*, London, Touchstone.

Barry, Brian; Goodin, Robert E. (1992) *Free Movement, Ethical Issues in the Transnational Migration of People and of Money*, New York, Harvester Wheatsheaf.

Barry, Tom; Wood, Beth; and Preusch, Deb (1983) *Dollars and Dictators, A Guide to Central America*, New York, Grove Press Inc.

Baudrillard, Jean (1995) *The Gulf War Did Not Take Place*, trans. Paul Patton, Bloomington, Indiana University Press.

Bauman, Zygmunt (1997) *Postmodernity and its Discontents*, Cambridge, Polity.

—— (1998) *Globalization, The Human Consequences*, Cambridge, Polity.

Beare, Margaret E. (2003) *Critical Reflections on Transnational Organized Crime, Money Laundering, and Corruption*, Toronto, University of Toronto Press.

Beckett, Andy (2002) *Pinochet in Piccadilly, Britain and Chile's Hidden History*, London, Faber and Faber.

Bello, Walden (1994) *Dark Victory: the US, Structural Adjustment, and Global Poverty*, London, Food First.

Bello, Walden; Cunningham, Shea (1994) 'The World Bank and the IMF', http://www.zmag.org/zmag/articles/july94bello.htm.

Benjamin, Walter (1973, 1992) *Illuminations*, London, Fontana.

Berdal, Mats; Serrano, Monica (2002) *Transnational Organized Crime and International Security, Business as Usual?*, Boulder, Colo., Lynne Rienner Publishers Inc.

Berman, Marshall (1982, 1988) *All That Is Solid Melts Into Air, The Experiences of Modernity*, New York, Penguin.

Bhattacharyya, Gargi; Gabriel, John; and Small, Stephen (2002) *Race and Power, Global Racism in the Twenty-First Century*, London, Routledge.

Bidwai, Praful; Vanaik, Achin (2000) *New Nukes, India, Pakistan and Global Nuclear Disarmament*, Oxford, Signal Books.

Bieber, Judy (1997) *Plantation Societies in the Era of European Expansion*, Aldershot, Variorum.

Binde, Jerome (2001) *Keys to the Twenty-First Century*, New York, UNESCO and Bergman Books.

Bishop, Ryan; Robinson, Lillian S. (1998) *Night Market, Sexual Cultures and the Thai Economic Miracle*, New York and London, Routledge.

Blackburn, Robin (1991) *After the Fall, The Failure of Communism and the Future of Socialism*, London, Verso.

Blejer, Mario I.; Skreb, Marko (2001) *Transition, The First Decade*, Cambridge, Mass., MIT Press.

Bogle, Lorilyn (2001) *Cold War Culture and Society*, New York, Routledge.

Bonanno, A.; Busch, L.; Friedland, W.; Gouveia, L.; and Mingione, E. (1994) *From Columbus to ConAgra, The Globalization of Agriculture and Food*, Lawrence, Kansas, University of Kansas Press.

Bondi, Loretta (1999) *Arsenals on the Cheap: NATO expansion and the arms cascade*, New York, Human Rights Watch.

Booth, Martin (1996) *Opium, A History*, London, Simon and Schuster.

Bracken, Paul (1999) *Fire in the East, The Rise of Asian Military Power and the Second Nuclear Age*, New York, Perennial.

Brah, Avtar; Hickman, Mary J.; and Mac an Ghaill, Mairtin (1999) *Global Futures, Migration, Environment and Globalization*, Basingstoke and London, Macmillan Press Ltd.

Brah, A. (1996) *Cartographies of Diaspora*, London: Routledge.

Braudel, Fernand (1977) *Capitalism and Material Life 1400–1800*, London, Fontana.

—— (1982) *The Wheels of Commerce*, London, Collins.

—— (1984) *The Perspective of the World*, London, Collins.

—— (1993) *A History of Civilizations*, London, Penguin.

Brennan, Teresa (2003) *Globalization and its Terrors*, London, Routledge.

Bretell, Caroline; Hollifield, James Frank (2000) *Migration Theory: Talking Across the Disciplines*, London, Routledge.

Broderick, Mick (1991) *Nuclear Movies, A Critical Analysis and Filmography of International Feature Length Films Dealing with Experimentation, Aliens, Terrorism, Holocaust and Other Disaster Scenarios, 1914–1989*, Jefferson, N.C., McFarland.

Brown, Louise (2001) *Sex Slaves: The Trafficking of Women in Asia*, London, Virago.

Buckley, Richard (1999) *Organised Crime: A Growing Threat to Democracy?*, Cheltenham, Understanding Global Issues.

Burkart, Oliver; Coudert, Virginie (2002) 'Leading Indicators of Currency Crises for Emerging Countries', *Emerging Markets Review*, Vol. 3, June 2002.

Buxton, Julia; Phillips, Nicola (1999) *Developments in Latin American Political Economy, States, Markets and Actors*, Manchester, Manchester University Press.

CAMPACC (2003) *A Permanent State of Terror?*, London, CAMPACC in association with Index Against Censorship.

Campbell, Bonnie K.; Loxley, John (1989) *Structural Adjustment in Africa*, Houndmills, Macmillan.

Campbell, Greg (2002) *Blood Diamonds, Tracing the Deadly Path of the World's Most Precious Stones*, Boulder, Colo., Westview.

Cardoso, Fernando Henrique (2001) *Charting a New Course, the politics of globalization and social transformation*, Lanham, Maryland, Rowman & Littlefield.

Carnoy, Martin; Castells, Manuel; Cohen, Stephen S. and Cardoso, Fernando Henrique (1993) *The New Global Economy in the Information Age, Reflections on our Changing World*, University Park, Pennsylvania: Pennsylvania State University Press.

Carr, E.H. (1970) *Socialism in One Country, 1924–1926*, Harmondsworth, Penguin.

Carter, Ashton B. (1999) 'Adapting US defence to future needs', *Survival, International Institute for Strategic Studies*, 41–43, winter 1999–2000.

Castells, Manuel (1989) *The Informational City: Information Technology, Economic Restructuring and the Urban-Regional Process*, Oxford, Blackwell.

—— (1996) *The Rise of the Network Society*, Oxford, Blackwell.

—— (1998) *End of Millenium*, Oxford, Blackwell.

—— (2000) 'Information Technology and Global Capitalism', in Will Hutton and Anthony Giddens, *On the Edge, Living with Global Capitalism*, London, Jonathan Cape.

Castles, Stephen (2004) 'Why Migration Policies Fail', *Ethnic and Racial Studies*, Vol. 27, No. 2, March 2004, pp. 205–27.

Castles, Stephen; Miller, Mark J. (1993, 2003) *The Age of Migration*, Houndmills, Basingstoke, Palgrave Macmillan.

Chanley, Virginia A. (1999) 'US public views on international involvement from 1964 to 1993: time-series analyses of general and militant internationalism', *The Journal of Conflict Resolution*, Vol. 43, No. 1, February 1999.

Chengappa, Raj (2000) *Weapons of Peace, The Secret History of India's Quest to be a Nuclear Power*, New Delhi, HarperCollins Publishers India.

Chomsky, Noam (1985) *Turning the Tide, US Intervention in Central America and the Struggle for Peace*, London, Pluto.

Chomsky, Noam; Herman, Edward S. (1979) *The Washington Connection and Third World Fascism, The Political Economy of Human Rights: Volume 1*, Boston, South End Press.

Chossudovsky, Michel (1997) *The Globalisation of Poverty, Impacts of IMF and World Bank Reforms*, London, Zed Books.

Choudhury, G.W. (1975) *India, Pakistan, Bangladesh, and the Major Powers, Politics of a Divided Subcontinent*, New York, Free Press.

Chua, Amy (2003) *World on Fire, How Exporting Free-Market Democracy Breeds Ethnic Hatred and Global Instability*, London, William Heinemann.

Chubin, Shahram (1995) 'The South and the New World Order' in Brad Roberts, *Weapons Proliferations in the 1990s*, Cambridge, Mass., MIT Press.

Cirincione, Joseph (2000) *Repairing the Regime, Preventing the Spread of Weapons of Mass Destruction*, New York, Routledge.

Clague, Christopher (1992) 'The Journey to a Market Economy' in Christopher Clague and Gordon C. Rausser *The Emergence of Market Economies in Eastern Europe*, Cambridge, Mass., Blackwell.

Clift, Stephen; Carter, Simon (2000) *Tourism and Sex, Culture, Commerce, and Coercion*, London, Pinter.

Cockburn, Alexander; St Clair, Jeffrey (1998) *Whiteout, The CIA, Drugs and the Press*, London, Verso.

Coerver, Don M.; Hall, Linda B. (1999) *Tangled Destinies, Latin America and the United States*, Albuquerque, University of New Mexico Press.

Cohen, Robin (1987) *The New Helots, Migrants in the International Division of Labour*, Aldershot, Avebury.

Coll, Steve (2004) *Ghost Wars: The Secret History of the CIA, Afghanistan, and Bin Laden, from Soviet Invasion to September 10, 2001*, New York, Penguin.

Cooper, Julian (1991) *The Soviet Defence Industry, Conversion and Reform*, London, Pinter.

Cooper, Neil (1999) *The Business of Death*, London, I.B. Tauris & Co.

Copetas, A. Craig (1991) *Bear Hunting with the Politburo*, New York, Touchstone.

Cordesman, Anthony H. (2002) *Weapons of Mass Destruction in India and Pakistan*, Washington, Center for Strategic and International Studies.

Cornish, P. (1995) *Controlling the Arms Trade: The West versus the Rest*, London, Bowerdean.

Cottam, Martha L. (1994) *Images and Intervention, US Policies in Latin America*, Pittsburgh, University of Pittsburgh Press.

Coyle, Diane (2000) *Governing the World Economy*, Cambridge, Polity.

Croft, Stuart (1996) *Strategies of Arms Control, a History and Typology*, Manchester, Manchester University Press.

Crook, Stephen; Pakulski, Jan; and Waters, Malcolm (1992) *Postmodernization, Change in Advanced Society*, London, Sage.

Curtis, Mark (1998) *The Great Deception, Anglo-American Power and World Order*, London, Pluto.

Dalforno, Steve (2003) 'Blowback and the Sorrows of Empire: An Interview with Chalmers Johnson', *Z Magazine*, November 2003.

Danaher, Kevin (1994) *Fifty Years is Enough, The Case Against the World Bank and the International Monetary Fund*, Boston, Mass., South End Press.

Darling, Arthur B. (1990) *The Central Intelligence Agency, An Instrument of Government, to 1950*, London, Pennsylvania State University Press.

Das, Gurcharan (2002) *India Unbound, From Independence to the Global Information Age*, London, Profile Books.

Dasgupta, Biplab (1998) *'Structural Adjustment', Global Trade and the New Political Economy of Development*, London, Zed Books.

Davis, Mike (2001) *Late Victorian Holocausts, El Nino Famines and the Making of the Third World*, London, Verso.

De Angelis, Massimo (2000) *Keynesianism, Social Conflict and Political Economy*, Houndmills, Basingstoke, Macmillan Press Ltd.

De Landa, Manuel (1997) *A Thousand Years of Nonlinear History*, New York, Zone Books.

De Rivero, Oswaldo (2001) *The Myth of Development, The Non-Viable Economies of the 21st Century*, London, Zed Books.

Dembele, Demba Moussa (2003) 'The Myths and Dangers of PRSPs', *Forum des Alternatives Africaines*, http://brettonwoodsproject.org/article. shtml?cmd[126]=x-126–19091.

Desai, Meghnad (2002) *Marx's Revenge, The Resurgence of Capitalism and the Death of Statist Socialism*, London, Verso.

Dhanapala, J. (1999) *Small Arms Control: Old Weapons New Issues*, Aldershot, Ashgate.

Dixit, J.N. (2002) *India–Pakistan in War and Peace*, London, Routledge.

Dollar, David; Svensson, Jakob (2000) 'What explains the success or failure of structural adjustment programmes?', *Economic Journal*, 110 (October), Oxford, Blackwell and Royal Economic Society, 894–917.

Douthwaite, Richard (1992) *The Growth Illusion*, Bideford, Devon, Resurgence.

Downie, Richard Duncan (1998) *Learning from Conflict, the US Military in Vietnam, El Salvador, and the Drug War*, Westport, Conn., Praeger.

Drescher, Seymour (1986) *Capitalism and Anti-Slavery*, Basingstoke and London, Macmillan.

Duffield, Mark (2001) *Global Governance and the New Wars, The Merging of Development and Security*, London, Zed Books.

Dunne, Paul (1999) *The Globalisation of Arms Production: Implications for the UK Economy*, London, Campaign Against the Arms Trade.

Eatwell, John; Taylor, Lance (2000) *Global Finance at Risk, The Case for International Regulation*, Cambridge, Polity.

Edwards, Adam; Gill, Peter (2003) *Transnational Organized Crime: Perspectives on Global Security*, London, Routledge.

Ellman, Michael; Kontorovich, Vladimir (1992) *The Disintegration of the Soviet Economic System*, London, Routledge.

Emelyanov, Tom (1983) *A Dangerous Business, The Arms Trade in the World Today*, Moscow, Novosti Press Agency.

Enloe, Cynthia (1990) *Bananas, Beaches and Bases, Making Feminist Sense of International Politics*, Berkeley, University of California Press.

Fann, K.T., Hodges, Donald C. (1971) *Readings in US Imperialism*, Boston, Mass., Porter Sargent Publisher.

Felsenstein, Frank (1995) *Anti-Semitic Stereotypes, A Paradigm of Otherness in English Popular Culture, 1660–1830*, Baltimore, Johns Hopkins University Press.

Felstead, Alan; Jewson, Nick (1999) *Global Trends in Flexible Labour*, Houndmills, Basingstoke, Palgrave Macmillan.

Ferguson, Niall (2003) *Empire: How Britain Made the Modern World*, London, Allen Lane.

Finckenhauer, James O.; Voronin, Yuri A. (2001) *The Threat of Russian Organized Crime*, Washington, National Institute of Justice.

Finkenauer, James O.; Waring, Elin (2001) 'Challenging the Russian Mafia Mystique', *National Institute of Justice Journal*, April 2001.

Fiorentini, Gianluca; Peltzman, Sam (1995) *The Economics of Organised Crime*, Cambridge, Cambridge University Press.

Fisher, William F.; Ponniah, Thomas (2003) *Another World is Possible, Popular Alternatives to Globalization at the World Social Forum*, London, Zed Books.

Fox-Genovese, Elizabeth; Genovese, Eugene D. (1983) *Fruits of Merchant Capital, Slavery and Bourgeois Property in the Rise and Expansion of Capitalism*, Oxford, Oxford University Press.

Frank, Andre Gunder (1978) *World Accumulation 1492–1789*, London, Macmillan.

Freemantle, Brian (1995) *The Octupus, Europe in the Grip of Organised Crime*, London, Orion.

Friman, H. Richard; Andreas, Peter (1999) *The Illicit Global Economy and State Power*, Lanham, Maryland, Rowman & Littlefield.

Galeano, Eduardo (1973, 1997) *Open Veins of Latin America, Five Centuries of the Pillage of a Continent*, London, Latin America Bureau.

Galeotti, Mark (1995) *The Age of Anxiety, Security and Politics in Soviet and Post-Soviet Russia*, London, Longman.

—— (2002) *Russian and Post-Soviet Organized Crime*, Aldershot, Ashgate.

Gambetta, Diego (1993) *The Sicilian Mafia: The Business of Private Protection*, Cambridge, Mass., Harvard University Press.

Gates, Henry Louis (1986) *'Race', Writing and Difference*, Chicago, University of Chicago Press.

Genovese, Eugene D. (1966) *The Political Economy of Slavery, Studies in the Economy and Society of the Slave South*, London, MacGibbon & Kee.

Gereffit, Gary; Korzeniewicz, Miguel (1994) *Commodity Chains and Global Capitalism*, Westport, Conn., Praeger.

Germain, Randall D. (2000) *Globalization and its Critics, Perspectives from Political Economy*, Houndmills, Basingstoke, Macmillan.

Gerner, Kristian; Hedlund, Stefan (1993) *The Baltic States and the End of the Soviet Empire*, London, Routledge.

Ghai, Dharam (1991) *The IMF and the South, The Social Impact of Crisis and Adjustment*, London, Zed Books.

Gilinsky, Victor (2001) 'Nuclear Proliferation After the Indian and Pakistani Tests' in Henry Sokolski and James M. Ludes, *Twenty-First Century Weapons Proliferation*, London, Frank Cass.

Gills, Barry K. (2000) *Globalization and the Politics of Resistance*, Houndmills, Basingstoke, Palgrave.

Gilman, Sander L. (1985) *Difference and Pathology, Stereotypes of Sexuality, Race, and Madness*, Ithaca, Cornell University Press.

Glover, Stephen et al. (2001) *Migration: An Economic and Social Analysis*, London, RDS Occasional Paper No. 67.

Goddard, C. Roe; Passe-Smith, John T.; and Conklin, John G. (1996) *International Political Economy, State-Market Relations in the Changing Global Order*, Boulder, Colo, Lynne Rienner Publishers.

Godnick, William; Vasquez, Helena (2003) *Small Arms Control in Latin America*, International Alert, Security and Peacebuilding Programme, Monitoring the Implementation of Small Arms Controls.

Goodin, Robert E. (1992) 'If people were money ...' in Brian Barry and Robert E. Goodin, *Free Movement, Ethical Issues in the Transnational Migration of People and of Money*, New York, Harvester Wheatsheaf.

Gootenberg, Paul (1999) *Cocaine, Global Histories*, London, Routledge.

Gray, Mike (2002) *Busted, Stone Cowboys, Narco-Lords and Washington's War on Drugs*, New York, Thunder's Mouth Press/Nation Books.

Green, Duncan (1999) 'A Trip to the Market: The Impact of Neoliberalism in Latin America' in Julia Buxton and Nicola Phillips, *Developments in Latin American Political Economy, States, Markets and Actors*, Manchester, Manchester University Press.

Greenaway, David; Upward, Richard; and Wakelin, Katharine (2002) *Trade, Investment, Migration and Labour Market Adjustment*, Houndmills, Basingstoke, Palgrave Macmillan.

Grimes, Kimberley M. (1998) *Crossing Borders, Changing Social Identities in Southern Mexico*, Tucson, University of Arizona Press.

Guardian, February 6, 2004, '"Supermarket" Trade in Nuclear Technology Alarms UN Inspector', Ian Traynor, James Astill, Ewen Macaskill.

Guardian, May 8, 2004, 'He Won, Russia Lost', Adrian Levy and Cathy Scott-Clark.

Guha, Ranajit (1997) *Dominance without Hegemony: History and Power in Colonial India*, Cambridge, Mass., Harvard University Press.

Guiraudon, Virginie; Joppke, Christian (2001) *Controlling a New Migration World*, London, Routledge.

Gupta, Amit (1997) *Building an Arsenal, The Evolution of Regional Power Force Structures*, Westport, Conn., Praeger.

Gustafson, Thane (1999) *Capitalism Russian-Style*, Cambridge, Cambridge University Press.

Guyatt, Nicholas (2000, 2003) *Another American Century? The United States and the World Since 9/11*, London, Zed Books.

Hables Gray, Chris (1997) *Postmodern War, The New Politics of Conflict*, New York, Guilford Press.

Hann, C.M. (2002) *PostSocialism, Ideals, Ideologies and Practices in Eurasia*, London, Routledge.

Harding, Jeremy (2000) *The Uninvited, Refugees at the Rich Man's Gate*, London, Profile Books.

Hardt, Michael; Negri, Antonio (2000) *Empire*, Cambridge, Mass., Harvard University Press.

Harris, Nigel (1996) *The New Untouchables: Immigration and the New World Order*, London, Penguin.

—— (2002) *Thinking the Unthinkable, The Immigration Myth Exposed*, London, I.B. Tauris.

Harvey, David (1989) *The Condition of Postmodernity*, Oxford, Blackwell.

—— (2003) *The New Imperialism*, Oxford, Oxford University Press.

Hatton, Timothy J.; Williamson, Jeffrey G. (1998) *The Age of Mass Migration, Causes and Economic Impact*, New York, Oxford University Press.

Haus, Leah (2001) 'Migration and International Economic Institutions' in Aristide R. Zolberg and Peter M. Benda, *Global Migrants Global Refugees*, New York and Oxford, Berghahn Books.

Hayter, Teresa (2000) *Open Borders: The Case Against Immigration Controls*, London, Pluto.

Held, David; Koenig-Archibugi, Mathias (2003) *Taming Globalization, Frontiers of Governance*, Cambridge, Polity.

Held, David; McGrew, Anthony; Goldblatt, David; and Perraton, Jonathan (1999) *Global Transformations, Politics, Economics and Culture*, Cambridge, Polity.

Henderson, Hazel (2001) 'The Global Financial Casino' in K.S. Jomo and Shyamala Nagaraj, *Globalization versus Development*, Houndmills, Basingstoke, Palgrave.

Higgott, Richard A.; Underhill, Geoffrey R.D.; and Bieler, Andreas (2000) *Non-State Actors and Authority in the Global System*, London, Routledge.

Hillman, Richard S. (2001) *Understanding Contemporary Latin America*, Boulder, Colo., Lynne Rienner Publishers.

Hobsbawm, Eric (1962, 2002) *The Age of Revolution 1789–1848*, London, Abacus.

—— (1994) *Age of Extremes, The Short Twentieth Century 1914–1991*, London, Abacus.

—— (2000) *The New Century*, London, Little, Brown and Company.

Hogan, Michael J. (1999) *The Ambiguous Legacy, US Foreign Relations in the 'American Century'*, Cambridge, Cambridge University Press.

Holland, Stuart (1994) *Towards a New Bretton Woods, Alternatives for the Global Economy*, Nottingham, Spokesman.

Holm, Hans-Henrik; Sorensen, Georg (1995) *Whose World Order? Uneven Globalization and the End of the Cold War*, Boulder, Colo., Westview Press.

Hughes, Donna M. (2001) 'The "Natasha" Trade: Transnational Sex Trafficking', *National Institute of Justice Journal*, January 2001.

Hutton, Will; Giddens, Anthony (2000) *On the Edge, Living with Global Capitalism*, London, Jonathan Cape.

Ignatieff, Michael (2003) *Empire Lite: Nation Building in Bosnia, Kosovo and Afghanistan*, London, Vintage.

Ignatiev, Noel (1995) *How the Irish Became White*, New York, Routledge.

International Monetary Fund (2001) 'Enhancing contributions to combating of money-laundering', IMF policy paper.

Jaipal, Rikhi (1986) *Nuclear Arms and the Human Race, To Die or Not to Die*, New Delhi, Allied Publishers.

Jamieson, Alison (2000) *The Antimafia: Italy's Fight Against Organized Crime*, Basingstoke, Macmillan.

Johnson, Chalmers (2000) *Blowback, The Costs and Consequences of American Empire*, London, Time Warner.

Jomo, K.S.; Nagaraj, Shyamala (2001) *Globalization versus Development*, Houndmills, Basingstoke, Palgrave.

Jordon, Bill; Duvell, Franck (2002) *Irregular Migration, The Dilemmas of Transnational Mobility*, Cheltenham, Edward Elgar.

Judd, Denis (2004) *The Lion and the Tiger, The Rise and Fall of the British Raj*, Oxford, Oxford University Press.

Jung, Dietrich (2003) *Shadow Globalization, Ethnic Conflicts and New Wars, A Political Economy of Intra-State War*, London, Routledge.

Kagarlitsky, Boris (1988) *The Thinking Reed, Intellectuals and the Soviet State from 1917 to the Present*, London, Verso.

Kaldor, Mary (1999) *New and Old Wars: Organized Violence in a Global Era*, Cambridge, Polity.

—— (2000) *Global Insecurity*, London and New York, Pinter.

Kapstein, Ethan (2001) 'A New Social Contract for a New Phase of Globalization' in Jerome Binde, *Keys to the Twenty-First Century*, New York, UNESCO and Bergman Books.

Kapur, Ashok (2000) 'India's Nuclear Weapons Capability: Convincing or Confusing?' in M.L. Sondhi, *Nuclear Weapons and India's National Security*, New Delhi, Har-Anand Publications.

Karp, Aaron (1995) 'The Arms Trade Revolution: The Major Impact of Small Arms' in Brad Roberts, *Weapons Proliferation in the 1990s*, Cambridge, Mass., MIT Press.

Keely, Charles B.; Tran, Bao Nga (1989) 'Remittances from Labor Migration: Evaluations, Performance and Implications', *International Migration Review*, XXIII (3), Fall, reprinted in Steven Vertovec and Robin Cohen, *Migration, Diasporas and Transnationalism*, Cheltenham, Edward Elgar.

Keh, Douglas I. (1996) *Drug Money in a Changing World: Economic reform and criminal finance*, Washington, United Nations Technical Paper No. 4.

Keller, Edmond J.; Rothchild, Donald (1996) *Africa in the New International Order, Rethinking State Sovereignty and Regional Security*, Boulder, Colo., Lynne Rienner Publishers.

Kennedy, Paul (1994) *Preparing for the Twenty-First Century*, London, Fontana.

Keren, Michael; Ofer, Gur (1992) *Trials of Transition, Economic Reform in the Former Communist Bloc*, Boulder, Colo., Westview.

Khilnani, Sunil (1997) *The Idea of India*, London, Penguin.

Khor, Martin (2001) *Globalization and the South, Some Critical Issues*, Mapusa, Goa, Other India Press.

Kiely, Ray; Marfleet, Phil (1998) *Globalisation and the Third World*, London, Routledge.

King, Anthony D. (1991) *Culture, Globalization and the World-System*, Houndmills, Macmillan.

Kiple, Kenneth F.; Beck, Stephen V. (1997) *Biological Consequences of European Expansion, 1450–1800*, Aldershot, Variorum.

Klein, Herbert S. (1999) *The Atlantic Slave Trade*, Cambridge, Cambridge University Press.

Klein, Naomi (2000) *No Logo*, London, Flamingo.

—— (2002) *Fences and Windows, Dispatches from the Front Lines of the Globalization Debate*, London, Flamingo.

—— (2003) 'Bring Halliburton Home', *The Nation*, November 24, 2003.

Koistinen, Paul A.C. (1980) *The Military-Industrial Complex, a historical Perspective*, New York, Praeger.

Kolodko, Grzegorz W. (2001) 'Postcommunist Transition and Post-Washington Consensus: The Lessons for Policy Reforms' in Mario I. Blejer and Marko Skreb, *Transition, the First Decade*, Cambridge, Mass., MIT Press.

Krugman, Paul (1999) *The Return of Depression Economics*, New York, W.W. Norton and Co.

—— (2000) *Currency Crises*, Chicago, University of Chicago Press.

Kundu, Apurba (1998) *Militarism in India, The Army and Civil Society in Consensus*, London, Tauris Academic Studies.

Kunkel, Benjamin; Kunkel, Lisa (2002) 'Who's Counting? U.S. plan to eradicate coca crops in Bolivia fails miserably', in *These Times magazine*, May 13, 2002, http://ww.thirdworldtraveler.com/South.America/Whos_Counting_Bolivia.html.

Kupchan, Charles A. (2002, 2003) *The End of the American Era, US Foreign Policy and the Geopolitics of the Twenty-First Century*, New York, Vintage.

Lafeber, Walter (1999) 'The Tension Between Democracy and Capitalism during the American Century' in Michael J. Hogan, *The Ambiguous Legacy, US Foreign Relations in the 'American Century'*, Cambridge, Cambridge University Press.

Lambert, Mick; Rattenbury, Judith; and Prichard, Ian (2003) *The Political Influence of Arms Companies*, London, Campaign Against the Arms Trade.

Laurence, Edward; Stohl, Rachel (2002) *Making Global Public Policy: The Case of Small Arms and Light Weapons*, Small Arms Survey, Occasional Paper No. 7.

Lavigne, Marie (1995) *The Economics of Transition, from Socialist Economy to Market Economy*, New York, St. Martin's Press.

Lens, Sidney (1971, 2003) *The Forging of the American Empire, From the Revolution to Vietnam: A History of US Imperialism*, London, Pluto.

Lessinger, Johanna (1992) 'Nonresident-Indian Investment and India's Drive for Industrial Modernization', in Frances Abrahamer Rothstein and Michael L. Blim (eds), *Anthropology and the Global Factory: Studies of the New Industrialization in the Late Twentieth Century*, New York, Bergin & Garvey.

Levering, Ralph B. (1994) *The Cold War, A Post-Cold War History*, Arlington Heights, Ill., Harlan Davidson.

Lindqvist, Sven (2001) *A History of Bombing*, London, Granta.

Linn, Johannes F. (2001) 'Ten Years of Transition in Central Europe and the Former Soviet Union: The Good News and Not-So-Good News' in Mario

I. Blejer and Marko Skreb, *Transition, the First Decade*, Cambridge, Mass. MIT Press.

Lumpe, Lora (2000) *Running Guns, The Global Black Market in Small Arms*, London, Zed Books.

Lusane, Clarence; Desmond, Dennis (1991) *Pipe Dream Blues, Racism and the War on Drugs*, Boston, South End Press.

Madeley, John (1992, 1996) *Trade and the Poor, The Impact of International Trade on Developing Countries*, London, Intermediate Technology Publications.

Mahajan, Harpeet (1982) *Arms Transfer to India, Pakistan and the Third World*, New Delhi, Young Asia Publications.

Maizels, Alfred (2003) 'Economic Dependence on Commodities' in John Toye, *Trade and Development Directions for the Twenty-First Century*, Cheltenham, Edward Elgar.

Makki, Sami (2001) *Private Military Companies and the Proliferation of Small Arms, Regulating the Actors*, London, Saferworld.

Mann, Michael (2003) *Incoherent Empire*, London, Verso.

Manning, Patrick (1996) *Slave Trades, 1500–1800: Globalization of Forced Labour*, Aldershot, Variorum.

Martin, Hans-Peter; Schumann, Harald (1997) *The Global Trap, Globalization and the Assault on Democracy and Prosperity*, London, Zed Books.

Mason, Mike (1997) *Development and Disorder, A History of the Third World since 1945*, Hanover and London, University of New England Press.

Max Planck Institute (2000) *Illegal Drug Trade in Russia*, Freiburg, Max Planck Institute for Foreign and International Criminal Law.

McClintock, Michael (1985) *The American Connection, Vol. 2, State Terror and Popular Resistance in Guatemala*, London, Zed Books.

McDonell, Nick (2002) *Twelve*, London, Atlantic Books.

McIntyre, Angela; Weiss, Taya (2003) 'Exploring Small Arms Demand, A Youth Perspective', *Institute for Security Studies*, ISS Paper 67.

McMahon, Robert J. (1994) *The Cold War on the Periphery, The United States, India and Pakistan*, New York, Columbia University Press.

McMichael, A.J. (1993) *Planetory Overload, Global Environmental Change and the Health of the Human Species*, Cambridge, Cambridge University Press.

Médecins Sans Frontières (1997) *World in Crisis: The Politics of Survival at the End of the Twentieth Century*, London: Routledge.

Melman, Seymour (1974) *The Permanent War Economy, American Capitalism in Decline*, New York, Touchstone.

Memmi, Albert (2000) *Racism*, Minneapolis, University of Minnesota Press.

Mertes, Tom (2004) *A Movement of Movements, Is Another World Really Possible?* London, Verso.

Mihevc, John (1995) *The Market Tells Them So, The World Bank and Market Fundamentalism in Africa*, London, Zed Books.

Milanovic, Branko (1998) *Explaining the Increase in Inequality During the Transition*, Washington, Development Economics Research Group, World Bank.

Miles, Robert (1987) *Capitalism and Unfree Labour, Anomaly or Necessity?* London and New York, Tavistock.

Mintz, Sidney (1997) 'Was the Plantation Slave a Proletarian?' in Judy Bieber, *Plantation Societies in the Era of European Expansion*, Aldershot, Variorum.

—— (1985, 1986) *Sweetness and Power, The Place of Sugar in Modern History*, New York, Penguin.

Mobius, Mark (1994) *The Investor's Guide to Emerging Markets*, London, Pitman.

Moggridge, D.E. (1976, 1993) *Keynes*, Toronto, University of Toronto Press.

Moon, Katharine H.S. (1997) *Sex Among Allies, Military Prostitution in US–Korea Relations*, New York, Columbia University Press.

Mueller, J. (1989) *Retreat from Doomsday: The Obsolescence of Major War*, New York, Basic Books.

Muggah, Robert; Griffiths, Martin (2002) *Reconsidering the Tools of War: Small Arms and Humanitarian Action*, London, Overseas Development Institute.

Musah, Abdel Fatau; Castel, Robert (1998) *Eastern Europe's Arsenal on the Loose: Managing Light Weapons Flows to Conflict Zones*, Washinton DC, Basic Publications.

Naik, N. (1999) 'Light Weapons Flows to and from Afghanistan' in Lora Lumpe, *Running Guns, the Global Black Market in Small Arms*, London, Zed Books.

Nelson, Joan M.; Kochanowicz, Jacek; Mizsei, Kalman; and Munoz, Oscar (1994) *Intricate Links: Democratization and Market Reforms in Latin America and Eastern Europe*, New Brunswick, Transaction.

Nelson, Joan M.; Tilly, Charles; and Walker, Lee (1997) *Transforming Post-Communist Political Economies*, Washington, National Research Council.

Nkrumah, Kwame (1965) *Neo-Colonialism, The Last Stage of Imperialism*, London, Nelson.

Omissi, David (1994) *The Sepoy and the Raj: Politics of the Indian Army, 1860–1940*, Houndmills, Basingstoke, Palgrave Macmillan.

Oppermann, Martin (1998) *Sex Tourism and Prostitution, Aspects of Leisure, Recreation, and Work*, New York, Cognizant Communication Corporation.

O'Prey, Kevin (1995) *A Farewell to Arms? Russia's Struggles with Defense Conversion*, New York, Twentieth Century Fund Press.

Oxfam (1998) *Small Arms, Wrong Hands*, London, Oxfam.

—— (2003) *Targeting Small Arms*, London, Oxfam Briefing Paper 8.

Oza, B.M. (1997) *Bofors, The Ambassador's Evidence*, New Delhi, Konark Publishers.

Pande, Savita (2000) 'The Role of Nuclear Weapons' in M.L. Sondhi, *Nuclear Weapons and India's National Security*, New Delhi, Har-Anand Publications.

Paranjpe, Shrikant (2000) 'India's Nuclear Tests of 1998 and Beyond' in M.L. Sondhi, *Nuclear Weapons and India's National Security*, New Delhi, Har-Anand Publications.

Pardo, Josecasas (1992) *Economic Effects of the European Expansion, 1492–1824*, Stuttgart, Steiner.

Pasinetti, Luigi L.; Schefold, Bertram (1999) *The Impact of Keynes on Economics in the Twentieth Century*, Cheltenham, Edward Elgar.

Pearce, Jenny (1981) *Under the Eagle, US Intervention in Central America and the Caribbean*, London, Latin American Bureau.

Pearson, M.N. (1996) *Spices in the Indian Ocean World*, Aldershot, Variorum.

Pettman, Jan Jindy (1996) *Worlding Women, A Feminist International Politics*, London, Routledge.

Pickles, John; Smith, Adrian (1998) *Theorising Transition, The Political Economy of Post-Communist Transformations*, London, Routledge.

Pieterse, Jan Nederveen (1998) *World Orders in the Making: humanitarian intervention and beyond*, Basingstoke, Macmillan.

Piirainen, T. (1994) *Change and Continuity in Eastern Europe*, Aldershot, Dartmouth.

Pirseyedi, Bobi (2000) *The Small Arms Problem in Central Asia, Features and Implications*, Geneva, United Nations Institute for Disarmament Research.

Plant, Sadie (1999) *Writing on Drugs*, London, Faber and Faber.

Prencipe, Lorenzo (2003) 'Migration and the Traffic in People, the Contradictions of Globalization' in William F. Fisher and Thomas Ponniah, *Another World is Possible, Popular Alternatives to Globalization at the World Social Forum*, London, Zed Books.

Prins, Gwyn (2002) *The Heart of War, On Power, Conflict and Obligation in the Twenty-First Century*, London, Routledge.

Puri, Balraj (1993, 1995) *Kashmir, Towards Insurgency*, New Delhi, Orient Longman.

Rahnema, Majid; Bawtree, Victoria (1997) *The Post-Development Reader*, London, Zed Books.

Rainnie, Al; Smith, Adrian; and Swain, Adam (2002) *Work, Employment and Transition, Restructuring Livelihoods in Post-Communism*, London, Routledge.

RAWA, Revolutionary Association of the Women of Afghanistan (2002) 'Afghanistan is again the world's largest opium producer, UN', October 25, 2002, http://www.rawa.org/opium-again.htm.

Report of the High Level Committee on the Indian Diaspora (2002), Delhi, Indiadiaspora.nic.in/contents.htm.

Roberts, Brad (1995) *Weapons Proliferation in the 1990s*, Cambridge, Mass., MIT Press.

Robinson, William I. (2003) *Transnational Conflicts, Central America, Social Change and Globalization*, London, Verso.

Rodney, Walter (1973) *How Europe Underdeveloped Africa*, London and Dar-Es-Salaam, Bogle-L'Ouverture Publications.

Rugman, Alan (2000) *The End of Globalization*, London, Random House.

Rupert, Mark (2000) *Ideologies of Globalization, Contending Visions of a New World Order*, London, Routledge.

Said, Abdul Aziz (1977) *Ethnicity and US Foreign Policy*, New York, Praeger Publishers.

Salt, John (2001) 'The Business of International Migration' in M.A.B. Siddique, *International Migration into the 21st Century*, Cheltenham, Edward Elgar.

Sampson, Steven (2002) 'Beyond Transition: rethinking elite configurations in the Balkans' in C.M. Hann, *Post-Socialism, Ideals, Ideologies and Practices in Eurasia*, London, Routledge.

SAPRIN (2002) *Structural Adjustment: The SAPRI Report, The Policy Roots of Economic Crisis, Poverty and Inequality*, London, Zed Books.

Sardar, Ziauddin (1998) *Postmodernism and the Other, The New Imperialism of Western Europe*, London, Pluto.

Sassen, Saskia (1998) *Globalization and its Discontents: essays on the new mobility of people and money*, New York, New Press.

—— (1994) *Cities in a World Economy*, Thousand Oaks, Calif., Pine Forge.

Schech, Susanne; Haggis, Jane (2002) *Development, A Cultural Studies Reader*, Oxford, Blackwell.

Schlosser, Eric (2003) *Reefer Madness and Other Tales from the Underground*, London, Penguin.

Schoultz, Lars (1998) *Beneath the United States, A History of US Policy Toward Latin America*, Cambridge, Mass., Harvard University Press.

Schroeder, William (2001) 'Money Laundering: A Global Threat and the International Community's Response', *FBI Law Enforcement Bulletin* 70 (5), May 1–9.

Schulz, William (2003) *Tainted Legacy, 9/11 and the Ruin of Human Rights*, New York, Thunder's Mouth/Nation Books.

Schvarzer, Jorge (1991) 'Opening up the Economy, Debt and Crisis: the Inescapable Relationship' in Dharam Ghai, *The IMF and the South, the Social Impact of Crisis and Adjustment*, London, Zed Books.

Schwartz, Warren F. (1995) *Justice in Immigration*, Cambridge, Cambridge University Press.

Scott, David (1995) 'Money-laundering and international efforts to fight it' in *At a Glance*, World Bank, May 1995, note no. 48.

Scott, Peter Dale; Marshall, Jonathan (1991) *Cocaine Politics, Drugs, Armies and the CIA in Central America*, Berkeley and Los Angeles, University of California Press.

Scraton, Phil (2002) *Beyond September 11, An Anthology of Dissent*, London, Pluto.

Seabrook, Jeremy (1996) *Travels in the Skin Trade, Tourism and the Sex Industry*, London, Pluto.

Shafer, Michael (1988) *Deadly Paradigms, The Culture of US Counterinsurgency Policy*, Princeton, NJ, Princeton University Press.

Shaw, Timothy M.; Quadir, Fahimul (1997) 'Democratic Development in the South in the Next Millennium: What Prospects for Avoiding Anarchy and Authoritarianism?' in Caroline Thomas and Peter Wilkin, *Globalization and the South*, Houndmills, Basingstoke, Palgrave.

Shawcross, William (2000) *Deliver Us From Evil, Warlords and Peacekeepers in a World of Endless Conflict*, London, Bloomsbury.

Shelley, Louise I. (1999) 'Transnational Organized Crime: The New Authoritarianism' in Richard H. Friman and Peter Andreas, *The Illicit Global Economy and State Power*, Lanham, Maryland, Bowman & Littlefield.

Shepard, Benjamin; Hayduk, Ronald (2002) *From Act-up to the WTO, Urban Protest and Community Building in the Era of Globalization*, London, Verso.

Short, John Rennie (2001) *Global Dimensions, Space, Place and the Contemporary World*, London, Reaktion.

Siddique, M.A.B. (2001) *International Migration into the 21st Century*, Cheltenham, Edward Elgar.

SIPRI (1982) *The Arms Race and Arms Control, Facts and Figures on the Arms Race and Arms Control Efforts*, London, Taylor & Francis.

Skidelsky, Robert (1995) *The World After Communism: a polemic for our times*, London and Basingstoke, Macmillan.

Skidmore, Thomas E.; Smith, Peter (1997) *Modern Latin America*, New York and Oxford, Oxford University Press.

Skrobanek, Siriporn; Boonpakdi, Nattaya; and Janthakeero, Chutima (1997) *The Traffic in Women, Human Realities of the International Sex Trade*, London, Zed Books.

Small Arms Survey (2003) *Small Arms Survey Yearbook*, Oxford, Oxford University Press.

Smith, Alan (1993) *Russia and the World Economy, Problems of Integration*, London, Routledge.

Smith, Chris (1993) *The Diffusion of Small Arms and Light Weapons in Pakistan and Northern India*, London, Centre for Defence Studies.

Smith, Neil (1984, 1990) *Uneven Development, Nature, Capital and the Production of Space*, Oxford, Basil Blackwell.

Sokolski, Henry; Ludes, James M. (2001) *Twenty-First Century Weapons Proliferation*, London, Frank Cass.

Sondhi, M.L. (2000) *Nuclear Weapons and India's National Security*, New Delhi, Har-Anand Publications.

Soros, George (1998) *The Crisis of Global Capitalism, Open Society Endangered*, London, Little, Brown & Co.

Spear, Percival (1965, 1990) *A History of India, Vol 2, From the Sixteenth Century to the Twentieth Century*, London, Penguin.

Stallings, Barbara (1995) *Global Change, Regional Response, The New International Context of Development*, Cambridge, Cambridge University Press.

Starr, Amory (2000) *Naming the Enemy, Anti-Corporate Movements Confront Globalization*, London, Zed Books.

Steger, Manfred B. (2003) *Globalization, A Very Short Introduction*, Oxford, Oxford University Press.

Stessens, Guy (2000) *Money Laundering: a new international law enforcement model*, Cambridge, Cambridge University Press.

Stewart, Frances; Wang, Michael (2003) 'Do PRSPs empower poor countries and disempower the World Bank, or is it the other way round?', Oxford, QEH Working Paper.

Stewart, Michael (1967, 1986) *Keynes and After*, Harmondsworth, Middlesex, Penguin.

Stiglitz, Joseph (2002) *Globalization and its Discontents*, London, Allen Lane.

—— (2003) 'Globalization and Development' in David Held and Mathias Koenig-Archibugi, *Taming Globalization, Frontiers of Governance*, Cambridge, Polity.

Strange, Susan (1998) *Mad Money*, Manchester, Manchester University Press.

Sturdevant, Saundra Pollock; Stoltzfus, Brenda (1992) *Let the Good Times Roll, Prostitution and the US Military in Asia*, New York, New Press.

Tarp, Finn (1993) *Stabilization and Structural Adjustment, Macroeconomic Frameworks for Analysing the Crisis in Sub-Saharan Africa*, London, Routledge.

Taylor, D.R.F.; Mackenzie, Fiona (1992) *Development from Within, Survival in Rural Africa*, London, Routledge.

Taylor, Ian (1998) *Crime and Political Economy*, Aldershot, Dartmouth.

Teitelbaum, Michael S.; Weiner, Myron (1995) *Threatened Peoples, Threatened Borders, World Migration and US Policy*, New York, W.W. Norton & Co.

Thomas, Caroline; Wilkin, Peter (1997) *Globalization and the South*, Houndmills, Basingstoke, Palgrave.

Thomas, Hugh (1997) *The Slave Trade, The History of the Atlantic Slave Trade, 1440–1870*, London, Picador.

Thomas, Vinod; Dailami, Mansoor; Dhareshwar, Ashok; Kaufmann, Daniel; Kisher, Nalin; Lopez, Ramon; and Wang, Yan (2000) *The Quality of Growth, World Bank 2000*, Oxford, Oxford University Press.

Thorpe, Richard; Little, Stephen (2001) *Global Change, The Impact of Asia in the Twenty-First Century*, Houndmills, Basingstoke, Palgrave.

Tirman, John (1997) *Spoils of War, The Human Cost of America's Arms Trade*, New York, Free Press.

Tomlinson, John (1991) *Cultural Imperialism, A Critical Introduction*, London, Pinter.

Toye, John (2003) *Trade and Development Directions for the Twenty-First Century*, Cheltenham, Edward Elgar.

Trebilcock, Michael J. (1995) 'The Case for a Liberal Immigration Policy' in Warren F. Schwartz, *Justice in Immigration*, Cambridge, Cambridge University Press.

Trocki , Carl A. (1999) *Opium, Empire and the Global Political Economy, a study of the Asian opium trade 1750–1950*, London, Routledge.

TUC (2003) *Migrant Workers – Overworked, Underpaid and Over Here*, London, TUC.

Turgeon, Lynn (1996) *Bastard Keynesianism, The Evolution of Economic Thinking and Policymaking since World War II*, Westport, Conn., Greenwood Press.

Ucarer, Emek M.; Puchala, Donald J. (1997) *Immigration into Western Societies, Problems and Policies*, London, Pinter.

Ul Huq, Mahmub; Jolly, Richard; Streeten, Paul; and Haq, Khadija (1995) *The UN and the Bretton Woods Institutions, New Challenges for the Twenty-First Century*, Houndmills, Basingstoke, Macmillan.

United Nations (1994) *Drugs and Development*, Washington, United Nations Technical Paper No. 1.

—— (2000a) *Convention against Transnational Organized Crime*, Geneva, United Nations.

—— (2000b) *UN Protocol to Prevent, Suppress and Punish Trafficking in Persons, Especially Women and Children*, Geneva, United Nations.

—— (2000c) *World Drug Report 2000*, UN Office for Drug Control and Crime Prevention, Oxford, Oxford University Press.

Vadney, T.E. (1987, 1992) *The World Since 1945*, London, Penguin.

Van Den Anker, Christien (2004) *The Political Economy of New Slavery*, Houndmills, Basingstoke, Palgrave Macmillan.

Van Doorn, Judith (2002) 'Migration, Remittances and Development', *Labour Education* 2002/4, No. 129, ILO.

Varese, Federico (2001) *The Russian Mafia: private protection in a new market economy*, Oxford, Oxford University Press.

Veenkamp, Theo; Bentley, Tom; and Buonfino, Alessandra (2003) *People Flow, Managing Migration in a New European Commonwealth*, London, Demos.

Vertovec, Steven; Cohen, Robin (1999) *Migration, Diasporas and Transnationalism*, Cheltenham, Edward Elgar.

Viano, Emilio C. (1999) *Global Organized Crime and International Security*, Aldershot, Ashgate.

Vidal, Gore (2002) *Dreaming War, Blood for Oil and the Cheney–Bush Junta*, New York, Thunder's Mouth Press/Nation Books.

Volkov, Vadim (2002) *Violent Entrepreneurs, The Use of Force in the Making of Russian Capitalism*, Ithaca, Cornell University Press.

Voronin, Yuriy A. (1997) 'The Emerging Criminal State: Economic and Political Aspects of Organized Crime in Russia' in Phil Williams, *Russian Organized Crime: The New Threat?* London, Frank Cass.

Wallerstein, Immanuel (1974) *The Modern World System I, Capitalist Agriculture and the Origins of the European World-Economy in the Sixteenth Century*, San Diego, Calif., Academic Press.

—— (1980) *The Modern World System II, Mercantilism and the Consolidation of the European World-Economy, 1600–1750*, San Diego, Calif. Academic Press.

—— (1999) *The End of the World as We Know It, Social Science for the Twenty-First Century*, Minneapolis, University of Minnesota Press.

—— (2003) *The Decline of American Power*, New York, New Press.

Wattanayagorn, Panitan; Ball, Desmond (1996) 'A Regional Arms Race?' in Desmond Ball, *The Transformation of Security in the Asia/Pacific Region*, London, Frank Cass.

Webster, William (1997) *Russian Organized Crime: Global Organized Crime Project*, Washington DC, Center for Strategic and International Studies.

Westerfield, Bradford H. (1995) *Inside the CIA's Private World, Declassified Articles from the Agency's Internal Journal 1955–1992*, New Haven, Yale University Press.

Willett, Susan (1999) *The Arms Trade, Debt and Development*, London, Campaign Against the Arms Trade.

William, Sue; Milani, Carlos (1999) *The Globalization of the Drug Trade*, UNESCO.

Williams, Phil (1997) *Russian Organized Crime: The New Threat?* London, Frank Cass.

Winant, Howard (2001) *The World is a Ghetto, Race and Democracy since World War II*, New York, Basic Books.

Winiecki, Jan (1988) *The Distorted World of Soviet-Type Economies*, London, Routledge.

Winters, L. Alan (2003) 'Trade Policy as Development Policy: Building on Fifty Years' Experience' in John Toye, *Trade and Development Directions for the Twenty-First Century*, Cheltenham, Edward Elgar.

Wisotsky, Steven (1986) *Breaking the Impasse in the War on Drugs*, New York, Greenwood Press.

Wolpert, Stanley (2000) *A New History of India*, Oxford, Oxford University Press.

Wrigley, Christopher (1999) *The Privatisation of Violence: new mercenaries and the state*, London, Campaign against the Arms Trade.

—— (2001) *The Arms Industry*, CAAT Goodwin paper 1.

Zolberg, Aristide R.; Benda, Peter M. (2001) *Global Migrants Global Refugees*, New York and Oxford, Berghahn Books.

Index

Compiled by Sue Carlton

'And you?'

'Sisterhood solidarity,' she replied.

'I mean it, Kaye,' I said seriously.

'Nothing. Don't be silly.'

'Ten,' I insisted.

'Don't be silly, Mara. I said nothing.'

'Ten.'

'Nothing.'

'Five.'

'Okay,' she gave in.

'To ensure you don't ever regret this help you've given me,' I added.

She laughed. 'Get ready. Your lawyer whore-payer will be here any moment.' As she was leaving the room she asked, 'How was Gerhardt?'

'The person or the detective?'

'Both.'

'Person, fine. Detective, I am yet to find out.'

'You won't be disappointed,' she said. 'In fact, you will marvel. He burrows and burrows. Some people even say he's got termites working for him.'

It took Gerhardt eight weeks, 'Because of inefficiences in Africa,' he informed me when he rang to make an appointment.

I packed two thousand Deutschmarks in an envelope – the rest of his fees – and set out for his office.

He received me more formally than the first time. 'Today is business,' he said, handing me a report. 'Do you want to read it yourself?'

'I don't read German very well,' I replied.

'In that case, you tell me, as we go along, which parts interest you and I will explain it simply. Ask questions and I'll give you the answers if I have them here . . . which I'm sure I do.'

'That would be better,' I said.

He took a pen and a block pad to note down which portions he would later put together and re-type for me, and said, 'You can begin.'

'He came here in June '75. Did you find that out?' I asked.

'It's here. With the help of an agent who brought him in through East Berlin. Do you want to know about the Ministry he worked for in Africa?'

'That is not necessary,' I said. 'How did he come to know Osey?'

'Osey is partner to the agent who brought him here from Africa. He lived with Osey for a while here in Hamburg when he first arrived.'

'You found all that out?' I asked.

'You are paying me for it,' he replied.

I wished he would be a little more informal. I wouldn't have minded at all giving him my services for free but he looked liked someone who kept pleasure and work apart.

'When did he leave Osey's?'

'When he met a woman by the name of Gitte in a disco. A shy, fat, young girl who was very aware she wasn't pretty. And who at nineteen had still not been kissed by a man. He gave her her first kiss and she fell madly in love with him. She had a one-room apartment and he began visiting her regularly. Two months later he moved in with her. Six months later they were a married couple. Soon after their marriage he got a job at a factory where he still works today. Then they moved to a two-room apartment in Scharlemann Strasse where they still live. About three months after he started work, Osey left for Africa. He returned with a woman called Comfort who used to work with Cobby Ajaman in the Ministries in Africa.'

'Did she live with them? Comfort? With Cobby and Gitte?'

'No. She lived with an African woman in Harburg, near Hamburg, until she got her own one-room apartment here in Hamburg. Cobby visited her daily. The hours and times varied according to his shift work. Sometimes he was there . . .'

'That doesn't interest me,' I interjected.

'Good. Cobby and Gitte took a joint loan from the bank. Two months later, Comfort married a German man, got her residency permit and began work at an Afro-Caribbean restaurant in Hanover, as a waitress. It can be concluded that the loan that Cobby Ajaman and his wife Gitte took out went into the financing of this arranged marriage of Comfort's. Most probably, Gitte was and still is in the dark about this fact. Comfort no longer works at the restaurant because of a fight Cobby had there with the brother-in-law of the owner of the restaurant. The owner is an African man with a German wife. The German brother-in-law was clearly interested in Comfort and Cobby was jealous.'

'And Comfort? Where does she work now?'

'She doesn't work. Cobby takes care of her.'

'Does she receive state help?'

'She doesn't. She doesn't qualify because the German man she married, a homosexual, has a job. This disqualifies his legal wife from state help. The welfare office, as you know . . .'

'That doesn't interest me,' I interrupted. 'So Comfort didn't find another job?'

'She didn't try. Cobby forbade her to, out of jealousy and fear of losing her to someone at the work place as he had nearly done at the restaurant.'

'So she is wholly dependent on Cobby?'

'Wholly.'

'And still lives in the apartment?'

'Yes.'

'And he still visits her?'

'Every day.'

'Good. Go on. Didn't you find out about anything in Africa? Is he building a house?'

'He is not building a house. He is renovating one, and extending it.'

'In the city? On the coast?'

'No. In a village.'

'Naka? A village called Naka?'

'No. In a village called Sumanyi.'

'What business has he got repairing an old house in Sumanyi?'

'Comfort comes from Sumanyi,' Gerhardt said.

I felt drained, so drained that I had to ask for a glass of water. My husband brings me from home to a foreign land and puts me in a brothel to work, and what money I make, he uses to pay the rent on his lover's apartment, and to renovate a house for her in her village back home. I came to Gerhardt expecting the worst, but this was even worse than I had conceived of.

Everything else that Gerhardt reported on, I only partly took in. When he had finished, I asked him to type out, in German, all the parts that had to do with Comfort and Akobi, including the information about the bank loan, which had most probably paid for Comfort's bogus marriage, and about the house Akobi was renovating and extending in Sumanyi. Then I paid Gerhardt the rest of his fees and left to go back to Peepy.

'My God, Mara, is everything all right?' Kaye exclaimed when she saw me on my return. 'You look awful.'

I told her all the new stuff I'd learned about Comfort and Cobby.

'So what are you going to do?' Kaye asked.

'When is Oves expecting me?' I asked.

'He is ready for you. We go to Schroeder's in four days' time. It's up to you.'

'Then tell Oves I am coming in four days' time. By the way, do you know anyone who will be travelling outside Germany soon? It doesn't matter where. Europe, Asia, Africa or America. It must be outside Germany.'

'Matou was talking about a cousin of hers going to visit her people back home soon. Why?'

Matou was one of the women at Peepy and I never found out whether this was her real name or not. She was a Thai.

'Thailand,' I reflected, 'that will do.'

'What do you want to do from Thailand?' asked Kaye.

'I want to post something from there to Gitte.'

That was a year ago now.

Comfort has been deported. I hear she is now in Nigeria and is the lover of some high-up army official there. I don't know any more details and don't want to know.

Akobi is in jail here in Germany. He attempted to sneak out while still owing money to the bank and a couple of mail order houses and was caught. I am sure that he was wanting to follow Comfort when she got deported. Everything he and Gitte owned

138

has been taken by the bank. Gitte has divorced him and returned to her family. I hear that she's grown thin with the anxiety but has decided it was luck in misfortune since God only knows how many diets she's tried and failed.

Sometimes I am not sure whether I did the right thing or not in coming here but thank God, here at Oves', I don't have time to worry and regret it. That doesn't mean that I consider myself totally blameless either. After all, I was also party to it all even if involuntarily. And I guess that my punishment for it is that I am stuck with Oves for the rest of my life. I have decided to stop thinking about ever going home. I just don't belong there any longer. Moreover, I have this fear that haunts me day in and day out, that if I show my face there one day, out of the blue that sex video Akobi made of me clandestinely will show up there, too. Worse still, I am now to be seen on a couple more sex videos. Home will have to remain a distant place.

Oves comes in holding his snow-white Siamese cat which he is stroking delicately. He's just come in to tell me about the two customers who are coming to me in the next hour.

At Oves' brothel, I have plunged into my profession down to the marrow in my bones. There is no turning back for me now. I am so much a whore now that I can no longer remember or imagine what being a non-whore is. I have problems recollecting what I was like before I turned into what I am now. I think a lot about my mother and my two sons. Recently I started getting so sad with the thought of them that I began pleasing my men less. And that nearly landed me in trouble with Oves, who is not as tolerant as Pompey and Kaye. And he has no wife in whom I can find a trusted friend as I did in Kaye. He only has his Siamese cat. So when I am down, when any of us is feeling down, Oves gives us 'snow' to sniff, to make us high. Now I can't go through a day without sniffing 'snow'. I am hooked on it. I am fast sinking into a place hotter than hell. But I know this. And that is why I have decided that before I sink too deep I will make as much money as possible for my mother and sons back home.

The only person I have contact with back home is Mama Kiosk. All the things I send to my family, whether money or goods, I send through her. She doesn't know the truth about me.

139

She thinks that I work in an African restaurant. I stole the idea, naturally.

I wonder a lot about what my mother is doing. What games my kids are playing. Where the soles of their little feet are standing. What they are thinking about. Maybe sometimes about me, I imagine.

I have sent my eldest brother who lives in the city a video set and television. And from time to time I record 'Sesame Street' and 'Tom and Jerry' and send the video tapes to him for my two sons. They stay with him most of the time because they have to go to school.

My third brother, too, I sometimes see in my daydreams, driving through the narrow pot-holed roads of the city and excitedly hooting the horn of the Datsun saloon I shipped to him. I am also financing a cement-block house for my mother in the village. They say that it has raised her esteem so much that it has even won her back my father. Trust my father! But I am pleased for her.

I have issued instructions to them to find a small cement house in town which I can buy for my two kids, so that when I sink too deep beyond help they will at least have a decent place to lay their heads. Material things are all I can offer them. As for myself, there's nothing dignified and decent left of me to give them.